EAGLE ANNUAL

THE 1950s

EDITED BY

DANIEL TATARSKY

This book belongs to:

EAGLE ANNUAL

THE BEST
OF THE
1950S
COMIC

FEATURES *DAN DARE*, THE GREATEST COMIC STRIP OF ALL TIME

First published in hardback in Great Britain in 2007
by Orion Books
an imprint of the Orion Publishing Group Ltd
Orion House, 5 Upper St Martin's Lane,
London WC2H 9EA
An Hachette UK Company

Printed and bound in China

The Orion Publishing Group's policy is to use papers that are natural, renewable
and recyclable and made from wood grown in sustainable forests. The logging and
manufacturing processes are expected to conform to the environmental regulations
of the country of origin.

Every effort has been made to fulfil requirements with regard to reproducing copyright
material. The author and publisher will be glad to rectify any omissions
at the earliest opportunity.

www.orionbooks.co.uk

EAGLE

When *Eagle* first hit the streets on 14 April 1950 it was, to paraphrase an infamous split infinitive of the next decade, boldly going where no strip comic had gone before. It cost 50 per cent more than its rivals but over half the pages were full colour and in Dan Dare, it was to create one of the most popular and most enduring heroes of them all.

Coming just five years after the end of the Second World War the *Eagle* landed in a United Kingdom still struggling with rationing and trying to cope with wide-ranging social changes. For the adults who had come through the war life was, in the main, still looking pretty grim. The economy was suffering, trying to recover from the large spending required for warfare, jobs were sparse, and the shops could not provide all that was required. Much of this though was outside the thoughts of the average child. The war brought stories of heroism and derring-do, and while a bombed out housing estate was just that to an adult, to a child it was an adventure playground. With a blast of colour, *Eagle* shone amidst the grime and while war has its devastating effects, it is also a time when invention

and technology thrives, and this spirit of discovery and limitless possibilities underpins every page of the comic.

If *Eagle* was the baby born on that spring day, then its parents were undoubtedly Marcus Morris and Frank Hampson. Many others were involved in what was a painful and protracted gestation period, but it was these two men with their unique drive and vision who are ultimately credited with bringing the *Eagle* into the world. Reverend Marcus Morris, to give him his clerical title of the time, had been serving his parish in Southport for just a few years when he decided to improve the efforts of his church magazine to spread the word. He changed its name to *Anvil* and, with the aim of it becoming a national mouthpiece for his views, set to work on redesigning its look.

Morris discovered Frank Hampson at the local school of arts and crafts. Having served with the Royal Army Service Corps during the war Hampson was trying to support his young family by making a living as an artist. Like most meetings of this sort – Lennon and McCartney, or Morecambe and Wise – there were no fireworks or bolts of lightning. Neither man could possibly have guessed that together they would change the face of the comic strip for ever.

Working first on *Anvil*, it was not long before Morris and Hampson turned their attention to the requirements of their younger readers. It has been well documented that Morris wrote an article for *The Sunday Dispatch* entitled 'Comics that bring horror into the nursery'. It was here that he, in effect, laid out his manifesto for what he thought was a suitable publication for young boys. While the American comics which Morris was so against brought death, destruction and low morals, his *Eagle* was to soar above that and take the high ground. 'Wholesome' is a word that has often been used to describe how *Eagle* would be different but a more accurate one is 'decent'.

Having met in 1947, it was two years before they had a dummy issue of *Eagle*, and Morris began to look for a publisher. The effort and detail that went into producing this blueprint for the comic should not be underestimated. To make the strips as detailed as possible, models were painstakingly built and costumes designed from which the artists could work. It is almost an insult to some of the work to merely refer to them as comic strips; many could be seen as works of art in their own right.

With the dummy under his arm, Morris pounded the streets of London, knocking on the doors of likely publishers. Eventually it was Hulton Press who took the risk on *Eagle*, and it was a risk. Taking on a publication with an editor whose day job was as a vicar, with artists and writers, many of whom had never worked on a published comic before, never mind one that would be a national magazine coming out every week, was going to be no easy task.

Hindsight allows 20/20 vision and so it can be easy to forget this risk. To devise, produce, and promote a comic with a circulation going from zero to nearly one million in its first week was a mammoth task, and it is a credit to all involved, that *Eagle* quickly established itself as a must have in the satchel of schoolboys up and down the country. Out of this effort came iconic characters and features which have held their place in the memories of millions of fans the world over. These include, just from the first issue, strips such as 'The Adventures of PC49', 'Seth and Shorty', and 'Rob Conway', L. Ashwell Wood's 'Cutaway', features about sport, nature and science and, last but not least, 'Dan Dare'.

Why was *Eagle* so successful? Vibrant colours, great stories, incredible detail all went into the mix, but maybe it was the very simple title of the first story, on the first page, of the first issue: 'Dan Dare – Pilot of the Future'. He and *Eagle* represented the unwritten future and the reader was part of it, right in the middle of it.

This collection from the Fifties attempts to bring together the best, the most beautiful and the most exciting elements of the *Eagle*. It's almost impossible to recreate the raw excitement of running down to the newsagent to grab the new issue off the shelves to see where Dan Dare and his crew were heading next, but it is hoped that these pages come mighty close.

Daniel Tatarsky

EVERY FRIDAY

THREEPENCE

EAGLE

14 APRIL 1950 No. 1

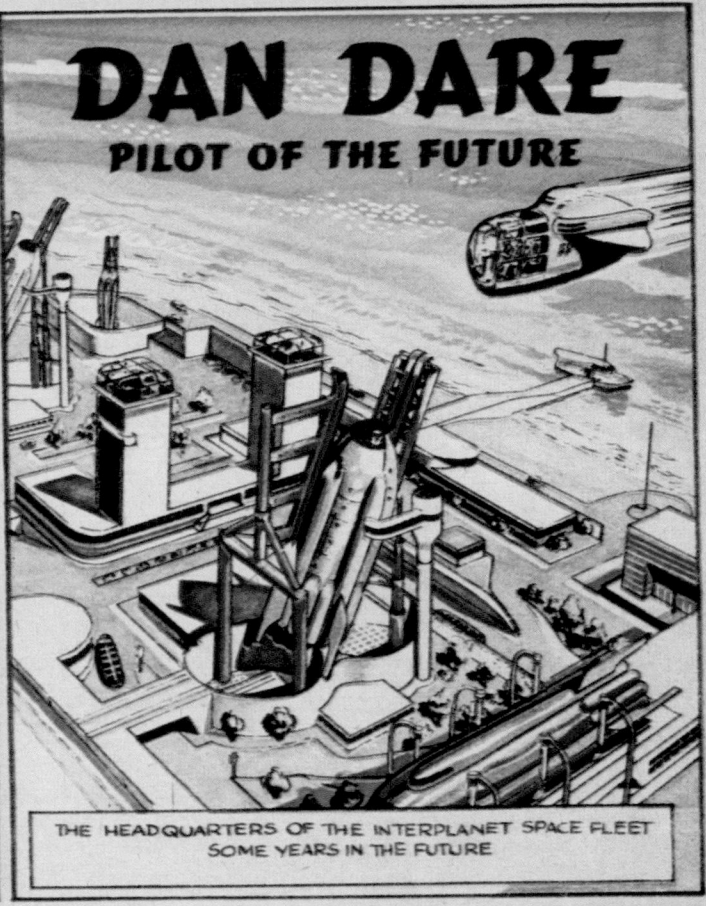

DAN DARE
PILOT OF THE FUTURE

THE HEADQUARTERS OF THE INTERPLANET SPACE FLEET SOME YEARS IN THE FUTURE

IN THE LAUNCHING CONTROL ROOM

"KINGFISHER'S READY TO GO, SIR HUBERT"

RIGHT DAN

HELLO KINGFISHER FLEET CONTROLLER HERE. WE'RE GOING TO GIVE YOU THE GUN NOW. GOODBYE AND THE BEST OF LUCK.

THEY'LL NEED IT!

AUXILIARY ROCKET BOOST

DANGER SPACE SHIP TAKING OFF DO NOT PASS THIS POINT

KINGFISHER

WELL, THERE SHE GOES, SIR — I WONDER IF SHE'LL EVER COME BACK?

SHE'LL NOT BE IN THE DANGER ZONE UNTIL THIS TIME NEXT WEEK, DAN— ALL WE CAN DO UNTIL THEN IS WAIT .....AND KEEP OUR FINGERS CROSSED.

THE EAGLE CLUB

AND EDITOR'S PAGE

14 *April* 1950

The Editor's Office
EAGLE
43 Shoe Lane, London, EC4

EAGLE, as you can see, is an entirely new kind of strip-cartoon paper – and it looks as if there is going to be a very big demand for it. So I suggest you ask your newsagent to order a copy for you each week. At the bottom corner of this page, you will find a form which you can cut out and hand to your newsagent. If you want to make sure of your copy fill it in straight away.

I'm sure you will agree that EAGLE is really good value for 3d. We are using only the best authors and the best artists.

The EAGLE CLUB is going to be one of the most important features in the paper and we've got a pile of ideas for making it a really good Club to join.

It has very definite aims and standards. To begin with, a member has to agree to the Club Rules. Here are the most important of them:- Members of the EAGLE CLUB will:

(*a*) Enjoy life and help others to enjoy life. They will not enjoy themselves at the expense of others.

(*b*) Make the best of themselves. They will develop themselves in body, mind and spirit. They will tackle things for themselves and not wait for others to do things for them.

(*c*) Work with others for the good of all around them.

(*d*) Always lend a hand to those in need of help. They will not shirk difficult or dangerous jobs.

The other main aims are: *First*, to link together those who read and enjoy EAGLE. *Second*, to organise meetings, expeditions, holidays, camps, etc., for members. *Third*, to make special awards to members who achieve anything really worthwhile.

This is what you do to join the Club. Send to the Editor at the above address, (1) your name and address; (2) your age and date of birthday; (3) your school and club (if you belong to one) and (4) a postal order for one shilling. Especially don't forget to tell us your birthday.

In return we will send you: (1) The EAGLE badge, in gilt, like the one drawn here. (2) A Charter of Membership. (3) The Club Book of Rules.

The badge is really first-rate – and all those who join the Club *within the next four weeks, i.e., before 14th May,* will be able to get it as part of the 1/- membership fee. After four weeks, new members will have to send an extra 6d. to pay for the badge. So send in your application right away.

The first 100 members to join will get a special prize. They are to be divided into four groups of 25 according to where they live. Twenty-five living in the South of England will be taken free to Farnborough Air Display on July 8th. Twenty-five living in the Midlands will go to Silverstone Grand Prix Races on May 13th. Twenty-five from the North of England to a Test Match against the West Indians; and twenty-five from Scotland to the Highland Games. The younger members will be invited to bring one parent or guardian free of charge.

The winners will be those 100 members whose applications for membership are opened first, on Wednesday, April 19th.

Then there will be, from time to time, special expeditions for selected members – for example, a trip to the T.T. races in the Isle of Man, to the Edinburgh Festival, to the Monte Carlo Rally, to the 1951 Festival of Britain, and to interesting places abroad. There will be something to suit all tastes and interests.

But joining the Club is only the first step. There's a second special kind of membership.

This second step is to become a MUG. That may sound a rather strange thing to become. This shortly is what it's all about.

There are really only two kinds of people in the world. One kind are the MUGS. The opposite of the MUGS are the Spivs – also called wide boys, smart guys, hooligans, louts or racketeers.

The MUGS are the people who are some use in the world; the people who do something worth-while for others instead of just grabbing for themselves all the time.

Of course the spivs snigger at that. *They* use the word Mug as an insult. " Aren't they mugs? " they say about people who believe in living for something bigger than themselves.

That is why someone who gets called a MUG is likely to be a pretty good chap. For one thing, he's got to have guts because he doesn't mind being called a MUG. He *likes* it. He's the sort who will volunteer for a difficult or risky job and say cheerfully, "Alright, I'll be the Mug." That doesn't mean he is stupid. It means he's got the right ideas and doesn't think it is at all clever to be a spiv-type, like the gentleman we have drawn here.

So when you join the EAGLE CLUB the next step is to become a MUG. We shall then send you a special badge to attach to the ring at the bottom of the EAGLE badge. And there are many special privileges arranged for MUGS which we'll tell you about another time.

But you cannot become a MUG just by writing to us. You have got to do something to earn it and someone – not yourself – has got to tell us about it. If someone who knows you – say, a school teacher, Club leader, and so on – writes to us and suggests your name, we shall go into it carefully and, if you really qualify, award you a badge and special certificate.

One of the privileges that MUGS will have is to be invited to take a hand in running the EAGLE CLUB and EAGLE. At regular intervals, we shall be calling an editorial conference in London, to which we shall invite selected Mugs. They will be able to meet the Editor and his artists and writers and discuss the whole policy of the paper.

Of course, there are thousands of Mugs already – the great Mugs of history. People like Scott of the Antarctic, who gave his life to discover new lands; or Michael Faraday – people said he was talking nonsense when he said that electricity could be used to serve man; or the Curies – people said they were wasting their time when they were working to isolate radium.

Here, for example, is a picture of one famous Mug:— J. L. Baird.

People laughed at him when he started to suggest that there could be such a thing as television. They wanted him to give up trying – but fortunately for us he didn't. .

Perhaps *your* picture may appear here one day. Each month we shall pick the MUG OF THE MONTH and publish his or her photograph. And at the end of the year, there'll be a special ' do ' laid on for the MUGS OF THE YEAR.

Don't forget to write and tell us what you think of EAGLE.

Yours sincerely
THE EDITOR.

CHICKO by thelwell

MUG OF THE MONTH

JOHN CHOWN

At the age of 16, as he went home from looking at the Christmas Tree in Trafalgar Square, at 9 o'clock on a dark windy night, a woman rushed out of a house in Paddington waving her slippers in her hand and shouting "Stop Thief!" Immediately ahead of him, in Craven Hill Gardens John Chown saw the figures of two men making off. He gave chase, caught up with the slower of the two men and tackled him. In a flash the man turned on him – with a knife. John Chown was stabbed in the chest and back. Both men made their escape, but John Chown was later able to give the police their description, and they were caught and tried at the Old Bailey. One got 8 years penal servitude, and the other 2 years imprisonment.

John Chown was awarded the British Empire Medal. As a result of his injuries he was in hospital for several days. He is still at school, a Boy Scout and Troup Leader; his ambition is to go into chemical research. The Scouts awarded him the Silver Cross. He is studying for the Higher Certificate, after which he is expecting to do his National Service.

MUG OF THE MONTH

As the title suggests, the Mug of the Month was a special Mug selected above all others for extra honour. Readers and their family and friends were invited to nominate young chaps. The nominee had to have done something special to deserve the award but that which made it special was really in the eye of the nominator and may not necessarily seem that outstanding to the cynical eyes of today. It may be that a young boy had saved a friend from drowning in the most heroic of circumstances. While at the other end of the spectrum it could be something as simple as always helping out at home, although this would generally require an added degree of urgency due to some family crisis happening as a backdrop. Whatever the reason for each month's award it was the highest honour available to a reader of *Eagle* and was much prized.

EAGLE CLUB

AND EDITOR'S PAGE

2 June 1950

The Editor's Office
EAGLE
43 Shoe Lane, London, EC4

WE have had a great many letters from parents, teachers, club leaders, etc., suggesting the name of a boy or girl who they think qualifies to become a MUG. We should like to thank them for their letters and to say that we shall be replying to each one in due course. The letters make very interesting reading and we have been greatly impressed to learn of all the fine actions that have been done – or are being done.

We are very tempted to elect them all MUGS straight away – but we can't do that, for several reasons. In the first place, we want to keep a very high standard for the MUGS Badge. If it is given too easily, it won't be the really valuable award we want it to be.

Secondly, every case suggested to us, which we think is at all likely to deserve a MUG's Badge, has to be personally investigated, to make sure there is no mistake.

And thirdly, a good many people haven't yet got quite clear what a MUG really is. We certainly take off our hat to almost all those whose actions have been reported to us – but many of them are not really actions which make a MUG.

Remember the test by which you can tell a MUG. He does something of such a kind that the other sort of person – the spiv – could, if he knew about it, jeer at him and say "You are a mug! Fancy wasting your time doing a thing like *that!*"

That is to say, it is something you wouldn't do if you thought only of yourself and what *you* would get out of it. It is not something which, if you had any sense, you would do in any case. For example, if you find your own house on fire and go for the fire-brigade, or if you find a burglar getting in through your kitchen window and try to stop him, that is *not* being a MUG. Of course, anyone would do that – because it's your own house. But if you spend a lot of time and trouble (and perhaps take a big risk) in helping *someone else* out of a jam – that is being a MUG. Because you needn't have done that – it doesn't help *you*.

But don't get us wrong – when we say you have to do something special we do *not* mean only acts of heroism and bravery – or acts which call for great physical strength. We have heard of a boy who said, "I can never become a MUG. I've done nothing special." By which he meant he had never saved anyone from a burning house or anything like that. But he had in fact done something to deserve the award. He had quietly helped someone out of a difficulty at great loss to himself. You don't necessarily have to do something spectacular and sensational and get your name in all the papers. Probably many people will be surprised when they hear they have been awarded a MUG's Badge!

So you don't need to go out of your way to find something very heroic to do. One boy we know of thought that the only way to become a MUG was by saving someone from drowning! So every evening he has been rushing down to the river near where he lives in the hope of finding someone who has fallen in – so that he can pull him out! That's not the idea at all. We shall have members pushing each other in rivers all over the place before long.

So, if you haven't yet heard anything from us about whether or not you are elected a MUG, that doesn't mean you won't hear sometime.

And now here is another famous MUG OF HISTORY – Marconi. He didn't (so far as we know) save anyone from drowning by pulling them out of the sea or the river. But he has certainly saved a great many people's lives by his discoveries and inventions. People said he was crazy to think that messages could be sent to the other side of the world by "wireless". They kept trying to get him to stop wasting his time, as they thought. But he decided to be a Mug – and kept on with his efforts until he succeeded – in giving us radio.

Yours sincerely,
THE EDITOR

MUGS OF THE MONTH *on their ski-ing holiday. They were guests of* EAGLE *Club at Sestrieres, Italy*

Exciting New Feature

EAGLE APPOINTS ITS OWN "SPECIAL INVESTIGATOR"

MOST of us can think of a dozen or so really thrilling and tough adventures we should like to have – if we got the chance. To ride with the Canadian Mounties, to do a parachute jump, to escape from a submarine, to walk on the bottom of the sea – which of us wouldn't like to experience things like that?

Because most of us don't get the opportunity, we have appointed an "EAGLE Special Investigator" who will do all these things – and many more – for us, and tell EAGLE readers all about it. He will undertake any daring or unusual adventure that we suggest to him.

He is Macdonald Hastings, War Correspondent, thriller writer, radio personality and sportsman. Mr. Hastings has crowded his life with exciting adventures. Fathers know him as the editor of the *Strand Magazine*; the Shooting Correspondent of *Country Life*, and War Correspondent of *Picture Post*.

As War Correspondent, he saw action in all three fighting services. With the R.A.F. he went on bombing raids and made parachute jumps. With the Navy he saw action in Destroyers, Assault Boats, Minesweepers, M.T.B's. With the Army he took part in the Normandy Campaign from the beach landings to the crossing of the Rhine.

As a magazine reporter he has travelled all over the world: in Canada, the United States and throughout Europe. As a sportsman he is a recognised authority on game shooting and country lore. He is a salmon and trout fisherman and expert horseman. He has published several books and written dozens of short stories, and his new thriller – being serialised in October and published in the spring – is called *Cork on the Water*.

His first report to EAGLE readers – *Journey into an Undiscovered World* – will appear next week. Don't miss it.

THE NEW GAS TURBINE-ELECTRIC LOCOM

THE CUTAWAYS

The cutaway quickly became one of the first pages that young boys, and their dads, turned to when *Eagle* hit the mat. Detailed drawings in vibrant colours exposed the inner workings of anything the imagination could desire. Trains, planes, boats and automobiles were staples but there really was no limit to what could be opened up to the cutaway's glare. The subjects chosen covered processes from oil production to ice-cream making, buildings such as the 1951 dome at the Festival of Britain, and vast projects including the London Underground and the imagined 'Avenue of the Future'. Several artists, or draughtsmen, really, were used but the most well known is L. Ashwell Wood. Whilst saying he is the most well known, very little is actually known about him. A quick search on the internet merely brings up references to work on *Eagle* and other comics of the time. One *Eagle*

EAGLE 14 April 1950

IVE

A new-comer to British Railways that will run on the Western Region Section
Length 70 ft. Weight 117 tons.

KEY TO CYCLE OF OPERATIONS

1. Air entry from grill at side of locomotive. 2. Turbine air compressor. 3. Compressed air pipe to pre-heater. 4. Compressed air passes through pipes of pre-heater which are heated by exhaust gases. 5. Oil fuel spray nozzle. 6. Air and fuel are mixed and fired in combustion chamber. 7. Igniter for starting up. 8. Flame tube. 9. Gas turbine, driven by expanding hot gases, drives the air compressor and generator through main shaft. 10. Hot exhaust gases passing upwards between tubes of pre-heater. 11. Exhaust gases to atmosphere. A. Reduction gears driving generator. B. Generator which produces electric power for driving the motors. C. Electric cables to motors. D.E.F.G. Electric motors and reduction gears driving the four main axles. H.H. Driver's control car each end.

18000

reader's father was lucky enough to meet Mr Wood. In a letter to the comic he explains that his father, a coalman, was delivering to an old lady and carried the coal into the front room. Who should he find on entering but none other than L. Ashwell Wood at his easel preparing another wonder of the cutaway world.

Harris Tweed, EXTRA SPECIAL AGENT

Harris Tweed

Harris Tweed was the product of John Ryan's vivid imagination. He is best remembered now as the creator of Captain Pugwash, the character that went on to feature in the popular show of the same name for children on the BBC. In fact 'Pugwash' first saw the light of day in the very first issue of *Eagle*, but his voyage on the high seas only lasted until Issue 19. The general consensus is that Marcus Morris felt it was aimed at too young an audience, but, not wanting to lose Ryan's input totally, he was encouraged to find another outlet for his bold style and slightly off-beat sense of humour. Three weeks before *Pugwash* walked the plank 'Harris Tweed, Extra Special Agent' appeared.

READERS' LETTERS

(A prize of 5/- is paid for each letter published)

I THINK Fox hunting is a very cruel sport and surely if people must hunt foxes they could shoot them instead of letting the dogs tear them to pieces. – Janice Allen, 9 Trurorean Terrace, Truro, Cornwall.

I AGREE with the reader who mentioned the way people treat coloured folk and cannot understand why, after admiring a coloured sportsman on the field, white people should refuse them a meal in a restaurant. We are told in the Bible all men are our brothers. – Peter Berridge (11), 39 Elmcroft Ave., Edmonton, London N.9.

WHEN I was in Egypt last year I visited a Museum; inside were Egyptian Mummies in cases and very old ornaments. In one case was some ancient jewellery – over a thousand years old – and in another, old carved knives and forks. – Moya Spencer (9), "Green Shutters", Barbrook, Nr. Lynton, Devon.

OUR SCOUT troop recently adopted a 13-year-old leper scout; we collected £5, the cost of a year's treatment and shall receive reports of his progress every six months. – Keith Wright, 17 Wynchcombe Ave., Penn.

I HAVE never walked except on crutches since I was born. I have a private teacher who comes to teach me every day. I have lots of hobbies. A few weeks ago in EAGLE in Readers' Letters someone asked if anyone had as many pen friends as she had. Well I have 189 pen friends all over England and other countries. – Anne Strettle, Fulwood, Preston.

EAGLE CLUB
AND EDITOR'S PAGE

The Editor's Office
EAGLE
43 Shoe Lane, London, EC4

WE have had a great many requests from readers that we should start a Pen Pals Group. We have now decided to do this and we invite any of you who would like to make full use of it. Anyone who is interested in having a pen pal should write to 'Pen Pals', 4 New Street Square, London, E.C.4, giving his full name, address and age and a note about the kind of hobbies and pastimes that he is interested in and the type of people to whom he wishes to write. Please put this information on a sheet of paper and then moisten one corner of a 2½d. stamp and attach it to the paper. Enclose also an envelope addressed to yourself (unstamped). It is important that you should not forget the 2½d. stamp because we cannot possibly run the pen pals group if we have to provide stamps for everybody.

HERE are the answers to the competitions in Issue 8.

1. In the *Shapes* competition, the sender of the first correct solution opened was Patricia Tomlinson, Wishanger, Willingdon, Sussex.

2. *Cartoons Wanted.* We had a big entry to choose from in this competition and some of the drawings sent were most entertaining and skilfully drawn. The winning cartoon for the title 'A Black Look' was submitted by D. Agg, 4 Radford Road, Lewes, Sussex, and we are reproducing his entry.

We are awarding a second prize to Frank Coulson, 22a Wellesley Road, East Croydon. The winning entry for 'A Brown Jumper' was Catherine Worth, 98 Polefield Hall Road, Prestwich, whose entry was delightfully simple and most amusing.

3. *The Noises They Make:* the first correct solution opened was submitted by Ian Barclay, 13 Maryfield Crescent, Leslie, Fife, Scotland, and the answers were:– Warble; Drone; Chirp; Squeak; Quaver; Pip; Chant; Cry; Yelp; Boom.

4. *To Make You Think:* Unfortunately there was a misprint in this competition which made the problem impossible to solve in round figures. The most ingenious attempt at a satisfactory solution, however, was made by John Woodruff, Police Station, Poulton-le-Fylde, Lancashire, and we are sending the prize to him. The problem should have read '3 sons were left £34 in their father's will.' Borrowing £2 and adding this to the £34 equals £36; of this, one half, to the eldest son, amounts to £18; one-third, to the second son, amounts to £12; and one-ninth, to the third son, amounts to £4 – total £34. The executor was then able to return the £2 borrowed.

5. *Do You Know:* The first correct solution opened was submitted by Elizabeth Watson, 30 Kirtleton Avenue, Weymouth, Dorset, and the answers were: Duck Billed Platypus; Guinea Pig; Penguin; Bat; Stickleback; Whale.

6. *Nine 'Ands' In A Row:* No competitor submitted the correct entry for this competition.

You remember that in Issue 5 we had a Test Selection Competition. No one submitted a list of the England team corresponding to the one selected officially. Even by eliminating Compton and regarding Bedser as twelfth man, no one got nearer than eight correct points. We have, therefore, decided not to award a prize for this competition. The prize money will be used to buy special prizes for another cricket competition which we shall be announcing shortly.

Yours sincerely,

THE EDITOR

SPORTING PERSONALITIES

J.A. PALMER-TOMKINSON

HERE ARE SOME OF HIS MAJOR WINS:
1936. The International Academic Ski-ing Championship.
1937. The Great Slilom in Switzerland.
1938. The Tempo Trophy.
1939. (With his sister) The British Ski Championship at Wengen.
1947. The Anglo-Swiss University Downhill Race.
1948. The Duke of Kent's Cup.
1950. The Davos Parsenon – in 15·45 seconds – a great performance for a racer of thirty-four.

AS YOU CAN SEE, HIS STYLE IS BOTH VIGOROUS AND GRACEFUL, AND HE IS A MASTER OF DIFFICULT TURNS. SUCH PERFECTION IN THIS SPORT CAN BE ACHIEVED ONLY BY RIGOROUS SELF-DISCIPLINE AND UNREMITTING PRACTICE.

PALMER-TOMKINSON, A BASINGSTOKE FARMER, IS A WORTHY CAPTAIN OF THE BRITISH SKI-TEAM, WITH A WONDERFUL LIST OF INDIVIDUAL SUCCESSES TO HIS CREDIT.
IN 1948, AT WENGEN WERE, HE RAN HIS SKI-STICK POINT INTO HIS THIGH DURING A PRACTICE RUN, AND HAD TO BE TAKEN TO HOSPITAL ON AN IMPROVISED AMBULANCE.

(Above) Sometimes, the *Eagle* did get it wrong. (Left) James competed as a skier at the Winter Olympics either side of the Second World War. His son Charles Anthony Palmer-Tomkinson competed as a skier in the Winter Games of 1964. Charles's daughter Tara Palmer-Tomkinson was runner-up in the 2002 series of *I'm a Celebrity Get Me Out of Here*; no skiing was involved.

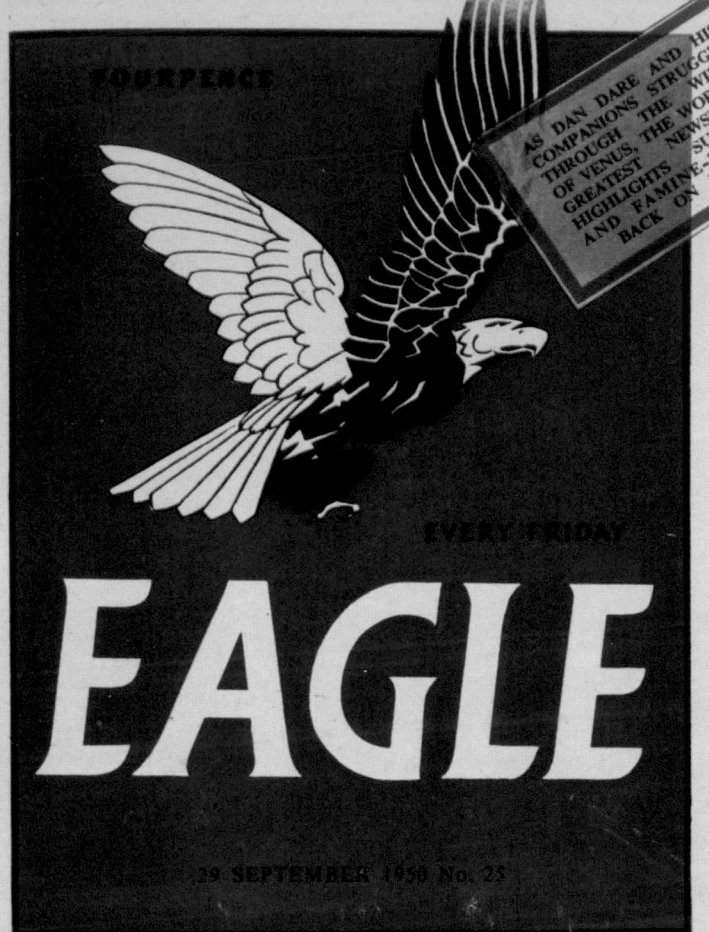

FOURPENCE

EVERY FRIDAY

EAGLE

29 SEPTEMBER 1950 No. 25

AS DAN DARE AND HIS COMPANIONS STRUGGLE THROUGH THE WILDS OF VENUS, THE WORLD'S GREATEST NEWSPAPER HIGHLIGHTS SUSPENSE AND FAMINE-THREAT BACK ON EARTH

DAILY WORLD POST

No. 17,777 · ONE PENNY EUROPE : TEN CENTS PANAMERICA : FOUR ANNAS ASIA : ONE SUT PANAFRICA

PUBLISHED SIMULTANEOUSLY IN LONDON, NEW YORK, SAN FRANCISCO, TOKIO, DELHI, BAKU, ROME, BULAWAYO, SYDNEY AND MARSVILLE

LIST. EDITION

MONDAY 28 SEPTEMBER 1995 · · · · · THE HULTON PAPER

LONDON

VETERAN SPACEMAN IN MISSING EXPEDITION

SIR HUBERT GUEST, *K.C.B., O.U.N.*, 65-year-old controller of the International Space Fleet, who accompanied the Space Expedition to find food on Venus. Sir Hubert, knighted in 1980 for his lifetime of service with the Fleet, was in the first ship to land on Mars in 1965. He has made over a hundred space flights.

STILL NO NEWS FROM VENUS

RADIO SILENCE BLANKETS DARE'S ROCKETS AS "RANGER" RETURNS TO EARTH

Space Station XI, Monday, 3 a.m.

SPACESHIP "Ranger" landed here an hour ago minus the three Rocket Ships which it carried to within 3,000 miles of Venus in the latest attempt to reach the mystery planet and find food to banish the threat of starvation from Earth.

Tired and worried-looking Captain Hunter, of the "Ranger", boarded a Helicar to the United Nations World Government Headquarters at New York. Thirty minutes later the following bulletin was issued from U.N.W.G.:–

COMMENT

DARE'S ROCKET THEORY JUSTIFIED?

There seem to be grounds for cautious optimism in the 'partial success' reported in the Government bulletin. The fact that the Rocket Ships built to Colonel Dare's specification did succeed in penetrating the mysterious Ray-screen which has taken such a terrible toll of previous attempts, is the first piece of good news which has come from the planet.

The sad fact that through a radio blunder this brave and brilliant officer and his equally courageous companions may have lost their lives must not be allowed to diminish the importance of their achievement for mankind.

"The Prime Minister regrets to announce that there is as yet no definite information of the success or otherwise of the Rocket Ship expedition to Venus.

In view of the partial success achieved in getting through the Ray-field, a further expedition will be fitted out with Rocket Ships.

The fate of the members of the present expedition is problematic. The *Ranger* will return to orbit the planet in case any kind of signal is sent out by survivors."

Captain Hunter arriving in New York

TENSION MOUNTS IN FAMINE TROUBLE SPOTS

PEKIN, SUNDAY (*delayed*). Central and Southern China is in an explosive condition tonight according to messages reaching here from Canton, Hong Kong and Shanghai. The Teleview communications system has broken down, presumably owing to deliberate interference and messages are being transmitted by radio. Rioting is reported from many provinces as a result of the complete collapse of the food rationing arrangements. Ration cards have not been honoured for over two weeks in some cities.

SENATOR DEMANDS VITAMINEAT PROBE

World Senator Hartwell of North England has called for a U.N. Congressional enquiry into the activities of Vitamineats Inc., the giant International Company which makes and markets the well known Vitamineat Food Substitute Tablets. Charging the Company with using inferior ingredients and making excessive profits, the Senator also hinted that the sabotage of food supply arrangements may be charged against the combine.

Mr. Lucius K. Kettlewell, Chairman and Managing Director of the Company, commented last night, "the Senator had better be careful."

Read

EAGLE

(Incorporating 'Lilliput')

EVERY FRIDAY 4d.

MRS. DIGBY SAYS "HE'S ALIVE ALL RIGHT"

Mrs. Digby and family at their Wigan home

OTHER NEWS

MASS CHANNEL SWIM BY EGYPTIANS

An entire company of the Egyptian Army entered the water at Cap Gris Nez yesterday evening to swim the Channel in formation.

SUCCESS IN EAST AFRICA— PEANUT ARRIVES IN LONDON

There was a touching ceremony at the Strachey Memorial in London yesterday when a whole unblemished peanut was handed to the Minister of Food by a delegation representing equally the native tribes in the groundnut area and the survivors of the Strachey scheme.

WIGAN, Monday

Interviewed in her Westbank St. home this afternoon, Mrs. Digby, wife of the only "Other Rank" member of the expedition, seemed very confident of her husband's safety. "He'll be all right," she said, when our reporter spoke to her in the parlour of this typically Lancashire home. "Albert's been in plenty of tight spots before with Colonel Dare."

DAN DARE
PILOT OF THE FUTURE

Although 'Dan Dare' is set in the future, the values of the characters are very much of the time in which it is was created. Of course, the main aim of the strip was to excite and intrigue the readers, but this did not mean that they could not be educated along the way. Here we see Sondar, not long after he has first met Dan, showing off his knowledge of Earth customs, and maybe even informing a few readers of something they never previously understood.

You can take a space traveller a gazillion miles from home but he never forgets the simple joy of a home cooked Sunday roast. At a time when very few, if any, of the readers were able to get their hands on roast pheasant, the food fantasies of the crew were probably mirrored in the stomachs of the readers.

AMAZ
FLYING AN

The Junction at Camden Town, Londo
crossover junctions. Trains pass under
allowing traffic a

L. ASHWELL WOOD

THE TUBE

EAGLE 13 *October* 1950

NDERGROUND
SSOVER JUNCTIONS

Underground railway lines meet is a wonderful example of flying and
out conflicting tracks in either direction in an ingenious layout, thus
a maximum frequency of 110 trains an hour.

KEY TO NUMBERS

1. Camden High Street
2. Drains and street mains
3. Camden Town Station
4. Booking hall
5. Escalator
6. Motors driving escalator steps
7. Subways to platforms
8. Northbound platform to Highgate
9. Southbound platform from Highgate to Moorgate or Charing Cross
10. Southbound platform from Edgware to Moorgate or Charing Cross
11. Northbound platform to Edgware
12. Flyover tunnel
13 and 14. Crossover tunnels
15. Subway between tunnels
16. Burrowing tunnels
17 and 18. Flying junctions
19. Southbound tunnel to Moorgate
20. Northbound tunnel from Moorgate
21. Southbound tunnel to Charing Cross
22. Northbound tunnel from Charing Cross

JUNCTION

EAGLE WISHES YOU A MERRY CHRISTMAS

FOURPENCE

EVERY FRIDAY

EAGLE

22 DECEMBER 1950 No. 37

DAN DARE
PILOT OF THE FUTURE

THE RANGER, MOTHER SHIP OF THE THREE ROCKETS, STILL CIRCLES VENUS, WAITING IN VAIN FOR SIGNALS FROM DAN AND HIS FRIENDS.

SEND A SIGNAL — "CAPT. HUNTER, O.C. "RANGER" TO EARTH SPACE H.Q. — NO SIGHT OR SOUND FROM DARE EXPEDITION — RATIONS ALMOST EXPENDED—TWO IMPULSE MOTORS U/S. CAN ONLY STAY HERE ONE MORE EARTH DAY.- ORDERS PLEASE."

POOR OLD DAN — IT'S HOPELESS — WHAT A WRETCHED BUSINESS.

FINE PLACE TO SPEND XMAS EVE — 150 MILLION MILES FROM HOME.

WON'T BE MUCH USE HANGING OUT OUR STOCKINGS UP HERE.

AND ON EARTH —

RANGER SENDS XMAS GREETINGS, SIR. STILL NO SIGN AND SHE'S OUT OF RATIONS

I'M AFRAID IT'S USELESS TO CONTINUE THE WATCH ANY LONGER TELL HER TO RETURN TO BASE.

... SPACE-FLEET H.Q. REGRETS TO ANNOUNCE THAT THERE CAN NOW BE NO HOPE FOR THE CREWS OF THE THREE ROCKET-SHIPS THAT RECENTLY ATTEMPTED A LANDING ON VENUS ... ... THE PRICE OF TURKEYS THIS YEAR REACHED A NEW ALL-TIME HIGH RECORD.

IT'LL SEEM QUIET THIS CHRISTMAS WITHOUT OUR ALBERT ON LEAVE, ANASTASIA.

HM, HE'LL BE ENJOYING HIMSELF, I'LL BE BOUND.

... AND AT THIS TIME LET US REMEMBER OUR ABSENT MESS-MATES. THE CONTROLLER, DAN, HANK AND PIERRE GOOD LUCK TO THEM — WHEREVER THEY MAY BE.

HEAR, HEAR.

EAGLE CLUB NEWS

A Grand Christmas Present

A great many of you may be wondering what to give as Christmas presents to your brothers, sisters, cousins, friends.

We have got a suggestion for something which would make a really fine Christmas present, and it is one that lasts all the year round. Why not give your friends EAGLE or GIRL every week? We will see it is posted regularly to whatever address you give us, and we will let you have a special Christmas card for you to send off personally to your friends, letting them know that they will be receiving the paper every week during 1952. We think you can be sure that any one would be very glad to get a present like this.

All you have to do is to send a cheque or postal order made out to "Hulton Press Ltd." for 26/- if you want EAGLE or GIRL to be sent every week for one year: 13/- if you only want it to last for 6 months, and 6/6d if you want it to last for 3 months.

Send your cheque or postal order to The Editor, EAGLE, 43 Shoe Lane, London E.C.4, giving your name, and address, and the name and address of the person to whom you wish the paper sent.

Eagle Carol Service
(See Editor's Letter)

Please send me .... admission tickets for the EAGLE Carol Service *(state number)* to be held at 3.30 p.m. on Saturday, 22nd December in Central London. I enclose stamped addressed envelope.

Your Name ....

Address ....

Readers' Letters
(A prize of 5/- is given for each letter published)

THANK YOU for the lovely service in St Paul's Cathedral on Saturday, December 22nd. I was very pleased to see so many people there and I am sure they enjoyed it as much as I did. I was also pleased to find so many of my favourite carols included. I thought the Christmas trees were very pretty outside the Cathedral and inside. – Judith Nuttall, 7 Red Cottages, Broadwater, Stevenage, Herts.

* * *

NOT VERY long ago I learned to drive a tractor. I can now drive it perfectly along the road and I can change all the gears for going round corners and through gates. – Peter Ewing (11), 3 New Houses, Papigoe, By Wick, Caithness.

EAGLE 25 *January* 1952

EAGLE CLUB NEWS
SALVO OF FUN AT STREATHAM

Balloon blowing takes some doing after such a big tea!

"Stick 'em up!" says cowboy Charles Chilton.

The Editor and the Mayor of Streatham stand up to a bit of friendly heckling.

The Mayor, with the Mayoress looking on, gets down to a friendly chat.

From the Editor

EAGLE, 4 New St Square, London EC4

21 December, 1951

ON this, your second Christmas as EAGLE readers, my staff and I want to send you our warmest greetings for a very Merry Christmas. May all of you enjoy a very happy time and have the good fortune to receive the Christmas present you most want.

Amidst all our Christmas fun and exchange of presents, I want you to remember especially the real spirit of Christmas, which we sometimes tend to forget. Christmas Day is the birthday of Jesus Christ, and we give each other presents in remembrance of the gifts brought to Him by the Wise Men from the East. But we have rather wandered away from the original idea of present-giving at Christmas time. Long ago, it was the poor and needy who were given presents and this is something, amid our exchange of gifts with our friends, which we should remember. I asked you a few weeks ago to try to spare a toy in nice condition for the children in your nearest hospital or orphanage. If you have done this, then you are helping to rekindle the true Spirit of Christmas and soon you will find others following your good example.

ON our back page, this week and next, we try to present to you the Christmas story as it might have appeared to someone living on the spot at the time. Among the shepherds on the hill side at Bethlehem, there was almost certain to have been a boy helping his father to tend the sheep and run errands. Our back page tells how the tremendous events of the first Christmas appeared to this boy, and how the birth of the baby Jesus affected his life and that of his family.

OUR Carol Service takes place in St Paul's Cathedral tomorrow, Saturday afternoon. **Will you please note that we have had to change the time of the Service from 3.30 to 2.30 p.m. Tell as many of your friends as possible about this change.** St Paul's, known and loved throughout the British Empire, is yours for that afternoon, and it is up to you, representing the youth of Britain, to fill it to overflowing. I want to hear *your* Christmas praises ring round the Cathedral in no uncertain manner. So come, all of you who can. If you haven't got an admission ticket, never mind – we can fit you in somehow. Your parents can come with you if they want to.

I WOULD like to thank you all for the good wishes and Christmas Cards which have already reached my staff and me. It is our wish that through these pages of EAGLE we shall continue to give you as much happiness as we possibly can.

Yours sincerely,

Marcus Morris

READERS' LETTERS
(A prize of 5/- is paid for each letter published)

READERS who go to church often will notice that every week the people and the Vicar say or sing the same prayers. Do you think that God gets tired of the same prayers every week? – Neil Upton, 52 Tennis Court Drive, Humberstone, Leicester.
[*No, I'm sure He doesn't. I think He would prefer a lot more people to do it. It's because the words are the same and well-known, that we can all join together in the prayers. – Ed.*]

ALL MALTESE readers are eagerly following "The Great Adventurer" as the story is now nearing the time when Paul will be shipwrecked on the rocks of Malta. This event is written in letters of gold in the history of Malta – we are all very proud of it. – Joe Camilleri, 101 Vinc. Bugeja Street, Hamrum, Malta G.C.
[*This incident is shown in this week's issue. – Ed.*]

MOST EAGLERS will know what a Dunce is, but I wonder how many will know what a Dunce was originally. The first Dunces were followers of Duns Scotus, a churchman opposed to the Renaissance. – M. Gough, Vicarage Lane, Swanmore, Southampton.

I AM a Chinese boy studying in an English School, and your magazine is very popular in my class. Everybody takes great interest in reading it and I like to read it also, for it deals with so many useful things. – Lew Chin Woon, 774 North Bridge Road, Singapore 7.

DO EAGLERS know that a clerk was once buried in the Bank of England? This man was an eight-foot giant whose name was Jenkins – he wanted to be buried there so that his body could not be taken by body-snatchers and sold, as a predecessor had been. – Pamela Thompson (15), 30 Ronald Drive, Denton Burn, Newcastle-on-Tyne 5.

I HAVE a set of jugs which belonged to my great, great, great, great auntie – she had them in 1786. – Maldwyn Rowland, 31 Brynhyford Terrace, Waunllwyd, Ebbw Vale, Mon.

Wherever Dan and the crew happened to be at Christmas, and whatever year it was, they always remembered to send a festive greeting back-in-time to the Fifties. The front covers of the late December issues were always decorated in some way to celebrate the time of year, and the crew always took time out from saving the universe to think of home.

EAGLE-BRITAIN'S NATIONAL STRIP CARTOON WEEKLY

The front cover of Issue 48 of Volume 1 (9 March 1951) highlights the sheer exuberance of the comic's artwork to a fantastic degree. It also, maybe, refers to the fighting that was raging in the East in 1951. The Korean War was close to reaching its first anniversary and was turning out to be the biggest global conflict since the end of hostilities in 1945. Was the *Eagle* trying to use this cover to convey images and iconography from this conflict?

DAN DARE

PILOT OF THE FUTURE

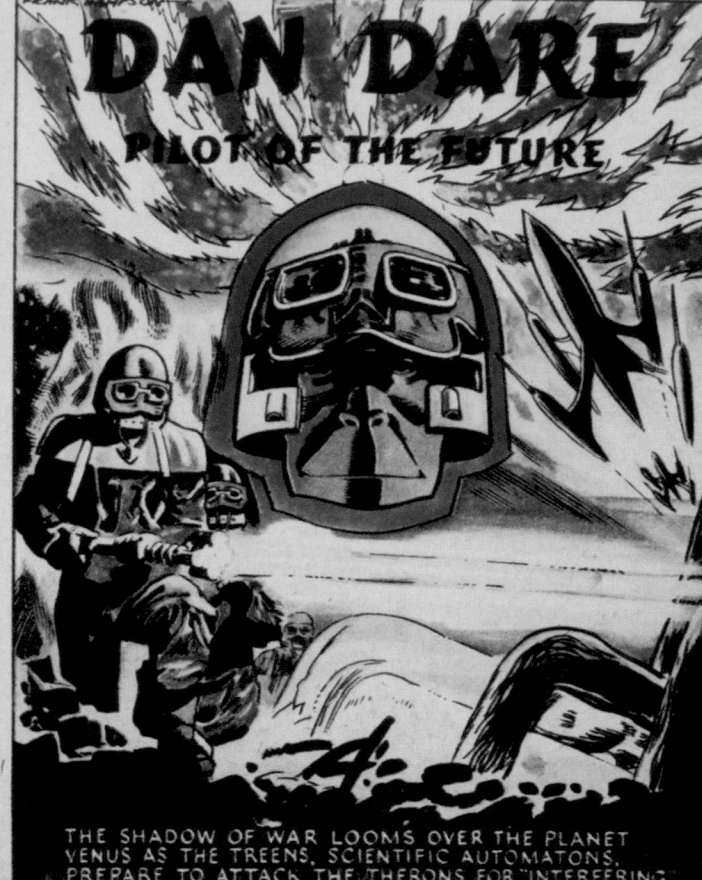

DAN DARE
PILOT OF THE FUTURE

THE SHADOW OF WAR LOOMS OVER THE PLANET VENUS AS THE TREENS, SCIENTIFIC AUTOMATONS, PREPARE TO ATTACK THE THERONS FOR INTERFERING WITH THE TREEN PLAN TO TAKE OVER THE EARTH.

FOR THE FIRST TIME IN CENTURIES THE TREENS SWITCH OFF THEIR RAY BARRIER OVER THE FLAME-BELT WHICH DIVIDES THE PLANET BETWEEN THE TREENS IN THE NORTH AND THE THERONS IN THE SOUTH.

HIGH FLYING TREEN RECONNAISSANCE TELEVIEW PLANES STREAK THROUGH THE STRATOSPHERE TOWARDS THE BORDER.

THROW SWITCH TWO ON NUMBER THREE — DOUBLE BANK CONDENSERS AND LINK RECTIFIERS FOR SECOND POWER STEP-UP. BRING IN MOTORS FOUR & FIVE.

IN MENONTA, THE TREEN CAPITAL WHERE MANY WAR MACHINES ARE BEING SET TO WORK, THE TELEZERO BEAM PROJECTORS BEGIN TO BUILD UP POWER TO STRIKE AT THERON CITIES.

TELEZEROS THREE AND SEVEN WILL REACH FIRST SHORT RANGE OPERATIONAL POWER LEVEL IN ONE TAMIT. WE SHALL THEN BOOST CONTINUALLY UNTIL WE REACH MAXIMUM RANGE. THE REFLECTOR SPACE — CRAFT HAVE BEEN ALERTED TO TAKE OFF AS SOON AS WE RECEIVE THE ORDER.

THE TINY MEKON, RUTHLESS LORD OF THE TREENS, REVIEWS THE PROGRESS OF HIS PLANS.

GOOD — HAS THE MOBILISATION OF THE ATLANTINE SERFS COMMENCED?

YES, O MEKON. MILITARY PARTIES ARE OUT COLLECTING THEM IN THE RESERVATIONS.

THE HELPLESS ATLANTINES — DESCENDANTS OF HUMAN SLAVES CAPTURED CENTURIES AGO, ARE ROUNDED UP TO ACT AS CANNON FODDER FOR THEIR INHUMAN MASTERS.

ADVICE ON YOUR PETS

Keeping Goldfish

By Professor Cameron

FUNGUS LOOKS LIKE STRANDS OF COTTON WOOL.

WATER PLANTS

12 GALLONS OF WATER

YOU CAN KEEP GOLDFISH EITHER OUTSIDE IN A POND, OR INSIDE, IN A SUITABLE AQUARIUM TANK— NOT IN A SMALL GOLDFISH BOWL. THE BEST TANKS ARE RECTANGULAR IN SHAPE BUT THEY NEED TO BE FAIRLY LARGE : THE RULE IS ONE GALLON OF WATER TO EVERY INCH (IN LENGTH) OF FISH. TWO GOLDFISH EACH SIX INCHES LONG NEED TWELVE GALLONS OF WATER. KEEP THE TANK AWAY FROM THE SUN AND HAVE SHADE OVER PART OF TANK.

WATER SNAILS

WIRE NETTING COVERING PROTECTING FISH FROM CATS & BIRDS

CROSS SECTION OF SUNKEN POND

SAND

THE TANK (OR POND) SHOULD BE KEPT CLEAN BY COVERING THE BOTTOM WITH SAND PLANTED WITH PROPER WATER PLANTS. YOUR LOCAL AQUARIST WILL SHOW YOU WHICH TO BUY PUT RAIN WATER IN AND ALLOW THE PLANTS TO GROW AND THE WATER TO GET REALLY CLEAR BEFORE INTRODUCING FISH.

GOLDFISH FOOD

Bread Crumbs

Chopped Earthworms

Prepared Food

Cooked Peas

Chopped Lettuce

Daphnia

FISH IN PONDS NEED LESS THAN THOSE IN TANKS, BUT SHOULD BE GIVEN A LITTLE PREPARED FOOD AND EARTHWORMS FROM TIME TO TIME. THOSE IN TANKS SHOULD BE FED REGULARLY EITHER WITH A COMMERCIAL FOOD OF GOOD QUALITY OR WITH BREADCRUMBS, CHOPPED EARTH WORMS, CHOPPED LETTUCE AND SMALL AMOUNTS OF COOKED PEAS. IF YOU CAN GET SMALL WATER CRUSTACEANS (SUCH AS DAPHNIA) THESE ARE EXCELLENT.

Golden Orfe

Water Snails

Cat Fish

GOLDFISH ARE 'LEATHER' MOUTHED AND HAVE NO TEETH AND DO NOT DAMAGE OTHER FISH. IT IS BEST TO KEEP THEM ON THEIR OWN OR WITH OTHER HARMLESS FISH SUCH AS THE GOLDEN ORFE OR CATFISH. DO NOT ON ANY ACCOUNT ALLOW STICKLEBACKS OR NEWTS IN THE SAME POND OR TANK. WATER SNAILS ARE USEFUL SINCE THEY ACT AS SCAVENGERS. *John Dyke*

GOLDFISH ARE NOW AVAILABLE AGAIN, BUT BE CAREFUL WHEN YOU BUY ONE TO SEE THAT IT LOOKS HEALTHY. DO NOT BUY ONE WITH DROOPING FINS OR DULL EYES OR WITH FUNGUS (WHICH LOOKS LIKE COTTON WOOL) ON ITS BODY. READ GOOD BOOKS ABOUT THE CARE OF FISH.

A LOCOMOTIVE DEPOT AT WORK

THE RAIL

EAGLE 16 *March* 1951

...ideal layout for a Motive Power Depot, as it is correctly called, of the ...road" type, that is, the tracks run parallel through the engine shed thus ...less space than the roundhouse type where the tracks radiate from a central

...heds the locomotive receives every attention necessary to keeping it in ...der. The numbered stages show the series of operations from the time the ...backs in from its last journey until it is ready again for the next. The types ...ives shown are the new standard ones of British Railways in three colour

KEY TO SEQUENCE OF OPERATIONS

(1) Acceptance road from main line. Fireman 'phones "On shed". (2) At the coaling tower. (3) Re-filling tender with water. (4) At the ash dropping pits. The ashes are taken in a hopper and hoisted to a discharge tower. (5) On the vacuum-operated turntable. (6) Engine now backs to inspection pits. (7) Enter shed – fitters take over. (8) Steam hydrants are used for smoke box cleaning and boiler washing. (9) Cleaning, lighting up and steam raising. (10) Exit shed, new crew take over and check water, coal, oil, etc., and vacuum brakes. (11) Fireman 'phones "Off shed" and engine is ready to enter main line to terminus. (12) Main line express out of terminus.

KEY TO OTHER NUMBERS

(13) Drivers' notice board for instructions. (14) Loco. superintendent's office. (15) Canteen and rest room. (16) Boiler house. (17) Empty trucks from coaling tower. (18) Full trucks for coaling tower move down slope by gravity and are hoisted to top of tower and emptied into a huge bunker. (19) Ash hopper discharge tower. (20) Ash trucks. (21) Running repair shops. Engine having wheels dropped. (22) Floodlights for night operations. (23) Staff allotments.

DEPOT

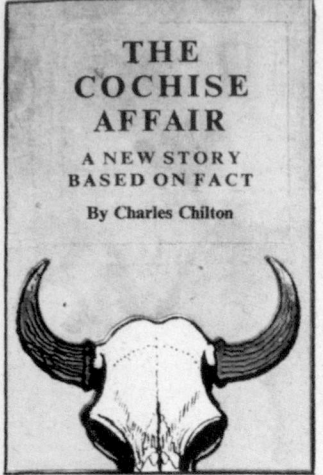

THE COCHISE AFFAIR

A NEW STORY BASED ON FACT

By Charles Chilton

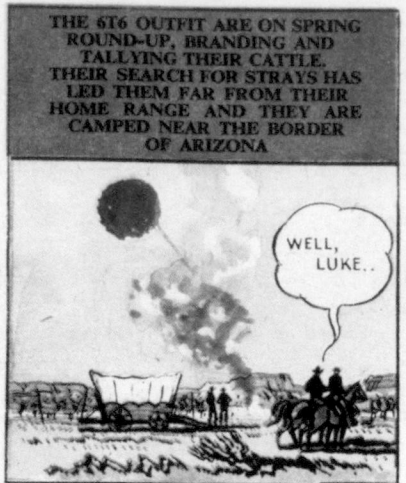

THE 6T6 OUTFIT ARE ON SPRING ROUND-UP, BRANDING AND TALLYING THEIR CATTLE. THEIR SEARCH FOR STRAYS HAS LED THEM FAR FROM THEIR HOME RANGE AND THEY ARE CAMPED NEAR THE BORDER OF ARIZONA

WELL, LUKE..

..JUST THAT MAVERICK TO DO AND THAT'S THE LOT.

YES, JEFF. HE'LL BE NEXT.

I'LL HEAD HIM OFF. YOU ROPE HIM.

YOU BET. GET UP THERE, BETSY. IT'S THAT CRITTER WITH THE WHITE FACE WE'RE AFTER.

KEEP AT HIM, RUSTLER.

GOT YOU!

CURIOUS CREATURES

BEETLES

THE HARLEQUIN BEETLE LIVES IN THE TROPICAL FORESTS OF ASIA AND SOUTH AMERICA. HE IS ABOUT ONE FOOT LONG FROM THE TIPS OF HIS HIND LEGS TO THOSE OF HIS ENORMOUS FRONT LEGS. THESE PROBABLY SERVE FOR TREECLIMBING. THE HARLEQUIN BEETLE IS A STRICT VEGETARIAN. HIS LARVAE LIVES ON THE WOOD OF TREES. THE BEETLE IS A QUIET, HARMLESS MEMBER OF THE LONGICORN FAMILY.

HARLEQUIN BEETLE (ACTUAL SIZE)

EAST AFRICAN TIGER BEETLE. (ACTUAL SIZE)

HERE IS ANOTHER MEMBER OF ABOUT 200,000 KNOWN SPECIES OF BEETLES, A CLOSE RELATIVE OF OUR TIGER BEETLE BUT VERY MUCH LARGER. ALL TIGER BEETLES ARE FIERCE ROBBERS AND FEED ON OTHER INSECTS. CATERPILLARS, ETC. THE ONE IN THE PICTURE IS ATTACKING A LONGHORNED GRASSHOPPER WHO IN HIS TURN LIVES ON SMALLER CREATURES.

LIKE ALL BEETLES, THE HARLEQUIN BEETLE HAS TWO PAIRS OF WINGS. THE FRONT ONES ARE HORNY CASES AND PROTECT THE BODY. THE BACK ARE FLIGHT WINGS. HARLEQUINS EYES FORM 'HORSESHOES' ROUND THE ANTENNAE AND CONSIST OF MANY 'COMPOUND LENSES' – ACTUALLY A COMBINATION OF MANY SINGLE EYES.

BACK WING

HORSESHOE SHAPED EYE.

FRONT WING

PART OF EYE (VERY MUCH ENLARGED)

BURYING BEETLE (ACTUAL SIZE)

YOU MAY HAVE SEEN THESE BEETLES (SPECIES NECROPHORUS) IN THIS COUNTRY. THEY DO USEFUL 'CLEANING UP' WORK BY BURYING SMALL DEAD BIRDS AND ANIMALS. THEY SCOOP THE EARTH FROM UNDER THE BODY UNTIL IT SINKS BY ITS OWN WEIGHT. THE BEETLES THEN REAR THEIR LARVAE IN THE REMAINS.

Charles Chilton created *Riders of the Range* for BBC radio. Set in the Wild West, it quickly built a big following in living rooms up and down the country. So it was a neat idea of *Eagle* to tap into an established market. To all intents and purposes Jeff Arnold was Dan Dare on horseback and it is interesting to see how much they resemble each other in both look and character.

Riders of the Range

Jiu-Jitsu for self-defence by MAZURE

Nº 8. NOSE-GRIP.

TO APPLY THE NOSE-GRIP, PLACE YOUR FLAT HAND ON OPPONENT'S FACE, WITH YOUR THUMB ON HIS UPPER LIP, AGAINST HIS NOSE, AND YOUR FINGERS ON HIS FOREHEAD.

DON'T JUST PUSH — YOUR THUMB SHOULD PRESS UPWARDS AGAINST OPPONENT'S NOSE, AND YOUR FINGERS SHOULD PUSH HIS HEAD DOWN AND AWAY.

... AND PUSH OUTWARDS AND DOWNWARDS.

Jiu Jitsu

The *Eagle* was keen to keep the youth of Britain active, healthy and fit for anything. Under the general banner of 'instructional sport' items came out on all aspects of physical activity. These covered vital skills such as the best fielding positions in cricket, how to improve your dribbling in football, and how to overcome an opponent by gripping his nose. On land and in the water the *Eagle* made sure that boys up and down the country would be at the forefront of all the latest techniques. This even extended to practising your swimming on dry land, in fact, on a table. Who needs water?

Practise your SWIMMING and DIVING with an Olympic Coach.

SWIMMING and DIVING

Swimming is a fine sport. It is useful and enjoyable, and it has great health value. The better you can swim the more fun you can have in the water, so why not learn to swim really well? Here is your opportunity. In this series we invite you to follow the activities of a crack junior team as they train for championship events in swimming and diving. Advice by the coach, and demonstrations by leading members of the team, will help you to develop speed and style in your strokes. You will also learn how to save life, how to play water games and how to dive.

We start this week with the CRAWL, fastest and most natural of all swimming strokes, so study the pictures below.

Introducing your instructor, *George Fryer*, the Southern Counties coach who won his first swimming championship at eleven years of age and is now busy coaching young swimmers in an Olympic training scheme. "You expend more energy in swimming badly than in swimming well," says George Fryer. "It's attention to detail that makes a champion."

Here are three of George Fryer's pupils who will demonstrate the strokes for you. On the left is *Ian Fraser*, 1950 Middlesex Back Stroke champion and Free Style finalist. In the middle, *Ken Smith*, 1950 Southern Counties and Middlesex Breast Stroke champion, and on the right, *Peter Alp*, 1950 English National Schoolboy Breast Stroke champion and 1951 Southern Counties champion and record holder. Peter will show you his successful butterfly stroke next week.

Your diving instructor *Harold Dixon*, A.S.A. Gold and silver medallist, one of the best divers in the south of England, and coach to the Olympic training scheme.

Here is the CRAWL demonstrated by *Michael Blanchard*, a young county champion. In this stroke, the arm action is a rhythmic circling movement, pulling under water and recovering out of water, while the legs maintain a steady, paddling action.

You can practise the CRAWL on land, as Michael is doing in the picture, but don't overdo it – water practice is best. Start the legs moving first in a steady beat, add the arm movements and then the correct breathing. Inhaling is done through the mouth, and exhaling through nose and mouth into the water on every complete arm circle, to the right or left side according to the swimmer's preference. Correct breathing is essential to a fast, smooth stroke.

Above you see the leg movement, which is a continuous flail up and down at unvaried speed. Depth of drive should be about twice the length of the foot, with knee slightly bent to increase whiplash, but foot fully flexed and instep in line with the shin.

Michael demonstrates a good stretching and suppling exercise for crawl swimmers.

HOW *EAGLE* IS PRODUCED

The complete story from a tree to your home

(3) At the mills the logs are cut into 39 in. lengths.

(5) The logs are stacked in immense piles, many as...

(4) DE-BARKING. The logs are now fed into huge inclined steel slatted drums rotating in shallow concrete tanks. The bark is knocked off by the logs rumbling one against the other and is washed away between the slats. The de-barked logs spill out into a conveyor.

(2) After felling and trimming the logs are (in Canada) floated down river to the mills.

(1) Spruce trees in enormous quantities come from Canada and the Scandinavian countries.

...ft. long (we sho... very eyes. (A) ... moisture drains; (D) Press ro... ing felts; (F) Calender rollers...

(12) Cut reel ready for printing.

(13) In the meantime a staff of 'Eagle' artists create the original drawings.

(17) The complete set of four colour cylinders are now fitted to the printing machine and a web of paper threaded up. Each cylinder runs in a bath of ink, yellow, red, blue and black, from which the excess ink is removed by a thin steel blade called a doctor.

(14) The drawings are photographed four times through a prismatic lens with four different colour filters for yellow, red and blue (the primary colours) and black.

(15) Positives are made from the retouched camera negatives and exposed, together with a fine screen to a sensitized pigment paper covered with soluble gelatine.

(16) The pigment paper, one for each colour, is transferred to one of the copper cylinders then stripped off, leaving the gelatine impression. This gelatine resist is etched, or engraved, by pouring iron perchloride in varying solutions over the cylinder. Hence the term photogravure.

L. ASHWELL WOOD

(7) BEATING. Here the pulp is circulated and is further disintegrated by bruising to produce ends to the fibres. (A) At this stage chemical sulphite pulp known as "half-stuff" is also beaten into the mixture; (B) Roller with blunt knives; (C) Concrete hill; (D) Water supply.

(8) The pulp is again screened and filtered and pressed into sheets like blotting paper for export to the British Isles.

(6) GRINDING INTO PULP. The logs are next conveyed to batteries of voracious grinders each driven by a 2,000 h.p. motor. (A) Operators slide the logs into the feed pockets; (B) Water supply; (C) Sandstone grinder roll; (D) Toothed pressure lead forcing logs against grinder. (E) Oil pressure piston cylinders. (F) Steaming ground pulp; more water is added and the pulp, after screening, is pumped to the beaters. This is called mechanical pulp.

(9) A continuous stream of freight ships bring the wood pulp to our shores.

...ACHINE. The liquid pulp (like porridge), is pumped ... Fourdrinier paper machine. These machines are 360 ...nvenience). Here the pulp turns to paper before your ... Web of wet pulp; (C) Wire screen through which the ... Main paper drying cylinders semi-encircled by dry-... paper; (G) Finished roll of paper; (H) Roll cutters.

(10) The imported pulp is shredded and fed to another beater; here is added a liquid proportion of china clay to improve the surface and resin as a size to prevent ink spread.

(18) ROTARY PHOTOGRAVURE PRINTING MACHINE. (A) Paper reel; (B) First colour printing, one side only; (C) Paper passes to the other end for colour printing on reverse side; (D) Ink scraper or doctor blade; (E) Printing cylinder and ink reservoir; (F) Impression cylinder holding paper against printing cylinder; (G) Second colour printing on reverse side; (H) Webb is now split by a cutter into page width and parts company on its way to the folder; (I) In the meantime, the black and white section is being printed on one side at the back of this machine and passes right over to the left to be printed on the other; (J) The black printing returns and is split; (K) The four split webs come together and are cut and folded into 8 sheets; (L) Delivery of copies.

...ready ...patch.

(21) Labelling and despatch.

(22) By road or express train to wholesaler.

(23) Wholesaler to retailer.

(24) Retail shop.

(25) EAGLERS

PAPER MAKING

This is the story of *Eagle*. How many of you realise that your favourite magazine started life in a forest in far away Canada?

This sequence of pictures depicts the huge organisation and planning necessary to place a copy in your hands.

The first stages of the breaking down of the wood into fibres is done in two ways, one wholly mechanical, as shown here, and the other chiefly chemical. The mechanical pulp contributes 80 per cent of the mass of finished paper but as the structure of the fibres is not strong, the remaining 20 per cent consists of chemical pulp of larger fibres which bind the others together.

The chemical pulp comes from similar wood but is boiled or digested by steam into which is added a solution of sulphur dioxide and bisulphate of calcium. After washing, the chemical pulp, known as "half-stuff", is mixed with the mechanical pulp.

The pulp is imported into this country and now has to be transformed into paper, the simplified principle of which, is passing water containing the pulp over a fine sieve or screen, when the water runs away and a thin layer of pulp is left behind. This layer, when removed from the screen, dried and glazed, is the finished sheet of paper. This finished paper 25 ft. wide comes out of the huge machines at the rate of 1,400 feet a minute.

PRINTING

This is done by a rotary photogravure process which is the most up-to-date in the country and the wonderful machine which prints it is shown in simplified form.

The basic principle of the photogravure process is its use of an engraved or indented surface from which the paper receives its impression, the cylinders being flooded with ink and scraped by a thin steel blade, termed a doctor blade, so that the surface is cleaned again and the ink left only in the engraved portions to make contact with the printing paper and so produce the image as you see it.

All the colours of the original drawings must be reproduced by four colours and their combinations, so that four cylinders are produced which will print yellow, red, blue and black respectively. The superimposition of these coloured printed images will reproduce the colours and tones (you learn at school that yellow and blue make green, etc.) seen in your copy of *Eagle*.

DISTRIBUTION

The distribution of the magazine is a system unto itself, involving careful marketing, finance and transport. At last you get it from your local shop and there is *Eagle* ready for your pleasure.

First Birthday!

EAGLE is one year old

MARCUS MORRIS, *Editor.*

FRANK HAMPSON, *creator and artist of 'Dan Dare'.* 32-year-old Lancashire born. Worked on EAGLE when it was first thought of. Hobby – playing with three-year-old son Peter.

ELLEN VINCENT, *Editorial Assistant.* Worked with advertising firm. Hobby – Music.

CHARLES GREEN, *Editorial Assistant.* Makes model ships and railways. Hobby – Amateur dramatics.

ERIC BEMROSE, *head of the firm who print EAGLE.* Hobbies – Photography and Radio.

"TELL them how the thing started," suggested someone.

"What *thing?*" asked the Editor coldly.

"EAGLE, of course – tell them how it began."

"And all that's happened since – up till now," put in someone else.

"Not all, I hope," commented the staff cynic. "There are some things best forgotten."

"Like the time you put in a wrong instalment of a strip, for example?" suggested my neighbour callously. "Though I will say this for you – nobody noticed, which just goes to show."

We were all together in the Editor's room at what we are pleased to call an Editorial Conference. That simply means that the editorial staff were scattered around the room in positions of varying inelegance, perched on the arms of chairs and the edges of tables – and arguing about what special features to put in the birthday issue.

Various suggestions had been put forward. An editorial suggester usually starts off full of enthusiasm and ends up rather lamely – withered by the glare of half a dozen pairs of critical eyes.

But this suggestion seemed to hit the nail on the head – at least the Editor thought so, and his decision is always final.

"Yes, I think that's a good idea," he said, "and we could put in photographs of you all – if the paper will stand it."

So that's how this story came to be written. We weren't at all sure whether you (our readers) would *want* to know how EAGLE started – still less what we all looked like. But we decided to risk it.

"Of course, it really all started in the bath – the idea of EAGLE I mean," went on the Editor. "But we'd better miss that part out – and how Hampson and I worked on the idea at home for nine months and then touted it round London, getting turned down by one publisher after another. Better start from when Hulton Press took it up, and decided to publish. Now who's going to write the story?"

The Editor looked round the room. We shuffled uneasily in our chairs.

"Better make it a combined effort," he said, in a determined voice. "All put down your impressions – and then we'll sort them out."

IT was towards the end of 1949 when EAGLE really got going – six months before the first issue came out. While the Editor and the staff contacted artists and writers, sorted out material, planned features and then scrapped them, and gradually battered the paper into shape, others carried out complicated research into what boys liked most to read, how much pocket money they got, and what they spent it on.

Others planned the advertising campaigns to launch the paper. Others again planned schemes for giving the paper publicity among those who were (we hoped) going to read it.

Some suggestions were more hare-brained than others. The Editor, one bright spark suggested, should parachute into Hyde Park dressed up as an eagle. Then someone thought of letting off 200,000 balloons in various parts of the country – until the thought of the time and puff required to blow up that many balloons put it out of court.

At last we decided on the *Hunt the Eagle* plan. Cars with giant effigies of golden eagles on them were engaged to tour the country. Inside the cars, loudspeakers announced "EAGLE is coming". Gift vouchers were hidden everywhere – the finder could claim a free copy at the nearest newsagent. And that nearly started a riot! We heard of one gang who gathered a handful of vouchers, collected their free copies from the shops, and then sold them at the street corner.

So the first number went off – and, back in the office, we held our breaths.

Then came the avalanche. Orders poured in from newsagents all over the country. EAGLE was selling like hot cakes.

But we needed more than a good start. We needed paper too. And of paper there seemed to be less and less every week – at a higher and

EAGLE *gets around – in fact, all over the world. Some of our keenest readers are the children of Tombstone, Arizona.*

Many thousands of letters reach us week by week. Here is the Editor and his secretary looking through some of them.

An EAGLE *reader takes a tumble while winter sporting in North Italy. The rest of the party tell him what he did wrong.*

EAGLE *readers inspect the latest Minic toys. A visit to this London toy factory was one of the outings organized recently by EAGLE Club.*

higher price. We had to take two bitter decisions. We must limit the size to sixteen pages, and that meant putting lots of ideas in cold storage. And EAGLE would have to go up to 4d. But our readers went on buying it in spite of that, in ever increasing numbers.

Meanwhile the rapid success of EAGLE Club almost overwhelmed us. Over 60,000 joined in the first week – and sixty thousand is a lot of letters to have about the place. An emergency staff worked all hours to get out the badges and membership cards – and each week the numbers increased.

That's how we began meeting some of our readers – at the trips and parties and prize-winning expeditions we arranged for Club members. That was the best part of all – meeting our readers.

The MUG's Badge took on too – though some people didn't understand the name at first. "A special badge for those who are especially helpful to others – that's the idea," we explained. "We call them MUGS because that's what the spivs call people who help others. So we'll turn the tables on the spivs by being proud of the title."

Some got the wrong idea about how to win a MUG's badge. They thought the only way was to rescue someone from drowning. "Bill spends all his time by the canal waiting for someone to fall in," one father wrote. We hurriedly explained some of the thousand other ways of earning a MUG's badge. And now the idea seems to have caught on.

Then there are the letters – hundreds of them every week – from readers, giving their views and criticisms and preferences. They are very frank and very helpful, and we keep a careful record of them all. We built up a staff of experts to answer the questions we received. "Please explain shortly Einstein's theory of relativity," one boy wrote. "Can you get me two tickets for the Cup final?" asked another. (We couldn't!)

Then we started a *Hobbies Advice Bureau* and a *Pen Pals Scheme* – and that brought in thousands more letters.

How does it all work? And who does the work? As well as our Editorial staff, we have our staff of full-time artists – some of whom you see here. Then we have many other artists and writers and ideas men working for us.

Here's how it usually goes. The script-writer sends in his script for a strip-cartoon – *Riders of the Range,* for example (in this case Charles Chilton). This goes off to the artist who draws it in rough pencil form, back it comes for editorial

ROSEMARY GARLAND, *Editorial Assistant,* writes children's books. Expert on lighthouses. Hobby – Painting pictures.

JAMES HEMMING, *Editorial Consultant.* Author of five books. Went round the world lecturing in 1949. Hobby – Tennis.

CHAD VARAH, *Editorial Consultant.* Reports on all manuscripts. Escaped after arrest by Nazis in 1934. Hobby – Photography.

RUARI MCLEAN, *Editorial Consultant,* expert typographer. Ex-submarine Officer. Hobby – Driving an Austin 7.

PHYLLIS WASEY, *Secretary.* Has been with EAGLE since the first issue came out. Hobbies – Swimming and Cycling.

JOHN RYAN, *artist and creator of 'Harris Tweed'*. Teaches art at big Public School. Hobby – Collecting Roman coins.

ASHWELL WOOD, *Centrespread artist*. Trained engineer, one-time draughtsman in aircraft company. Hobby – Cricket.

JACK DANIEL, *'Riders of the Range' artist*. Was a newspaper cartoonist. Ex-Desert Rat. Hobbies – Sculpture and Squash.

NORMAN WILLIAMS, *'Great Adventurer' artist*. Trained in Sheffield. Was a newspaper strip-cartoonist. Hobby – Stamp Collecting.

STROM GOULD. *'P.C. 49' artist*. Has 'panned' for gold, caught sharks and snakes. Hobby – Collecting New Guinea carvings.

HAROLD JOHNS, *Assistant artist on 'Dan Dare'*. Born in Devon, trained at Southport School of Art. Hobby – Photography.

...re are Miss Peabody, Sir Hubert and Digby ...ng in EAGLE studio for artist Frank Hamp...n in a dramatic scene from DAN DARE.

approval; back to the artist to do the finished artwork. Then when the balloons are lettered, the page is ready – some time in advance, we hope, of press day. Similarly the great number of stories sent in to us are vetted by one of our Readers, approved or rejected – and if approved, sent to an artist to be illustrated.

At last all the material is ready and up it goes to Liverpool by train in a special sealed satchel. A week later we get back a pasted-up "dummy" of the issue for our corrections and alterations. And so the issue goes to press, and the copies roll off the machine, 12,000 an hour, 200 a minute, 3½ a second. Our centrespread this week shows how it is done.

And meanwhile our EAGLE Club staff are busy arranging the holidays and outings, and despatching the Club badges, the MUG's badges, the articles of one kind or another that EAGLE Club produce.

It's a busy life and it never stops.

How about the future? Well, we've got plenty of ideas and plans – but it would rather spoil things to tell you about them now. Our aim is "Bigger and Better" – and we hope to make use of many of the ideas you have sent in to us.

Meanwhile, thank you for all your letters, encouraging and congratulating us. Although its our birthday, not yours, we still want to wish you – and ourselves – "Many happy returns" of EAGLE birthdays.

JOHN RUSSELL, *Club Staff*. In charge of outside activities. Served in the Navy. Hobbies – Squash and Swimming.

DAN DARE, *Colonel*, Chief Pilot of International Inter-planet Space Fleet. Hobby – Jet Cricket.

When EAGLE was first started, we sent out cars bearing these huge golden eagles to all the most important towns in the country, to announce "EAGLE is coming".

A FLYING WING JET AIR-LINE

L. ASHWELL WOOD

FLYING

THE FUTURE

Our artist's impression of a flying wing aircraft is based on scientific data and is quite within the realms of possibility. In fact an American 8 jet-propelled bomber – the Northropp YB-49 – is already built but still on the secret list. In the air-liner the whole of the cabin and cargo space is pressurized for high altitude flying at high speeds.

Eight super-jet engines give adequate power. New type combined elevator-aileron controls counteract the tendency to a nose-down movement when the take-off and landing flaps are used. An aircraft of this type would fly non-stop by night to America or India with sleeping passengers.

KEY TO NUMBERS

(1) Rudder and fin (port and starboard). (2) Side-slip indicator. (3) Exhaust vents for de-icing warm air. (4) Corrector for horizontal trim. (5) Aileron – elevator controller. (6) Trim tab. (7) Hydraulic operating gear. (8) Main spar. (9) Outer fuel tanks. (10) De-icing pipe from engines and air corrugations in leading edge of wing. (11) Air intakes to jet engines. (12) Four port super-jet engines. (13) Port undercarriage (retracted). (14) Inner fuel tanks. (15) Passengers' observation windows. (16) Lounge. (17) Galley and pantry. (18) Radio operator and navigator. (19) Captain and first officer. (20) Flight engineer. (21) Dining room. (22) Four starboard super-jet engines. (23) Starboard undercarriage (retracted). (24) Two berth cabins. (25) Skylights and emergency exits. (26) Gentlemen's dressing room and toilet. (27) Ladies' dressing room and toilet. (28) Main entrance under wing. (29) Mails. (30) Freight. (31) Slotted flaps to assist take-off and landing. (32) Double skin of pressurized wing.

WING

DAN DARE
THE RED MOON MYSTERY

BE STILL, WILLY!

Dan and Co's plan to lure the Red Moon away from Earth with a chlorophyll light has succeeded and now, having met the Treen Fleet, they are transferring to Sondar's ship to watch the Treens attack the asteroid with their projectors.

DAN DARE

THE RED MOON MYSTERY

AND:
EAGLE CHRONICLERS
A JOB FOR EVERYONE

We feel that EAGLE and its readers should play their full part in the Festival of Britain this year. We are, therefore, launching on a nation-wide scale, a brand new scheme to enable *you* to play *your* part, and we hope that all of you will join in. Our EAGLE *Chroniclers Scheme* is something which can last for a very long time, and which can be of real benefit to future generations.

This is how it works:—

How is it that you know that King Alfred burnt the cakes, and that Lady Godiva saved Coventry from excessive taxation? It is only because someone at the time who lived near where these incidents happened took the trouble to write them down, and their records have been passed on to us. But thousands of similar events, which would have been of great interest to us, have been lost because there was no one to chronicle them.

During this Festival of Britain year especially, a great deal of local history may be made. Need the record of all this be lost, or can we EAGLE readers help in chronicling it for the future?

Forming a Group

We suggest that *Eaglers* in the same school or the same district should form a group, and together plan to produce a Chronicle of their own town or district or village. They should invite some one older (perhaps their headmaster or headmistress) to act as Editor-in-Chief, and give advice.

Then each member of the Group, who would be known as EAGLE Chroniclers, should be entrusted with one particular part of the Chronicle. Here are some of the subjects into which it could be divided:—

1. Brief historical notes on your District, including local Notables and Folk Lore.
2. Interesting Architecture of the Distr
3. Local Government activities.
4. Plans of your District (with details population, rates, roads, transport, et
5. Social Life of District (Youth Organi tions, Institutes, Literary Societies, et
6. Local Flora and Fauna.
7. Local Art (drawings of beauty spots, et
8. Local Sport (1951 records, teams, et
9. Festival Activities of the District. Not visitors, etc.

These subjects could easily be divided into smaller sections, or you may be able think of many more subjects to deal wi Every section could be illustrated with pho graphs and drawings.

Twelve Prizes

When you have collected all the mate together, you should then hand it over to one in your school or district who is the "pen-man", who could write it out nea EAGLE will give a prize to the 12 groups w produce the best Chronicle.

This scheme of EAGLE Chroniclers is so thing in which almost everyone can take p because it does not matter how big y group is. All you have to do in the first p is to call a meeting of EAGLERS you know a make your plans.

When you have formed your group, one of you who is appointed as Chairm should write in to me telling me what dis you are going to cover. We will give you the advice and help we can. Later on shall make arrangements for all the Chronicle produced to be judged to find the 12 pr winners. We shall, of course, give you ple of time to make your Chronicle and s not start the judging until the autumn.

READERS LETTER

(A prize of 5/- is paid for each letter published)

TWO SUMMERS ago my brother found a baby crow that had fallen out of its nest, brought it home, fed it on milk and glucose and kept it warm in a box with straw and a hot water bottle. He grew to be a very large bird — we never caged him and he flew about all day and slept in a large tree. He always tapped on the window for meals and liked to be fed by hand. He was very naughty and as soon as clothes were pegged on the line he flew down and pulled out the pegs. He became so cheeky that my brother put him in a box and took him up to the heath. As the crow circled the sky my brother said "We will never see him again – he has lost faith in us because we put him in a box" – and we never did! – Robert West (9), 117 Mayplace Road East, Branhurst, Kent.

MY HOBBY is searching the countryside and collecting all manner of country-g pressing them in a thick book an fastening them in a scrap book and la them. – Raymond, 11 Newthorpe Norton, Doncaster, Yorks.

MY GRANDMOTHER has an orange w 35 years old. She gave it to my gran when he went over to France in 1916 the first World War. He carried it pocket until 1919 when he returned t land. It is now inedible, and of cours hard. – H. W. Burningham, 48 Th Road S.E.9.

I HAVE tried many times to understa journeys of St Paul when reading my but failed. Now, thanks to EAGLE, his jo and adventures are being explained to way I can understand. – John Win Kirkpatrick Road, Mile Cross, Norwic

EAGLE CHRONICLERS

Here are some more notes for *our* Chronicle of the *imaginary* town of Hulton Pressborough. Remember, these notes are only *examples* of the sort of things you should be looking for to include in your *real* chronicle of the district or place in which you live.

A.10. The Hulton Pressborough district is rich in dialect words and sayings not commonly encountered elsewhere. They are especially to be found among the older inhabitants of the surrounding villages. The following is a list of some of these sayings, with their more generally known equivalents. The last two seem to be most rarely used in modern times, but they were remembered by Mr William Longfurrow, an 81-year-old retired farmworker of Great Ravenscroft, who recalls hearing them as a boy.

Local saying	Equivalent meaning
Don't pick your flowers and expect a showy garden.	You can't have your cake and eat it.
Open mind – shut mouth.	Wise men keep still tongues in their heads.
A crumb o' comfort's worth an oven full of dreams.	A bird in the hand's worth two in the bush.
Kind words often granite soften.	A soft answer turneth away wrath.
Rust, and you'll eat crust, Wear, and you'll better fare.	It's better to wear out than to rust out. (Through laziness).
Half-aquartern's still bread.	Half a loaf is better than no bread.

READERS' LETTERS
(A prize of 5/- is paid for each letter published)

I WAS most interested in your illustration of the "Vanguard", as I was lucky enough to spend an afternoon on board her when she was anchored in Portland Harbour. We were not allowed to visit all the parts you illustrated, but the afternoon included a visit to the Admiral's Bridge. – Patricia Mason, 80 Woodfield Road, Birmingham 12.

I WONDER if any other family has a Nature Club? We have: it is called the Secrets of Nature Club, and all of us – Daddy, Mummy and six children – belong. It is run on strictly business-like lines; we pay weekly subscriptions which help to pay for outings or new equipment, have a small library to which we

hope to add as it pays for itself (½d. a d book), keep a log book of all outing hold meetings to discuss the Club's pro – Mary Ward, 46 Brighton Road, Bris

A FEW weeks ago in EAGLE there picture strips of Ray playing cricket, article "Cricket with the Masters". I an old book, cut out the strip pictures a time, and stuck them on the corner o page, making sure they were in the order. When this was done, all I had was to flick the pages of the book, could see Ray actually playing cric Arthur Gilbert, 21 Nearcroft Road, Oak Est, Wythenshawe, Manchester.

I BECOME A KNIFE-THROWER'S TARGET

by MACDONALD HASTINGS, *Eagle Special Investigator*

WITHOUT wasting any precious time, I asked the knife-thrower if he ever missed. Thoughtfully, he tested the steel point of one of his wicked-looking weapons on the tip of his finger.

"It's like this," he said. "I'm not going to pretend to you, Mr Hastings, that I'm anything that I'm not. No man is infallible. That's right, isn't it? And what I always say is that a man who never makes a mistake, if you get my meaning, never makes anything."

"That's Hal Denver all over," said the girl who usually stands at the business end of the Sensational Denver's Knife-Throwing performance. "Modest, that's him."

"What I'm anxious to learn," I said, "is what he's got to be modest about. You ought to know, if anybody does."

"Tell him," said the knife-thrower. "Go on, I haven't got any secrets. Tell him about the time when I pinned you by your hair to the board."

"Was it an accident?" I enquired feelingly.

"I'll say it was an accident," said the girl. "When I pulled out the knife, it took half my hair with it."

"Still, you've got a lot of hair," I said hopefully. "Not like me."

"Yes," said the knife-thrower, "but, apart from her curls, my partner doesn't take up much room. She's built the way I like my targets to be, on the small side. When she stands up against the board, there's plenty of space to miss all around her."

"What are you looking at me for?" I said.

"Can't help it. Ever since I saw you, I've been thinking to myself: 'He's a very big man. When we put him up against the board, he'll fairly well cover it'."

"Have you ever thought up any way of overcoming the difficulty?"

"Nothing much we *can* do about it, is there? You'll just have to squash up and make yourself as small as you can. My partner'll show you what to do."

The girl smiled encouragingly. I smiled wanly back.

"You'd better take your coat and waistcoat off," she said. "A little while ago, Hal threw a knife which went right through the sleeve of a man's coat, and his shirt as well."

"Did he do it on purpose?" I said.

"Of course he didn't do it on purpose."

Slowly – as slowly as I could anyway – I stripped off my jacket and loosened my collar and tie. I wished, as I've wished so often before, that I had the courage to tell the knife-thrower to go away and practise on somebody else. But the Editor had sent a photographer to get the pictorial record of my impending execution. Hal Denver was already bracing up his shirtsleeves with elastic bands and arranging his weapons of torture in patterns on the floor. And his partner was gently backing me up against the board.

LOOKING desperately for an excuse to delay the fatal moment, I noticed that the top of the board came below my head.

"It's no use," I said triumphantly. "I'm too tall."

For a moment the knife-thrower was baffled. He'd got to admit that I had presented him with an unexpected snag.

"The best part of the act," he explained in a worried voice, "is when I throw two hatchets which land on either side of your head."

"Hatchets?"

"Sure. That's the climax."

"When he throws the hatchet at me," said his partner, "he aims straight at the middle of my forehead. As the hatchet spins through the air, I duck and it hits the board where my head ought to be."

"Tell him about last week – remember? – when I threw a bit low," said the knife-thrower.

"Don't," I said.

"Oh, it's all right," said the girl. "He didn't hit me with the blade. It was just the handle that got me on the back of the neck. But it did make me feel funny."

"Funny! It sounds very serious to me."

"You're quite right," said the knife-thrower. "It *is* serious."

I felt that I couldn't agree more.

While they were talking, Hal Denver and his partner, were man-handling the heavy board, pitted and scarred with knife slashes. With devilish ingenuity, they were raising it another foot from the ground by balancing the board on the top of the property box used to carry the tools of the knife-throwing trade.

"O.K." said Hal.

Stepping back from the board, he gathered up a bunch of long knives, like a hand of cards and, selecting one, crouched down and flourished it at me in the air.

"Hold your arms in," said his partner. "You want to make yourself as insignificant as you can. Lean your head back and, whatever you do, DON'T MOVE."

I felt like a specimen beetle pinned to a collector's tray. With hypnotised attention, I watched the knife-thrower working himself up for his task.

After several preliminary scares, he was dissatisfied with the set-up. He told me to relax while he produced an enormous tape-measure and carefully measured out the ground.

"Just an extra precaution," he said. "I'm not going to pretend, Mr Hastings, that I don't feel a bit nervous myself working on you. You know what I mean. I usually throw my knives at a particular point of the board. No offence meant, but, with you, you sort of get in the way."

"As it's me, couldn't you shorten the distance at which you throw the knives?"

"That'd be a certain short cut to trouble. I only throw at one distance, eighteen feet exactly, and no mistakes."

"Or else . . ." echoed the girl.

"That's how they bill us on the halls," said the knife-thrower proudly. "The Sensational Denvers. No mistakes, or else . . . Sounds good, doesn't it?"

I tried to agree.

"All right. One to be ready, two to be steady . . . and a few knives just to get us both used to it."

Hal, who was wearing a sort of Spanish outfit with bell-bottomed trousers and a short bolero jacket, tossed back the black locks of hair off his nose, spread his legs, crouched down on one knee, and, holding one of his long knives by the tip of the blade, sighted me carefully.

"Aim to miss, that's the secret," he said.

I agreed heartily.

"What part of me are you going to start on?"

"Always begin at the legs, and work upwards."

"I'm glad it's legs first."

"Doesn't follow," said the girl. "Hal's last partner had to have five stitches in her leg once."

"That's right," said the knife-thrower. "Cut her about dreadfully."

As he spoke, the knife left his hand. I watched the flash of it and heard it hiss as it span through the air. Then there was a sullen thump close to my legs which made the board I was leaning on vibrate against my back.

A moment later, another knife and then another, cut through the air and landed trembling in the wood round my thighs and waist. Three more followed, the last one landing neatly within six inches of my ear.

"I threw wide that time so you wouldn't get the wind-up," said the knife-thrower. "Now we'll give you the whole dozen, six up one side, six up the other."

As he explained, he wrenched the knives out of the wood. The blades were about eleven inches long, the handles another six inches. They were very heavy, and the point sunk deep through the wood of the three inch thick board.

I asked Hal if it was possible to get knives like them.

"I wouldn't know," he said. "This set belonged to an old fellow who worked in my father's circus. When I was a boy it used to be my job to clean the rust off them. I got to throwing them myself and, one day, when the old fellow was ill, I went on and did the act. I've done it ever since, with these same knives."

"How long have you been a knife-thrower?"

"About sixteen years."

"Do you ever practice?"

"Not unless I meet someone like you. It isn't easy to get targets in this business, you know. And throwing at playing cards, the way they do in story-books, teaches you nothing. You've got to work on the real thing, as you might say."

I shall never forget the swish of those hatchets

Getting my own back !

EAGLE 4 May 1951

Natural centre of interest at the Festival of Britain is the Dome of Discovery which, by its great size and unique shape, dominates the whole place. It has been designed by Ralph Tubbs, the young British architect. The great dome, the largest in the world, is supported by a circular ring girder of steel and this in turn is borne by a series of steel struts. Inside there are three vast galleries and the largest of these, seen on the right in the picture, is supported by a series of concrete fins. The drum wall is also of concrete and is so thick at its base that it can contain many of the staircases and stores. Above the wall and reaching outward to the edge of the dome, is the apron which, like the dome, is made of sheet aluminium. The height of the building is 93 feet and its diameter between bases and struts is 365 feet. The story told in the Dome of Discovery is of Britain's pre-eminence in discovery and exploration, not only by land and sea, but into the very nature of the living world and the Universe. Alongside the achievements of such men as Cook and Livingstone there are other displays on such subjects as nuclear energy; polar exploration; and methods of combating disease, to name only a few.

THE DOME O

LAWRENCE DUNN

(1) Aluminium dome	(8) Centre gallery	(15) Fin supporting gallery
(2) Portholes	(9) Lower gallery	(16) Main entrance
(3) Exit	(10) Control room	(17) Wall broken to show entrance
(4) Drum wall	(11) Escalator	(18) Roof girders
(5) Supporting struts	(12) Top gallery	(19) Electrical contact breaker (Exhibit)
(6) Aluminium apron	(13) Store	(20) Skylon
(7) Ventilating chambers	(14) Staircase to top gallery	

F DISCOVERY

ADVICE ON YOUR PETS

TRAINING YOUR FOX-TERRIER PUPPY

by Professor Cameron

GAIN YOUR PUPPY'S CONFIDENCE BY HOLDING HIM FIRMLY AND COMFORTABLY. SUPPORT HIS WEIGHT AND REMEMBER IN ALL TRAINING THAT A FEW WORDS OF PRAISE AND ENCOURAGEMENT ARE QUITE AS IMPORTANT AS SCOLDING.

GROWING PUP'S TIME TABLE (ROUGH GUIDE ONLY)

7 AM Let out.	12·30 PM Meal.
8·30 AM Light Meal.	3 PM Afternoon Walk.
9 AM Morning Walk.	6 PM Evening Meal.
	7 PM Let out and so to bed.

REGULARITY IS THE MOST IMPORTANT THING IN TRAINING. GIVE MEALS AND EXERCISE REGULARLY AS POSSIBLE AND SEE THAT YOUR PUP GOES TO BED AT ABOUT THE SAME TIME EACH NIGHT. DON'T BE TOO RIGID, BUT REGULAR HABITS LEARNED IN PUPPY-HOOD WILL MAKE LIFE MUCH EASIER FOR BOTH OF YOU.

YOUR COMMANDS SHOULD BE FEW AND SIMPLE, BUT THEY **MUST** BE OBEYED; NEVER 'PLAY' AT HITTING A DOG—A HALF-HEARTED PAT IS WORSE THAN USELESS. ON THE RARE OCCASIONS WHEN CHASTISEMENT IS NECESSARY IT—

—SHOULD BE FOR A REASON WELL UNDER-STOOD BY THE PUPPY. DON'T HIT HIM OR SCOLD HIM AFTER HE HAS COME BACK TO YOU OR DECI AT LAST TO OBEY.

BE FIRM BUT SENSIBLE ABOUT 'HOUSE TRAINING' SCOLD FOR ANY MESSES MADE IN THE HOUSE, BUT BE SURE TO LET YOUR PUP OUT FREQUENTLY—AND SHOW HIM WHERE TO GO IN THE GARDEN. WHEN OUT ON WALKS TRAIN HIM TO USE THE GUTTER—THIS IS QUITE EASY WITH PATIENCE, AND IT HELPS TO AVOID THE NASTY NUISANCE OF FOULED PAVEMENTS.

EXERCISE SHOULD BE REGULAR AND IS BEST PROVIDED BY TWO GOOD WALKS A DAY. WHEN YOUR PUP WANTS TO 'LET OFF STEAM' HE CAN LEARN TO RETRIEVE A RUBBER BALL BUT **DON'T** TIRE HIM OUT AND **NEVER** THROW STONES, WHICH WHEN SWALLOWED CAN CAUSE OBSTRUCTION THAT MAY BE FATAL.

John Dyke

MOST DOGS TAKE READILY TO CAR-TRAVEL, BUT HELP YOUR PUP TO BE A WELL-BEHAVED PASSENGER BY LIFTING HIM PROPERLY INTO THE CAR AND SEEING THAT HE IS COMFORTABLE WHILST TRAVELLING. IF YOUR PUP IS ONE OF T UNFORTUNATE SUFFERERS FROM 'CAR SICKNES' YOUR VET CAN SUPPLY TABLETS BEFOREHAND, PREVENTING TROUBLE ON THE JOURNEY. WRITE TO PROFESSOR CAMERON % 'EAGLE' I YOU HAVE ANY QUESTIONS OR PROBLEMS

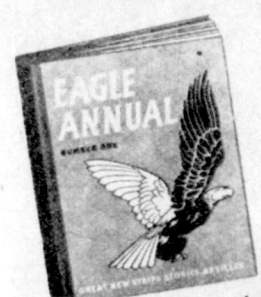
The Adventures of P.C.49

PC49 was created for radio by Alan Stranks and told stories in the everyday life of Police Constable Archibald Berkeley-Willoughby. As well as being broadcast over the airwaves and getting picked up by *Eagle*, there were two films made featuring the popular PC. In the first, snappily titled 'The Adventures of P.C. 49: Investigating the Case of the Guardian Angel', our hero was played by Hugh Latimer. He had a long career as a jobbing actor. In 1957 Latimer appeared in an episode of *Dixon of Dock Green*, in 1972 he showed up in *New Scotland Yard*, and in 1980 he saw how times had changed when he was cast in *Juliet Bravo*.

A NEW
P.C. 49 ADVENTURE

THE CASE
OF
KILLER'S KEEP.

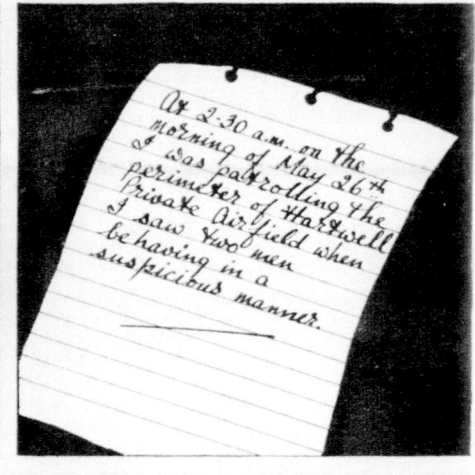

At 2-30 a.m. on the morning of May 26th I was patrolling the perimeter of Hartwell Private Airfield when I saw two men be having in a suspicious manner.

?

UP YOU COME, PIMPLE. WE'VE GOT NO TIME TO WASTE.

O.K. SCORPIO. ALL CLEAR— HAUL AWAY.

THIS IS THE JOB. THEY MUST HAVE LEFT HER OUT READY FOR THE TRIAL FLIGHT AT DAWN.

BUT WHEN THEY ARRIVE THEY FIND THE BIRD HAS FLOWN, EH?

I HOPE YOU KNOW HOW TO HANDLE THIS HUSH-HUSH KITE.

DID NOT I, SCORPIO CARLOTTI, HELP TO BUILD THIS EXPERIMENTAL MODEL? PULL THE CHOCKS AWAY AND COME ABOARD.

HEY! WHAT'S THE CAPER?

LUMME — IT'S A COP!

COME DOWN OUT OF THERE, CHUM! I'M TAKING YOU BOTH INTO CUSTODY.

THAT'S WHAT YOU THINK!

COP THIS!

CONTINUED

EAGLE-BRITAIN'S NATIONAL STRIP CARTOON WEEKLY

Travelling the universe, saving the world and the human race, time and again Dan Dare and his crew always fall back on home comforts. In this penultimate instalment of 'the Venus story', the team are desperate for the basics of life, and maybe their choices tell the reader a little about each one. Sir Hubert desires a bath; Dan, food; Professor Peabody (the only regular young female character), clothes; and good old Digby, sleep. The central panel, signed by Frank Hampson himself, shows the crew tucking in to a Theron feast.

H.M. THE K

1. The Royal microphones, signal lights, and script board.

2. B.B.C. engineers' room with G.P.O. land line connections to Broadcasting House.

4. Permanent land line from Bi

7. Musical recordings can be introduced where necessary.

6. Continuity Room. Here the various items of the programme are fitted into the hole at the right moment. Equipped with loud speaker.

3. Broadcasting House, London.

8. Announcing room with red, blue and white signal lights. Announcer has loud speaker, head phones and microphone. These two rooms are connected to amplifiers through control.

5. Control room, which i nerve centre. Here the in ing impulses are amplified before being distributed by plifiers C to the transm Their course is pre-set fre control desks. Amplifiers B are controlled from the and used for studio pr mes, signal lights, fade-ou

L. ASHWELL WOOD

THE KING

CHRISTMAS BROADCAST

N Christmas Day, subject to circumstances, the King speaks to his loyal subjects throughout the world.

his special EAGLE feature we endeavour to show, in a very simplified manner, what ens when His Majesty speaks and how you receive it on your set almost simulously.

ild the King speak from Sandringham, his voice will impinge on the moving coil ophones and be transformed into electrical impulses of audio frequency. Two ophones are used as a precaution.

se impulses are conveyed to Broadcasting House over G.P.O. land lines.

e the incoming microphone impulses are amplified (or boosted up) and distributed antaneously to all the B.B.C. Transmitting Stations, and also by G.P.O. land wire. e, again, the microphone impulses are further amplified and superimposed on a g carrier wave current, generated at the station by the transmitter.

modulated current is fed to the aerial wire from some of which it is radiated to the sh Isles and from the others to the four corners of the Empire, to be reconverted sound by millions of radio receivers.

waves travel through the ether with the same velocity as that with which light is smitted from the sun. This velocity is 186,000 miles per second, so that His esty's voice travels once round the earth in one-seventh of a second.

CANADA AND NEWFOUNDLAND

PACIFIC ISLANDS AND THE FAR EAST

SOUTH AFRICA

ALL EMPIRE SHIPS AT SEA

Amplified microphone current being borne along on transmitted carrier wave.

AUSTRALIA AND NEW ZEALAND

⑨ Distribution panel to transmitting stations by G.P.O. land lines.

⑩ Transmitting station. Here the impulses are (the following numbers refer to drawing on the right): (1) Further amplified; (2) Super-imposed on carrier waves; (3) Oscillated to high frequency; (4) Controlled; (5) Power amplified; (6) Finally transmitted to (7) feeders and (8) aerial feeder. (9) In the Diesel-electric generating plant; (10) Generators supplying current to transmitting valves, etc.

⑫ And so to everybody in the British Isles and the Empire overseas.

SPEAKS

PILOT OF THE FUTURE

DAN DARE

Large of head, and therefore enormous of brain, The Mekon was Dan Dare's most enduring enemy. Intelligent beyond the wildest imaginings of Man he had an ego to match the size of his dome and, of course, like all the best villains, it was this that enabled him to be defeated. Floating around on what looks like a Subbuteo base, The Mekon ruled the Treens with an iron will. Dan came up against him on many occasions and, although he was always defeated in the end, he always came back for more, the ultimate recidivist.

The occasional use of real photographs in the 'Dan Dare' stories added to its allure. It brought a sense of reality to the adventures that had never been seen before. From the reader's point of view, it meant that these people were real, they must be, there's a photograph of Sir Hubert. It's actually Frank Hampson's dad, but don't tell anyone.

DAN DARE
PILOT OF THE FUTURE

THE MEKON, LORD OF THE TREENS, SUMMONS THE THREE CAPTIVES TO HIS PRESENCE.

THEY SHOULD DECEIVE THE EARTH ALL RIGHT AND BEING ARCHAIC SINGLE PLANE PHOTO—GRAPHS THEY WON'T GIVE ANYTHING AWAY ABOUT OUR TECHNICAL SUPERIORITY.

MM—QUITE A TOUCHING SPECTACLE OF KINDLY TREENS OVERFLOW WITH GOODNESS TO THEIR LITTLE HUMAN FRIENDS

Left to right: Mr. H. Berkeley Hollyer; Mrs Grimes; Alderman F. J. March, Father of the Torquay Council; and John Grimes, Mug of the Year, taking tea during the EAGLE holiday that John spent with his mother at Torquay.

READERS' LETTERS

(A prize of 5/- is paid for each letter published)

I RECENTLY polished my EAGLE badge and was surprised how dirty it had become over the past year. After I had finished it was shining like a new pin. Don't you think it would be a good idea if all *Eaglers* polished their badges fairly regularly and kept them clean and smart? – Alexander Parkinson, Thomlea, 14 Seafield Road, Aberdeen.

WE LIVE at the foot of a snow-capped mountain, the highest mountain in Africa. They say that at the top is a leopard embedded in ice. No one knows how long it has been there or how it ever reached the snow line – climbers say they have really seen it. – Peter Guy, Box 97, Moshi, Tanganyika.

I FIND it very interesting to walk round a ploughed field looking for things that have come to the surface in ploughing. Yesterday I found a whelk shell, and a lot of oyster shells. As I live 70 miles from the sea can these be relics of the time when the sea covered this part of England? – Christopher Knowles, 1 Woodside Road, Burton Joycee.

HE'S WON A BIKE

Michael Lager (10) of Westbury, Norwich, is the proud winner of Bike-a-Week Competition No. 11. Michael is looking forward to lots of summer cycling.

Readers' Letters

I WONDER how many *Eaglers* know that at the top of Big Ben above the clock faces is a bright light known as the Ayrton Light or Clock Tower Lantern. At sunset the Speaker of the House of Commons presses a switch near his chair, and the lantern lights up. It is to tell Londoners that Parliament is at work – it often burns far into the night until the House adjourns. – Ernest Brown, 107 Ringstead Crescent, Sandgate, Sheffield 10.

IN THE cricket match between Nether Wallop and Picrust Parva you have shown four stumps for the wicket. Is this a mistake? – Edwin Vale, 5 Arbroath Road, S.E.9.

(*Originally, two stumps were used – later a third was introduced in order to speed up the game. Many people consider that cricket today is still inclined to be rather slow, causing matches to be drawn, so we assume that a fourth wicket will be introduced by 1996. – Ed.*).

LOOK OUT FOR THESE EAGLE CARS!

Watch out for the Humber cars with the dummy gold Eagles on their roofs! Watch out for them wherever you go! They are handing out free leaflets which give you advance news of the next exciting Dan Dare adventure. These leaflets also include special EAGLE coupons which we hope you will fill up and take round to your newsagent. We are sending out this fleet of cars all over Britain in order to remind you to make sure you're in at the *start* of the

new Dan Dare serial: and also to remind you that there is only one certain way of getting EAGLE every week – and that is by placing an order with your newsagent. There are, by the way, a few more copies of EAGLE available now; and so, if until now you have had to borrow or share with a friend, now's the time to get your own copy while the chance is still there.

Readers' Letters

(5/- is paid for each letter published)

I AM twelve years old and have lived in twenty-eight different houses. Can any reader beat that? – V. Kilner, 46 Clock-House Road, Beckenham, Kent.

· · ·

I THINK it is a deplorable hobby for boys to throw messages inside bottles into the sea. When they reach the shore they invariably break, and can thus cause many accidents. – David Irving, "Park House", Rayleigh Road, Hutton, Essex.

· · ·

THE MIDDLE stump in cricket first came in 1775. A match was being played between Hambledon and Kent. Hambledon wanted 14 runs to win when the last man came to the crease. A player named "Lumpy" Steven was bowling fast, underhand lobs. Three times the ball passed under the bail and between the stumps – the law was "If ye wicket is bowled down it is out" – so there came the middle stump. – *Eagler* 127037, 64 Kimbolton Road, Bedford.

· · ·

UP NORTH here are some exceedingly strange place-names, such as Quaking Houses, Pity Me, Johnny Dab, Shiny Row, Windy Nook and Windy Ridge – neither of the latter are very much more windy than any other place. There are also Philadelphia, New York, Washington, Hollywood and Quebec. These are only a few of the queer and cosmopolitan names of this district. – Michael Shields, 27 Valley View, Primrose, Jarrow, Co. Durham.

I BECOME A LIVING FIREWORK

By MACDONALD HASTINGS, EAGLE Special Investigator

I EXPECTED him to wear a cloak and a conspirator's hat, but, although he didn't dress the part, Mr Brock was as businesslike as Guy Fawkes on November the Fifth.

"We'll wait until it's quite dark," he said ominously. And he peered out of the window of his office as suspiciously as if he had a cask of gunpowder under each arm.

I'd have felt much better about it if the plan had been to blow up somebody else. But that wasn't the idea at all. Yes, you've guessed it. The plot was to make a firework out of me.

Mr Brock, in dark whispers with the editor, had arranged an assignment for me at his works at Hemel Hempstead. So when everybody else had gone home, when the owls were hooting and the witches were warming-up their broomsticks, I stumbled through the gloom into Mr Brock's cellar. Well, it wasn't quite a cellar. It was one of a series of isolated sheds. But, as I waved my torch to light my way, the beam lit on notices warning me at my peril to leave all "smoking materials" at the gate. Sitting on barrels of gunpowder is Mr Brock's business.

He assured me that it was quite safe. These days the manufacture of fireworks is so carefully regulated that accidents scarcely ever happen. But what Mr Brock had planned for *me* scarcely ever happens either.

We marched off, like an execution squad, with a man pushing a herse-like barrow in front of us. It was a moonless night with a high wind, and Mr Brock had to guide my faltering footsteps over the fields.

"We're going to the trial ground," he shouted in my ear. "It's the place where we try out our new ideas."

So that was it.

"Will it hurt?" I asked.

"What hurt?"

"When you light me up?"

"Good heavens no. In the old days at the Crystal Palace we used to put on a show like you every week."

"But the Crystal Palace was burnt down," I said.

"Not by us," replied Mr Brock, firmly.

We had come to a place which, in the light of our electric torches, reminded me of a battlefield in the war. It was littered with the burnt-out remains of explosives. There was a sort of wire enclosure, studded about with posts, and the ground had been churned into sour and blackened mud.

"This'll do, Woodie," said Mr Brock.

The shadowy figure of the man in charge of the barrow came to a halt. Using my torch, I looked to see what he'd got aboard.

"This is a living piece," said Mr Brock, "which we call the boxers. It's one of our best effects and it ought to make a good picture. Woodie will show you what to do."

"Is Woodie in this?" I asked.

"Woodie's the other boxer," said Mr Brock.

My heart warmed to Woodie. At any rate, he stood as good a chance of being blown up as I did.

"What's it like?" I whispered.

"O.K." said Woodie hoarsely. "All you have to look out for is the bang-pop-bang when you're lit up."

I said I could quite believe that.

"Never you mind," said Woodie comfortingly. "When you've been in this business as long as I have you won't feel really well unless you've got a burn or two. Anyhow you'll be all right in this."

Woodie dragged off the barrow something that looked like a divers suit, with a square headpiece and a rectangular window in front.

"Asbestos," he said.

I took off my coat and jacket and, sitting on the barrow, hauled on the gear. When the headpiece was attached, I was so isolated from the others that they had to give me a tap to attract my attention.

The next phase was that Mr Brock hooked on to my shoulder a life-size cut-out of a man mounted on wood. After that, he strapped another device on my arm.

Through my window, I could see that the outer side of the frame was outlined in paper-tubing, mounted on rows of cylinders about the size of a cigarette.

As I stood there in my suit, with the gear weighing down on my shoulder, Mr Brock tapped my headpiece to remind me to move very carefully. At the same time, he worked busily with a pair of scissors, splitting up the paper tubes, pocketing the ends together, and joining them up into a continuous line from my top to my toe.

I know now that the paper tubes are what are called quick match. The cylinders on which they are mounted are small fireworks named la .ces. What Mr Brock was doing was joining up the tubes of quick match to fire the priming in the lances, and to make sure that I burned properly from head to toe.

While Mr Brock was dealing with me, Syd was also being serviced. At last, we were both moved rather stiffly into position.

"Are you ready?" shouted Mr Brock through the asbestos suit.

I WASN'T ready – who would be? – but, if I'd raised any objection from the inside of my armour, nobody would have heard me. So I just stood there, holding up my arms, as Mr Brock had instructed me, in a boxing position. Heaven knows, at that moment nobody could have felt less in a fighting mood than I.

I didn't see Mr Brock strike the match. All I can tell you is that, a moment later, I found out what it feels like to be inside an explosion. Woodie said I was to look out for the bang-pop-bang. That was a memorable understatement.

Inside my suit, the whole world was suddenly eclipsed in a blinding fiery burst of hiccups. Woodie was blowing up too. We were both popping and crackling like a couple of chickens roasting on a spit.

It didn't last long. As the quick match fired the lancework, we both settled into a warm glow. Much too warm. After a moment or two, I felt very hot. By the time we'd burnt out, I'd decided that there must be a crack or two in my asbestos suit.

When they got me out, I was smelling like milk that's boiled over. My face was blackened with powder and, sure enough, I'd baptised myself as a pyrotechnist by collecting a burn on my arm.

But Mr Brock made it better by saying that I had now qualified as a firework type. If I liked, he said, I could come as an apprentice and help his people in the burning of one of their big displays. So, of course, I went.

As a preliminary, Mr Brock gave me a first lesson in the business. For example, he told me that real operators never talk of letting off fireworks. The old hands say: When do we burn?

Next, I found out that burning a firework display is a very different matter from touching off a few squibs or catherine wheels. It's an art, of which Mr Alan St Hill Brock is certainly the greatest master in the world. For six generations, his family have made fireworks. And, in that time, fireworks have developed from mere showers of flame-coloured sparks and fire, to the complicated devices and colour effects which you can see in a display today.

Up to the beginning of the last century, all fireworks were flame-coloured. Then the manufacturers introduced Chlorate of Potash. Chlorate of Potash, mixed with various metal salts, is the method by which fireworks are now tinted in colour. Chlorate of Potash is dangerous stuff, improperly used, but it's the secret of the red, yellow, green and blue stars which burst out of Roman Candles, Shells and Rockets today. The discovery of the uses of magnesium, and later aluminium, have also played a big part. In fact, you can say that, although the Chinese used saltpetre, charcoal, and sulphur to make the first fireworks a thousand years ago, fireworks as we know them have been perfected only in the past hundred and fifty years.

You can't compare the sort of fireworks that come out of a box at home with the enormous shells, rockets, set-pieces and revolving devices which are burnt at a big display. On one occasion, a former Mr Brock actually let off a revolving wheel which was fifty feet in diameter. When it was fired, the effect spread more than a hundred feet.

I didn't let off a firework myself as big as that. But I didn't do badly. Mr Brock put me in charge of some enormous frames of rockets. They were joined together with quickmatch, so that a touch set off three, five, or twenty at a time.

I was given a pocketful of "port-fires" to light my flights of rockets. My job was to let them off, when I got a shout from the chief operator in charge of the display.

Letting off a single rocket is good fun. But, when you set off five rockets at a time, they go off like a sock in the jaw. There's a roar and a bang, and if you're not careful, you sit down on your backside in surprise.

But, although firing flights of rockets is exciting, they're nothing to the big shells. Shells are fired out of mortars like small iron cannon sunk in the ground. The effect they give in the air is like a mushroom of sparks. And, if you are near them on the ground when they go off, the rush of the explosion as they lift is something quite terrific.

When we fired our display, I almost fell flat on my face when the first shell went off behind me. Afterwards, I got wise.

Whenever our chief operator (Mr Harry Austin) said: "Right, Harold," to his other assistant, I knew that was the moment to expect a big shell. And I ducked.

They didn't ask me to be a living firework again. But I burnt two holes in an old suit firing flights of rockets. So, one way and another, Mr Brock has no reason to be ashamed of me as his assistant. I've learned how to burn, and I've burnt.

The end

Mr Brock put me in charge of some enormous frames of rockets

The plot was to make a living firework out of me

EAGLE CLUB
AND EDITOR'S PAGE

The Editor's Office
EAGLE
4 New St. Square, London, E.C.4

I DO not know which magazine, if any, your father or mother read, but whatever it is I think you will find that it has gone up in price just recently. At any rate a large number of magazines have had to increase their price because of another rise in the cost of paper, which took place the other day.

Paper now costs nearly a third more than it did six weeks ago, and this, of course, has hit every magazine very hard. The cost of paper is one of the most expensive items in producing any publication.

Among others, EAGLE has also been very hard hit. Our paper now costs nearly twice as much as it did when EAGLE started a year ago. So we have had to do what many others have had to do. We have had to decide to increase the price of EAGLE to 4½d. If we did not do this, either EAGLE would run at a serious loss, or we would have to cut out many of the features you like best.

I am very sorry to have to tell you this, but I am sure you will understand the position since you will know well enough that in these difficult days the cost of everything is going up. You may think the extra halfpenny is a strange amount to charge. It's because we have kept the increase as low as possible.

I hope you will still agree that EAGLE is good value for money, and that you will go on reading it just as regularly. This increase in price will take place with the next issue.

Paper rationing began during the Second World War and continued until the middle of 1953, and Marcus Morris was not afraid to go into detail about the effects this had on the size and cost of *Eagle*. While the high price of *Eagle* was for the most part justified by it having so many colour pages, Morris was always at pains to make sure his readers knew why the cost increased, or the number of pages reduced.

Within the first six weeks of its launch the Reverend was pleading with young boys all over the country to share their comic, as it was difficult in these times of deprivation to make enough copies to go around. Was this just a clever way of him making readers think it was more popular than it was? Or maybe he was employing a clever form of word-of-mouth advertising. Regardless of his motivation, readership continued to grow and they had to reduce the size of the magazine to accommodate the extra demand. Obviously some people just weren't sharing enough.

PROFESSOR BRITTAIN EXPLAINS

takes everyday objects or topics – a clock, a television, molecular physics – and explains how it works in mind-numbing but somehow beautiful detail.

A *prize for every*
EAGLE CHRONICLER

A year ago today we invited our readers to compile, if they cared, a Chronicle of Events taking place in their district during the Festival of Britain Year – and we promised twelve prizes to the senders of the twelve best Chronicles. Many of you have now completed and sent in these Chronicles and to them we say, "Well done for staying the course!" All efforts sent in are excellent and obviously the result of much time and effort. Each one, we feel, deserves recognition and because of this we have decided to give everyone a prize who has sent in a Chronicle. They will be receiving, in the course of the next few weeks, a special letter and a book autographed by the Editor.

The Chronicles will be returned very soon now to the readers who sent them.

This has been a job well done.

The Chroniclers project lasted for the whole of *Eagle's* second year. Every now and then new ideas were given to encourage readers. The first big one of these was the invention of the town of Hulton Pressborough. In doing this *Eagle* was able to give examples of how Chroniclers up and the down the country could go about their business. This was followed, a week later, by a map of the town with accompanying notes such as 'The Chairman of the Urban District Council is Major Rhode a Head.' It was then suggested that you split your chronicle into (a) general history, past and present and (b) day-to-day happenings. They even went so far as to make up some local sayings. Favourites include: 'Don't pick your flowers and expect a showy garden'; 'Open mouth, shut mind'; and the rather obscure, 'half-aquartern's still bread'. After a whole year of this and many promises of great prizes, the *Eagle* Chronicling Project went out with a whimper on the 10 April 1952, when everyone was told they would get a prize. All entries, apparently, were excellent. Or maybe no one bothered. We never really knew as, unlike many other *Eagle* competitions, we were never shown any of the efforts. Shame.

HOW ELECTRICITY IS DISTRIBUTED
(By the National Grid Network)

A typical primary line tower carrying a double three-phase circuit.

(A) Arcing horns
(B) Insulating strings
(C) Steel cord aluminium conductors carry current at 132,000 volts.

ELECTR

We have seen, in last week's EAGLE, how electricity is generated at 11,000 volts. Here we show how this current is stepped up in pressure, and made available to city, town, village and isolated farm in every part of Great Britain. A National network of transmission lines link the main power stations with local undertakings. There are nearly 3,000 miles of primary transmission lines altogether, carrying 132,000 volts.

Main Grid Rooms are in touch by private telephone with all the power stations in their area, and with each other, so that power can be switched from one to another in case of failure. The supply of each section can be increased, diminished, or cut off according to the requirements of the load.

KEY TO NETWORK

(1) Main power station. (2) Boiler house. (3) Turbo-generating room. (4) 11,000 volt current from turbo-alternators is stepped up to 66,000 volts by transformers. (5) Switch house. (6) Cable tunnels. (7) Power house control room distributing the current in various ways. (8) 66,000 volt underground feeder cables to city sub-stations. (9) 66,000 volt underground cables to transformers. (10) Primary step-up transformer station. Here the current is stepped up to 132,000 volts for primary transmission lines. (11-11) Primary transmission lines carrying 132,000 volts and connected up to other main power stations throughout the country. (12) Primary step-down transformer station. Here the current is stepped down to 66,000 volts for secondary transmission lines. (13) 66,000 volts underground cables to town sub-station. (14) Town sub-station. Here the current is stepped down again to 400 or 250 volts for town supply. (15) 250 volt underground cables for house to house distribution. (16-16) Secondary transmission lines carrying 66,000 volts round sections of the countryside. (17-17) Secondary step-down transformer stations. Here the current is further reduced to 11,000 volts for rural transmission. (18) 11,000 volt underground cables to electric railways. (19) Transformer stations for railway. (20-20) 11,000 volt lines for rural transmission. (21-21) Local transformers again reduce the current to 250 volts for village supply. (22-22) 250 volts transmission lines. (23) 250 volt supply to farm. (24) 250 volt supply to country hotel. (25) 250 volt supply to quarry. (26) 11,000 volt supply to factory. (27) 250 volt underground cables to houses from factory transformers. It will be noticed that the whole system is interchangeable. Should the main power station fail or be overloaded the supply can be maintained from other main power stations or vice versa.

L. ASHWELL WOOD

ICITY

PICTURE REVIEW OF EAGLE'S SECOND YEAR

Dan Dare Recording. At Star Sound Studios in London, Frank Hampson, with son Peter, explains to *Eaglers* how the machine works. This was the first recording of Dan Dare.

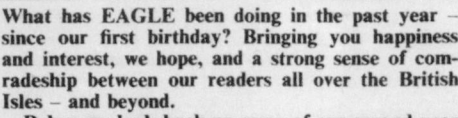

What has EAGLE been doing in the past year — since our first birthday? Bringing you happiness and interest, we hope, and a strong sense of comradeship between our readers all over the British Isles — and beyond.

Below we look back on some of our second year activities in pictures and hope you will enjoy them.

Visit to the T.T. Races at the Isle of Man. The Editor and competition winners are photographed before they take their seats in the plane to fly them over to the Isle of Man.

Mug of the Year for 1951. EAGLE sent John Grimes, last year's No. 1 MUG, to Torquay with his mother for a summer holiday. Here you see John with Mr Hollyer and Mr March of Torquay Corporation.

Chat with an Engine Driver. Which is better – to be a passenger or the driver? Here you see the driver and fireman exchanging views with EAGLE readers at Waterloo.

The Daily Splash! On your mark . . . ready . . . and into the swimming pool was just part of the fun at our holiday camp at Little Canada, Isle of Wight, last summer.

Sampling the soup. Seeing round hotel kitchens can be a hungry business and when the cook says, "Try this, son," *Eaglers* are apt to form a quick queue! It tasted good, too!

See that up there? Cadet W. P. Embleton of the Canadian Pacific *Beaverdell* shows an EAGLE party round the vessel at London Docks.

After Dinner. A good time for quiet reading or for exploring the "log cabin" at our Holiday Camp at Little Canada, Isle of Wight.

On the way to Lords. England's cricketers Denis Compton, Godfrey Evans and Alec Bedser stopped to have a friendly chat with *Eaglers* before the Test last June.

Film Premiere of *Tom Brown's Schooldays*. John Howard Davies, who played Tom Brown and who is also an EAGLE club member, chats to other *Eaglers* before they see the film premiere at the Gaumont Theatre, Haymarket.

Iceland Visit. Sponsored by EAGLE, Richard Lawrence and Michael Keen went with the British Schools Exploring Society's Expedition to Iceland. Their parents and EAGLE representative greet them on their return to London.

Christmas Carols at St Paul's. What better end to the year of 1951? St Paul's was filled to overflowing by EAGLE readers and their parents. Our collection was given to the Children's Society and Dr Barnardo's Homes.

Trip in a Helicopter. One of the high spots of our past year was a helicopter trip between Birmingham and London for prizewinners. *Eagler* Terence Ball finds the dashboard pretty exciting, especially with an interested pilot there to explain it all clearly.

A quiet corner. Robin Holloway's father was exhibiting at the Festival Exhibition of the Royal Society of British Artists. Half way round, Tony thought a rest was indicated so settled to read his EAGLE.

GLIDING AN

Gliding flight may be divided into three categories. First comes ordinary gliding, and then soaring and sailplaning. The first two must be learned before a pilot can undertake long, cross-country sailing flights.

Ordinary gliding or 'air tobogganing' consists of taking off from the top of hills or downs and gliding to earth. The machines used are more robustly constructed and not so refined in design as the sailplanes. Sailplaning itself is a much more skilled art and is performed with aircraft of the highest aerodynamic efficiency, one of which is shown here. On the right are depicted some of the tactics employed.

Both gliders and sailplanes are really aeroplanes without any means of self-propulsion. They fly without losing height, or actually gain height, by supporting themselves on air which is moving upwards. The pilot knows by experience the best places to find such air currents. For example, when a wind strikes a hillside the air is deflected upwards to a considerable height above it. Or again, warm air will always rise, forming what are known as thermal up-currents. As cumulus clouds owe their formation to the condensation of moisture due to ascending warm air, the experienced sailplane pilot uses these clouds, covering considerable distances by passing from one to the other.

KEY TO HOW IT WORKS

(1) Towing hook and quick-release. (2) Rubber landing skid. (3) Single under wheel. (4) Rudder pedals. (5) Cable to quick-release. (6) Pressure tube for air speed indicator. (7) Variometer flask connected to gauge. Used to register state of change in atmospheric pressure and tells pilot instantly when he is in a rising air current. (8) Instrument board. (9) Control stick. Backwards and forwards for elevator, and sideways for ailerons. (10) Elevator trim control. (11) Baragraph. (12) Oxygen bottle for great heights. (13) Aileron operating rods. (14) Control wires to rudder and elevator. (15) Main wing spar. (16) Dive brake operating rods. (17) Port ailerons. (18) Port diving brakes. (19) Starboard diving brakes, upper and lower, to prevent too steep a diving angle. (20) Starboard ailerons; these are divided to prevent distortion when the wing tips move in heavy air gusts. (21) Aileron control wires. (22) Fabric covered wing. (23) Plywood covered leading edge. (24) Plywood covered fuselage. (25) Tail skid. (26) Elevator control. (27) Fabric covered one-piece elevator. (28) Fabric covered rudder. (29) Elevator trim.

Launching: Gliders and sailplanes a car with a winch on back axle a can also be launched by man-powe

THE GLIDER

ING FLIGHT

How a sailplane pilot uses up-currents in the atmosphere.

(A) Pilot losing height.
(B) Up-current caused by hill.
(C) Pilot circling in rising air.
(D) Pilot losing height.
(E) Pilot using cumulus cloud.
(F) Pilot losing height until next cloud is reached.
(G) Pilot again using cloud.

L ASHWELL WOOD

EAGLE HAS ITS OWN SONG !

SPREAD YOUR WINGS

Words and Music by John Jerome

SPREAD YOUR WINGS, —————— SPREAD YOUR WINGS,

C   G7   C7   F   F   F♯ DIM

Copyright MCMLII by John Fields Music Co., Ltd.,

IT has been in our minds for a long time that EAGLE should have a song of its own. And, at last, it is ready! There's a catchy tune, easy to pick up, and words to fit.

The cost of the sheet music, which has a coloured EAGLE cover, is 1/3 and if you would like a copy, send a postal order for 1/3d made out to Hulton Press Ltd. and crossed "&/Co." to EAGLE Reader Services, Long Lane, Liverpool 9. Please also enclose a fairly large stamped addressed envelope in which we shall send you the music.

You'll find *Spread Your Wings* a rousing song for your camp fires, hikes and Club meetings. Hum it, whistle it or shout it – it sounds good any way!

Tea Party For Mugs

Towards the end of March a very successful get-together of "MUGS" in the Manchester area was held. Here is what George Hancock of Fallowfield, Manchester, had to say about it.

'I arrived at the Hulton Press offices in Mosely Street and found quite a number of the other "MUGS" already there. Mr Rover of Hulton's made us all feel at ease and we were soon talking to each other, discussing the latest copies of EAGLE, GIRL and the other Hulton publications which were on the table in his office.

'Mr Rover took us next door, to Lewis's Restaurant for tea. We soon decided what we wanted to eat, and within ten minutes we were all tucking into a lovely tea of plaice, chips, cakes, jelly and cream, and, of course, ginger pop!

'During the meal we discussed EAGLE, the articles in it and the various EAGLE products. The one thing we all agreed on was: that EAGLE, the EAGLE Club and everything to do with EAGLE is, well, just tops!'

Readers' Letters

(A prize of 5/- is paid for each letter published).

ABOUT TWO years ago our dog brought in a young jackdaw which had been pushed from a nest. He is full-grown now, but he is not as big as other jackdaws of his age. He has never been caged and he roams about the house and garden and so is great friends with Pip, our dog. – Martyn Spence, 8 The Grove, Felpham, Sussex.

* * *

WE HAVE all been proud in our town as Private Speakman, V.C., lives here. We had a half holiday the day he came home and everybody turned out with flags to welcome him. He rode in an open car, with the Mayor. Now he has gone back to Korea to his regiment. He was the first man to be decorated by Queen Elizabeth as he received his medal at the first Investiture. – Keith Dodds, The Rookery, 1 Woodlands Park Way, Timperley, Cheshire.

* * *

I WELL remember the day I first visited Wales. We stopped at Conway for an hour. What a lot I did in that short hour! I had my dinner and went to see "The Smallest house in Great Britain." It was certainly small, but the downstairs brasses were polished till they shone like gold. I saw and crossed the bridge. I sailed in a motor boat and I bathed. I was very impressed by the majestic castle. It stood out clearly against the skyline, but what struck me about all of Wales, was the Welsh people's hospitality, kindness and understanding. – J. Coppock, 3 Hillside Road, Offerton, Stockport, Cheshire.

Wings of the Morning

A 'Table-Top' model, made from his EAGLE Club badge and two lumps of coal, by R. W. TAYLOR (aged 13), 87 Westbury Road, Edgbaston, Birmingham 17.

Ever eager to extol the virtues of healthy, outdoor activity, *Eagle* ran regular features encouraging readers to get out and about. These covered everything from basic tips on how to enjoy hiking, through to how to get the most out of your Zoomerang. Remember, in the days before television and Playstations, it really was necessary to come up with your own entertainment.

ENJOY THE OPEN AIR — *Hiking (1)*

When going on a hike always wear loose clothes – open-neck shirt and shorts. A wind-cheater or sweater is useful. Roll-neck sweaters should be avoided. Woollen underclothes are most suitable for all weathers and the wearer is less likely to catch a chill. *Tips* – Two thin layers of clothes are warmer than one thick. To make an effective 'windcheater' on cold nights – wrap a few layers of newspaper round your chest inside a shirt.
Don't set out in new boots. Wear heavy boots, double-soled for strength, with hobnails in the sole and clinkers at the side to prevent slipping. The leather should be strong and waterproof, yet pliable. Treat the uppers with oil and dubbin to keep them waterproof and in good condition. Leave the top two holes unlaced and wear two pairs of socks to prevent chafing.

Before setting out, harden the skin by using Methylated spirit. On the road, wash the feet daily to keep them fresh and free from perspiration. If they tend to sweat dust them with talcum powder. *Tip* – to give relief to sore feet, use the 'magic' cure: dissolve some permanganate of potash in a bucket of warm water and soak the feet in this. Walk on the ball of the foot, just skimming the ground. Keep up a regular pace – it's easier and quicker. Whenever you rest, lie down (don't sit) and put your feet up on your rucksack.

A frame rucksack with pockets is best. It distributes weight evenly. Shoulder pads, waist strap, blanket and tent straps make the rucksack easier to carry. Pack soft articles against the back and shoulders. Cloth or plastic containers take less room than tins or boxes, are lighter; have no sharp edges. Raincoat and sweater should be easy to get at; food, cooking-equipment, maps and the first-aid outfit should preferably be carried in the side and front pockets. Then they can be got at without disturbing the rest of the kit. Before setting out, see that the rucksack sits easily on the shoulders.

Kit: (limit: 20 lbs.) Rucksack; groundsheet; sleeping-bag or blankets; sweater; towel; soap; tooth-paste and brush; comb; mirror; pyjamas; underclothing; socks; rain-cape; cotton; pins; needles; twine; swimming-pants; canvas shoes; aluminium canteen; knife; fork; spoon; tin-opener; mug; plate; canvas bucket; torch; matches; maps; first-aid outfit.

If a sleeping-bag is used instead of blankets, this should weigh between 2 and 5 lbs; if camping the tent should weigh about 2 lbs. It is better to use an ordinary sleeping-bag than a rubberized one, to avoid the inside being soaked with sweat every morning.
Never leave the finding of accommodation or a camping-ground until too late. Always stop about seven o'clock.

ENJOY THE OPEN AIR — *Learn to fly the EAGLE ZOOMERANG with JOHN McCALLUM*

John McCallum, well-known British film star, meets for the first time the EAGLE Zoomerang. Australian inventor, Frank Andrews, points out details to be observed when throwing. The Zoomerang is designed to fly from 70 to 100 yards, rise up to about 60 feet, perform a half barrel roll and return to the thrower.

John demonstrates how to hold the Zoomerang for throwing. Note that he is holding the end of the blade firmly. Any blade may be used but it is important that the labelled side faces towards the thrower's body. If reversed, the principle of flight is reversed also, and the Zoomerang would veer off and not return.

These two pictures illustrate the different angles at which the Zoomerang is held and thrown when the wind varies in strength. The Zoomerang must be thrown into or against the wind, as it is air pressure acting on the curved blades which causes it to perform the barrel roll and return. On the left the angle illustrated is for a fair to strong wind. On the right is the angle to be used for light air. The curve of the blades can be clearly seen in these photographs.

Having followed all the instructions carefully, John McCallum is ready for his first throw. Here he is about to launch the Zoomerang. He looks confident that he will get it right back!

This view shows John McCallum throwing at a slight upward angle. The wind is light so he holds the EAGLE Zoomerang flat when throwing, as shown in illustration 4 for light air.

This drawing shows how the EAGLE Zoomerang gradually rises and then performs the unusual barrel-roll before sweeping around in a wide arc to return to the thrower. Remember, it *must* be thrown *into* the wind.

WIND DIRECTION

A perfect throw and back comes the Zoomerang to be caught as it hovers gently down. John has thrown an Australian boomerang, but he finds the EAGLE Zoomerang much easier to control.

Here, Peter Barker of EAGLE, Frank Andrews and John McCallum discuss points of design and construction. The EAGLE Zoomerang is very strong, and can be obtained for 4/11d at most stores.

H.M.S. EAGLE

THE NEW WONDER AIRCRAFT CARRIER OF THE ROYAL NAVY

It is fitting that in the second birthday number of EAGLE we introduce the first and exclusive drawing of Britain's latest and largest aircraft carrier, with some of her crew spelling out her name on the flight deck.
H.M.S. Eagle has a displacement of 45,000 tons and the four sets of steam turbines give her a speed of 31½ knots. She is 803 ft. 9 ins. long and 112 ft. 9 ins. wide. The enormous area of flight deck is equivalent to over two acres.
The great hangars can accommodate over 100 aircraft. This space could stow 263 double-deck buses. The full crew is 2,750 men.
Armament consists of 16-4.5 in. high-angle dual-purpose guns and 60-40 m.m. Bofors anti-aircraft guns. The ship has the first operational squadron of jet aircraft to go into service with the Navy-Supermarine Attackers of 800 Squadron.
H.M.S. Eagle is indeed a fine ship. *In another issue of EAGLE we shall show one of the Attackers.*

HMS

KEY TO ABOVE DECKS

(1-1) Aircraft catapults. (2-2) Forward 4.5 in. guns. (3) Forward aircraft lift. (4-4) Multiple 40 m.m. anti-aircraft guns. (5) 5 ton mobile crane. (6) Flight control bridge. (7) Navigating bridge. (8) Fire control director towers. (9-9) Radar gun control apparatus. (10) Tripod mast with radar navigating scanner. (11) New type funnel. (12) Funnel uptakes from boiler room. (13) Single 40 m.m. guns. (14) Aircraft safety barriers lowered (six in all). (15) Aircraft safety barrier raised. (16) Single 40 m.m. guns. (17-17) Gunnery directors. (18) Multiple 40 m.m. anti-aircraft guns. (19) Fire control director towers. (20) Aerial masts. These are lowered outboard when flying is in progress. (21) Life saving Carley floats. (22) Flight deck centre line, marked off every 20 feet. (23) Supermarine Attacker jet aircraft parked on flight deck. (24) Aircraft and boat crane. (25) After aircraft lift (lowered). (26-26) After 4.5 in. guns. (27) Arrester wires (16 in all), to assist in pulling up landing aircraft, engage them with a hook on the tail. (28) Round down landing lights.

KEY TO BELOW DECKS

(29) After upper hangar. (30) After lower hangar. (31) Twin balanced rudders (port side). (32) Port propellers. (33) After port engine room. (34) Forward port engine room. (35) Ward room. (36) Officers' baths. (37) Torpedo room. (38) After boiler room. (39) Oil fuel tanks. (40) Forward boiler room. (41) Auxiliary machinery. (42) Aero-engine room. (43) Bakery. (44) Forward lower hangar. (45) Forward upper hangar. (46) Crew space and wash places.

THERE IS A SPECIAL MESSAGE FOR READERS ABOUT H.M.S. EAGLE ON PAGE 11

EAGLE

Flight to Adventure!

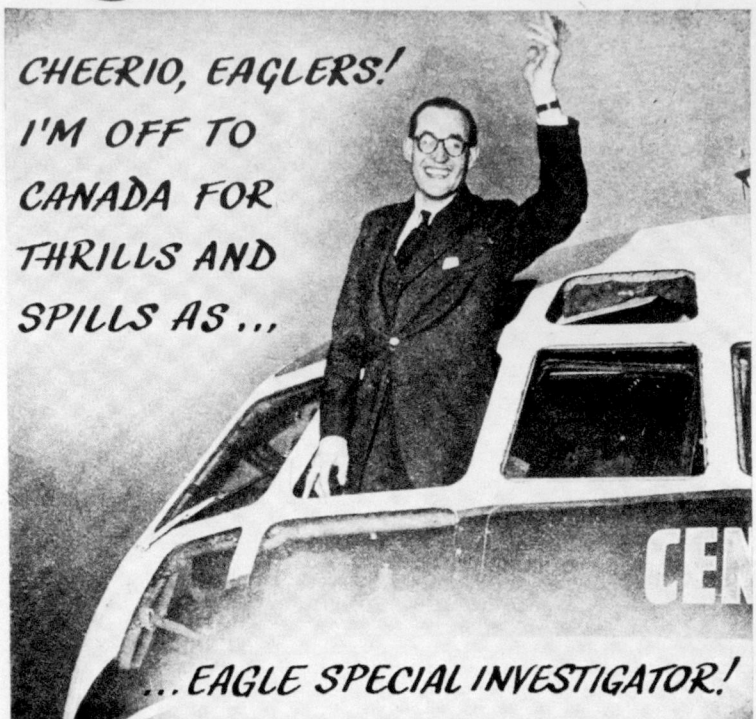

CHEERIO, EAGLERS! I'M OFF TO CANADA FOR THRILLS AND SPILLS AS ...

... EAGLE SPECIAL INVESTIGATOR!

Headline News! EAGLE has sent its own Special Investigator to Canada to provide *you* with first hand, thrilling accounts of adventure on that vast and varied Continent. Macdonald Hastings is going to drive a loco through the Rockies, pan for gold, visit a logging camp, travel by dog team to the remote posts of the Royal Canadian Mounted Police. He will also take a good look at the cockpit of a BOAC stratocruiser during his flight to Canada.

Thrills in plenty are in store for you during the following weeks. See that you're 'in' on EAGLE Special Investigator's Canadian adventures – they're going to be talked about by all the boys in Britain who read EAGLE. Be sure you don't miss them! Order your EAGLE now!

YIPPEE!

MACDONALD HASTINGS, Our Special Investigator, rides the range.

YIPPEE!

I FLY THE ATLANTIC

On the Flight Deck of a B.O.A.C. Stratocruiser
by MACDONALD HASTINGS

In the 20 June 1952 issue Macdonald Hastings began a report on one of his greatest early adventures. Travelling 15,000 miles in just 15 days, the self-styled *Eagle* Special Investigator (ESI) had been set a major task by his editor. His 1,000 mile-a-day journey would see him riding with cowboys, investigating with the Mounties, racing a dog-team in the frozen north and travelling through the Rocky Mountains on the Canadian Pacific Railway. Squeezed in between all of this, he had to go logging, and mining for gold.

Such a trip was an expensive outlay for the *Eagle*, but they made sure they got their money's worth out of it by spreading Hastings' reports over 16 weeks. The final instalment came on the 19 September, with Macdonald being hunted by a Grizzly Bear. When it was all over he needed, in his words, 'a stiff double milkshake'.

From the Editor

EAGLE, 4 New St Square, London EC4

14 March, 1952

BECAUSE EAGLE goes to press a few weeks before it reaches your newsagent, it was not possible for us to pay tribute in these pages to His Majesty King George VI at the time of his death. I feel, however, that you would not want me to let the passing of our beloved King go by without my talking to you about him.

King George VI stood for all the ideals which I hope are the aims of each one of you. Here was a man who, although afflicted with ill-health, strove to overcome his handicaps so completely that he became one of the most sincerely loved monarchs of our history. Here was a man, good, kind, courageous – and who, for all his Crown of State, was imbued with the humility of the truly great, thus endearing himself to the old and young, the rich and poor, the strong and the weak. May we all learn from his gracious example.

As head of a great Empire our young Queen Elizabeth has a heavy and arduous task before her. The devotion of the youth of the country can be a great help to her and I am sure all of you will serve her with wholehearted loyalty.

CONGRATULATIONS to the following on winning the MUG's Badge: Twelve-year-old *Noel Spreadbury* of 16 Bells Orchard, Wareham, Dorset, has received high recommendations from both home and school for his sound common sense and quickness to be of service whenever he can. He was going to dinner with two or three of his school friends when a nasty accident occurred involving an old lady who was badly hurt. Noel had never seen a bad accident before; nevertheless he was in action at once and the speed with which he got through to the police and the help he gave to the old lady, assisted by Georgina Barnes, another pupil, marks him out as a true MUG.

Yours sincerely,

Marcus Morris

NATURE INVENTED IT FIRST

SECONDARIES

PRIMARIES

A BIRD'S FLIGHT DEPENDS MAINLY ON ITS PRIMARY AND SECONDARY FEATHERS. IF THESE QUILL FEATHERS, AS THEY ARE CALLED, BECOME DAMAGED, THE ABILITY TO FLY IS LESSENED, AND MAY EVEN BE LOST UNTIL THE DAMAGE IS REPAIRED.

THE BARBS ON EACH SIDE OF THE QUILL ARE BOUND TOGETHER BY A SERIES OF HOOKS WORKING IN A WAY SIMILAR TO A ZIP FASTENER. A RUFFLED FEATHER CAN BE RESTORED TO SHAPE BY A SLIDING PRESSURE OF THE FOREFINGER AND THUMB ALONG THE BARBS, MOVING FROM THE QUILL OUTWARDS. A BIRD PREENS ITS QUILL FEATHERS IN THE SAME MANNER, ITS BEAK TAKING THE PLACE OF THE FOREFINGER AND THUMB.

BARBS

QUILL

QUILL

BARB

BARB

A DIAGRAM OF THE HOOKS OR BARBULES (NOT TO SCALE). CLAWS OF THE DISTAL BARBULES HOOK ON TO THE RACKS FORMED BY THE PROXIMAL BARBULES. THE HOOKS ARE MIN LIKE FINE HAIRS, PACKED CLOSE TOGETHER, KNITTING TH BARBS INTO A FLEXIBLE, WIND-PROOF SURFACE. IN THE PICTURE A SPACE HAS BEEN LEFT BETWEEN THE BARBU AND THEIR SHAPE SIMPLIFIED IN ORDER TO SHOW THEIR ARRANGEMENT AND THE METHOD OF WORKING.

ONE DRY SPRING, A HOUSE MARTIN, SEEKING MATERIAL FOR ITS NEST, BECAME ENTRAPPED IN THE MUD OF A HALF DRY POND. WHEN RESCUED, ITS PLUMAGE WAS COVERED WITH THICK SLIME.

TOLD AND DRAWN BY BACKHOUSE

TO PREVENT IT CAKING ON THE PLUMAGE, THE SLIME WAS RINSED OFF. THE MARTIN, ITS PLUMAGE SOAKING AND BEDRAGGLED, AND UNABLE TO FLY, BEGAN PREENING ITSELF USING A SLIDING ACTION TO RESTORE THE ALL IMPORTANT WING FEATHERS, NEARLY TYING KNOTS IN ITSELF TO REACH THE TIPS OF THE WING AND TAIL.

AFTER MANY STOPS FOR A REST, THE MARTIN T OFF TO REJOIN ITS COMPANIONS, ITS PLUMAG RESTORED TO SHAPE, THE BARBULES OF THE W FEATHERS RE-HOOKED. NEXT TIME YOU SLIDE T TAG OF A ZIP-FASTENER, REMEMBER THAT NA WORKED OUT THE IDEA FIRST.

Occasionally, *Eagle* would run a series which appeared to be based on one or two great ideas, but then expatiated on the subject matter for too long. 'Nature Invented It First' and 'Their Names Made Words' are two classic examples.

'Nature Invented It First' appears to be a fantastic concept when it compares the zip fastener with the barbs on the feather of a bird's wing, but when it compares a whale to a submarine, it's time to move on.

Similarly, '*Their Names Made Words*' is quite marvellous when relating the story of the Earl of Sandwich and his bread meal which he created to avoid having to stop playing cards to eat. The creation of the Cardigan (thank you James Thomas Brudenell, 7th Earl of Cardigan) is also a treasure, as are the tales of Plimsoll, Macadam, Wellington, and … actually they're all really good.

THEIR NAMES MADE WORDS — *Cardigan*

James Thomas Brudenell 7th Earl of Cardigan (1797-1868)

THE 7th EARL OF CARDIGAN LIVED AT A TIME WHEN COMMISSIONS IN THE ARMY COULD BE BOUGHT. HE WAS AMBITIOUS AND WEALTHY AND BOUGHT HIS WAY STEADILY UP UNTIL, IN 1832, HE PURCHASED THE COMMAND OF THE 15th HUSSARS, AS HE WANTED TO WEAR THEIR SPLENDID UNIFORM.

HIS BROTHER OFFICERS HATED HIM FOR BUYING HIS WAY OVER THEIR HEADS, AND HIS FIERCE TEMPER DID NOT MAKE THINGS ANY EASIER. IN 1840 HE WOUNDED ONE OF HIS OFFICERS IN A DUEL ON WIMBLEDON COMMON. DUELLING WAS ILLEGAL SO LORD CARDIGAN WAS ARRESTED AND TRIED IN THE HOUSE OF LORDS HE WAS FOUND "NOT GUILTY" ON A TECHNICAL POINT.

IN 1854 THE CRIMEAN WAR WITH RUSSIA BROKE OUT AND LORD CARDIGAN WENT OUT WITH THE ARMY IN COMMAND OF A CAVALRY BRIGADE.

AT THE BATTLE OF BALACLAVA ON OCTOBER 25th, 1854, A MISUNDERSTOOD ORDER LED TO THE FAMOUS CHARGE OF THE LIGHT BRIGADE IN WHICH LORD CARDIGAN, GALLOPING IN FRONT OF HIS MEN, LED THEM IN THE ILL-FATED ATTACK ON THE HEAVILY-DEFENDED RUSSIAN BATTERIES.

WINTER IN THE CRIMEA WAS SO HARD AND BITTER THAT IT WAS SAID THE RUSSIANS HAD TWO EXTRA GENERALS FIGHTING FOR THEM — GENERALS JANUARY AND FEBRUARY. OUR TROOPS SUFFERED SEVERELY FROM THE COLD AND WRAPPED THEMSELVES IN EVERY BIT OF CLOTHING THEY COULD FIND. ON THEIR HEADS THEY WORE WHAT BECAME KNOWN AS "BALACLAVA HELMETS" — STILL IN USE TODAY.

LORD CARDIGAN INVENTED FOR HIS OWN USE AGAINST THE COLD WHAT HE DESCRIBED AS "A LONG WOOLLEN OVER-WAISTCOAT". OTHER OFFICERS COPIED HIM AND ORDERED WHAT THEY CALLED "CARDIGANS" AFTER HIM.

EAGLE 7 November 1952

THEIR NAMES MADE WORDS — *Sandwich*

John Montagu 4th Earl of Sandwich (1718-1792)

JOHN MONTAGU SUCCEEDED HIS GRANDFATHER AS EARL OF SANDWICH IN 1729. HE WAS EDUCATED AT ETON AND CAMBRIDGE, AND TOOK HIS SEAT IN THE HOUSE OF LORDS IN 1739 AS A FOLLOWER OF THE POWERFUL DUKE OF BEDFORD.

THANKS TO THE INFLUENCE OF THE DUKE OF BEDFORD HE HELD MANY IMPORTANT AND WELL PAID POSTS, ALTHOUGH HE WAS INTERESTED IN NONE OF THEM. HE WAS FIRST LORD OF THE ADMIRALTY FROM 1771 TO 1782, WHILE THE AMERICAN WAR OF INDEPENDENCE WAS BEING FOUGHT, AND IT WAS PARTLY DUE TO HIS BAD ADMINISTRATION THAT BRITAIN LOST THE WAR.

NEVER BEFORE HAD THE ROYAL NAVY BEEN SO BADLY RUN. BRIBES WERE TAKEN, STORES STOLEN, SHIPS SENT TO WAR UNSEAWORTHY AND WITHOUT ENOUGH AMMUNITION, FOOD OR STORES. THE "ROYAL GEORGE" SANK IN STILL WATER AT SPITHEAD, WITH HEAVY LOSS OF LIFE, BECAUSE A GREAT PIECE OF HER BOTTOM FELL OUT.

HIS ONLY GOOD ACTION WAS HIS ENCOURAGEMENT OF CAPTAIN COOK IN HIS EXPLORATIONS. IN RETURN, WHEN COOK DISCOVERED SOME ISLANDS IN THE PACIFIC, HE CALLED THEM THE SANDWICH ISLANDS. (THEY ARE NOW CALLED HAWAII.)

CHART OF THE SANDWICH ISLANDS

LORD SANDWICH PREFERRED GAMBLING TO ANYTHING ELSE AND WOULD SPEND LONG HOURS AT THE CARD TABLE. ONE DAY, HE WAS SO BUSY PLAYING CARDS AT HIS CLUB THAT HE DID NOT WANT TO STOP FOR DINNER, SO HE TOLD THE WAITER TO BRING HIM A SLICE OF MEAT BETWEEN TWO SLICES OF BREAD.

OTHER MEN FOLLOWED SUIT AND TOLD THE WAITER TO BRING THEM A "SANDWICH". SO THE CUSTOM SPREAD UNTIL TODAY MORE "SANDWICHES" ARE EATEN THAN EVER BEFORE.

EAGLE 22 June 1956

THE ROUTEMASTER
THE WORLD'S MOST UP-TO-DATE BUS

The prototype of London's 'Bus of the future', the 64-seater *Routemaster*, has recently gone into public service.

The new bus, which is of revolutionary design, will be produced in quantity in about three years' time and will replace London's trolleybuses as they become worn out.

Between 1,600 and 1,700 of the new buses will be built, at an approximate cost of £8,000,000.

The *Routemaster* is of chassis-less design, with the front and rear mechanical units carried on sub-frames which are attached to the body. The engine is an A.E.C. 9.6-litre Diesel, developing 125 h.p., and the radiator is mounted under the main floor. Gear selection is by electro-hydraulic valves operated by a lever on the steering column, thus providing only two foot-pedal controls, accelerator and brake.

Additional comfort for passengers is provided by the coil springs on the front wheels and very large hydraulic shock-absorbers on the rear sub-frame — the first bus in the world to have 'private car' independent springing.

L. ASHWELL WOOD

RM1

SLT 56

The detachable parts of the front portions of the *Routemaster* make for easy maintenance.

(A) Air intake to radiator fan.

(B) Side-lights.

(C) Head-lights.

(D) Adjustable fog-light.

THE ROUT

EAGLE 22 June 1956

KEY TO PARTS

(1) Inlet to air-conditioning system. (2) New-type direction indicator. (3) Route-number panel. (4) Gear selection lever on steering column. (5) Hand-brake lever; rear wheels only. (6) Accelerator and foot-brake. (7) A.E.C. 9.6-litre Diesel engine. (8) Fuel injection pump. (9) Independent front coil springs. (10) Track rod from worm and nut steering gear. (11) Fluid flywheel transmission. (12) Radiator header tank. (13) Radiator with air intake on top, mounted under the floor. The fan and water-pump is at the forward end. (14) Front sub-frame member. (15) Point of attachment to body frame (either side). (16) Fuel tank; 25 gallons. (17) Universal joints of driving shaft. (18) Electrically-selected and hydraulically-operated, direct transmission four-speed gearbox. (19) Four-wheel, hydraulic foot-brake supply cylinders. (20) The entire central section is arranged under the floor. (21) Exhaust silencer. (22) Point of attachment to body frame (either side). (23) Rear sub-frame member. (24) Universal joints of driving shaft. (25) Spiral bevel final drive to back axle. (26) Rear sub-frame carrying back axle. (27) Offside hydraulic shock-absorber. (28) Nearside hydraulic shock-absorber. (29) The conductor has a special recess in which to stand, giving a clearer way for passengers getting on and off the bus.

1856 – 1956

The London General Omnibus Company was formed a hundred years ago. This interesting comparison shows the winning design in a contest for the best horse-bus when the company began operations.

It seated twelve passengers inside, six a side, facing each other (like 'trussed fowls', as a critic said) and room for ten more on the roof, sitting back to back. From 2-horse power to 125-horse power a hundred years later, London Transport's latest, the Routemaster, seats sixty-four passengers in well-upholstered comfort.

EMASTER

MAN ABOUT THE HOUSE

SMASHED THE CROCKERY? THEN MEND IT!

CLEAN, SIMPLE BREAKS LIKE THESE CAN BE MENDED WITH SUCCESS, BUT NOT THE VERY SPLINTERY KIND LIKE THIS.

CLEAN ALL BROKEN SURFACES WITH SOAP AND HOT WATER. ALLOW TO DRY OUT THOROUGHLY.

APPLY A THIN FILM OF WATERPROOF GLUE OR CHINA CEMENT TO THE SURFACES TO BE JOINED AND PRESS HOME FIRMLY.

KNOT AND TIGHTEN BY TWISTING A STICK BETWEEN THEM.

TWIST

PRESSURE — WHEREVER POSSIBLE, PUT ON A TOURNIQUET FOR 24 HOURS. TO DO THIS TAKE TWO TURNS OF STRING ROUND THE OBJECT.

KNOT UNDERNEATH

THE TOP BREAK IS HELD BY TWISTED STRING. GUMMED STRIP KEEPS THIS PIECE IN PLACE UNTIL SET.

MAN ABOUT THE HOUSE

BLEEP, BLOP! IS THAT TAP DRIPPING?

THE INSIDE OF A TAP. WHEN THE TAP IS TURNED OFF, THE JUMPER AND WASHER COME DOWN AND SEAL THE PASSAGE.

A WORN WASHER CAUSES THE TAP TO DRIP.

BEFORE YOU START, TURN OFF THE WATER BY THE MAIN STOPCOCK. THIS WILL BE IN THE HOUSE OR BOXED IN THE GROUND OUTSIDE. IF THE TAP IS FED FROM A TANK, SHUT OFF THE TANK STOPCOCK.

JUMPER   WASHER

UNSCREW

ANOTHER KIND OF TAP

1. WITH A WRENCH OR ADJUSTABLE SPANNER, UNSCREW TOP AND LIFT OUT.

3. FIT NEW WASHER. REPLACE NUT. SCREW ON TAP AGAIN AND TURN ON WATER.

2. USING PLIERS, UNDO SMALL NUT (A) WHICH HOLDS OLD WASHER (B) TO JUMPER (C). REMOVE OLD WASHER.

ENJOY THE OPEN AIR *Cooling Off*

When out for a hike, or a cycle ride, you'll enjoy a swim. Wait until you have cooled down. Don't swim in *extremely* cold water because it will sap your energy; and don't bathe for at least half an hour after a meal.

Make enquiries locally that the attractive, "unknown" spot you have chosen is SAFE. Don't swim where there is a sudden drop at the bottom. Deep holes and ledges are dangerous. Bathe in the sea only when the tide is coming in.

When wading into unfamiliar water, keep your arms do at water level. If you hold them straight in the air a step into an unsuspected hole you will sink like a sto Duck your head as soon as you enter the water to equ ise body temperature. Out of all the various swimm strokes the Crawl or the Breast-stroke are probably most useful for all-round swimming in pool river or s

Scull on the back for quiet and restful enjoyment. To do this, simply lie flat on your back with your eyes looking at your toes as they peep out above the surface. Thrash your legs steadily up-and-down and, with hands held to your sides, let them scull gently from the wrists, pushing the water towards your feet.

From sculling on your back next try the Back Crawl. In the same position, and with the same leg action, move your arms backwards alternately in windmill fashion, allowing each to enter the water, little finger first, almost in line with the shoulder. As each arm enters the water pull it vigorously forward under water as far as the thigh.

Don't swim in strange places by yourself. If you cramp, turn on your back and float. If it is seri your friend can help you by approaching you fr the rear, passing his left arm over your left sho der, and holding your chin in his left hand. W your shoulders resting on his chest, he can then you to safety by swimming on his back. If you bathing from a boat, always remember to ge and out over the stern or it may capsize.

YOU CAN TAKE THE REVEREND OUT OF THE PARISH BUT...

EDITOR --------

From the EDITOR

EAGLE, New St. Square, London, E.C.4.

15 August, 1952

AS I write this, it is a warm summer afternoon, and I have turned my office chair round towards the window to catch any breeze that is blowing. Through my open window, the first object that catches the eye is the steeple of the Church of St Bride's, Fleet Street's own particular church, of which I have the privilege to be an honorary chaplain.

St Bride's is a church of unusual interest. Burned down in the Great Fire of London in 1666, it was rebuilt by the famous architect, Sir Christopher Wren in 1680. In 1701 he added its famous tall steeple of 234 feet. After a severe storm in 1764 the steeple was damaged and reduced in height by 8 feet. Then came the Nazi bombing of the recent war and in December 1940 the church was burned out completely, but still the steeple remained standing.

The church is now in process of being rebuilt and during present excavations many remarkable discoveries have been made, notably some Roman remains, ancient pieces of pottery and even some seven-foot skeletons! With such a wealth of history behind it, you can understand that St Bride's is a landmark to be proud of. I have asked our artist to draw a picture of the steeple as it looks from our office windows and you can see it in the first column of this letter.

EAGLE Club members and readers alike will, I know, feel very proud of Barry Woods, August's MUG of the Month, whose story and photograph you see on this page. It was a very fine effort indeed.

Barry's father was in hospital when this incident happened and he was amazed, and proud, when a fellow patient drew his attention to a newspaper report on the rescue and said, "Is this your son?"

We want to know more about boys who have done something worthwhile, whether it be an act of bravery or a difficult situation tackled with courage and determination.

Yours sincerely,

Marcus Morris

* * *
Try This One

I TIME the aeroplanes passing over my house every night in the week, then check them the following week. If they are on time I tick them, if they are not, I put a little cross by them and wait for the following week.

Has any other reader of EAGLE a hobby like this? — Raymond Crompton, Glamorgan, S. Wales.

EAGLE 15 June 1956

THE GERMAN POCKET-BAT

The 10,000 ton German Pocket-Battleship *Admiral Graf Spee*, out-shot and out-manoeuvred by three British cruisers at the Battle of the River Plate in 1939, was one of three Pocket-Battleships serving in the German Navy during World War II. Ingenious in design, these ships were the first of such size to have electrically welded hulls, and to be propelled by Diesel engines. *Graf Spee's* engines gave her a remarkable speed of 26 knots !

KEY TO NUMBERS: (1) Quarter deck. (2) Rudder. (3) Starboard propeller. (4) Quadruple torpedo tubes. (5) Officers' quarters. (6) Ship's office. (7) Three 11-inch Krupp guns; maximum range, 30,000 yards. (8) After gun-turret. (9) Fresh-water tanks. (10) Torpedo room. (11) 11-inch magazine. (12) Operating theatre. (13) Sick bay. (14) 5.9-inch magazine. (15) Auxiliary machinery. (16) Gun trunk. (17) Engineers' mess. (18) After starboard 5.9-inch guns. (19) After twin 4.1-inch anti-aircraft guns. (20) After main director-tower and range-finder. (21) Reconnaissance seaplane. (22) Catapult. (23) Secondary armament director-tower. (24) Mainmast. (25) Engine exhaust vents. (26) Searchlight platform. (27) Admiral's barge. (28) Starboard twin 4.1-inch anti-aircraft guns. (29) After starboard M.A.N. Diesel engines. (30) Forward starboard M.A.N. Diesel engines. Altogether there are eight sets of these engines employed, developing some 54,000 h.p. It was reported, at the time, that the high speed produced by these Diesels resulted in a vibration so severe as to interfere with accurate shooting during the River Plate action. (31-31) Vulcan clutch. (32-32) Oil fuel tanks in double hull. (33) Starboard gear-box. (34) Torpedo bulge. (35) 5.9-inch magazine. (36) Petty Officers' mess. (37) Seamen's mess. (38) Fans. (39) Stores. (40) Forward starboard 5.9-inch guns. (41) Armourer. (42) Foremast. (43) Upper control top and range-finder. (44) Searchlight platform. (45) Control tower. (46) Conning tower and range-finder. (47) Forward gun-turret. These turrets are fitted with bomb-deflecting crowns. (48) Three 11-inch Krupp guns; maximum range, 30,000 yards. (49) Main ammunition trunk. (50) Magazines and handing rooms for 11-inch guns. (51) Compressors. (52) Seamen's mess. (53) Breakwater. (54) Capstan gear. (55) Pronounced chine. (56) Chain locker. (57) Paint store. (58) Bulbous bow to reduce wave resistance.

THE POCKET

HIP ADMIRAL GRAF SPEE

EAGLE 15 June 1956

WEIGHT OF SHELL AND BROADSIDE OF THE SHIPS ENGAGED IN THE BATTLE OF THE RIVER PLATE COMPARED

"GRAF SPEE"   "EXETER"   "AJAX & ACHILLES"

CAST STEEL
SHELLITE
EXPLODER
BASE FUSE
DRIVING BAND

11 IN. SHELL—670 LBS.   8 IN. SHELL—256 LBS.   6 IN. SHELL—100 LBS.

The total broadside of the *Spee* weighed 4,708 lbs. The COMBINED total broadside of *Exeter, Ajax* and *Achilles* weighed 3,136 lbs!

RIVETING AND WELDING COMPARED

ANGLE PIECES
RIVETED
WELDED
JOINTS

This diagram illustrates how angle pieces and rivets considerably increase weight as compared to welded joints. By using the latter method in the construction of the *Graf Spee*, it effected a saving of 550 tons.

BATTLESHIP

EAGLE GALLERY
OF FAMOUS SPORTSMEN

No. 36   FRED TRUEMAN
(Yorkshire and England)

This 21-year-old ex-miner from Stainton, Yorkshire, who is at present serving in the R.A.F., made a sensational Test debut for England this season when he took four India wickets for 27 runs, three of them in eight balls without conceding a run. Already he is being called a second Larwood because, in short spells, he is the fastest bowler England has had since the "Nottingham Express" was in his prime. Fred, who is strongly-built, and also a hard-hitting batsman, made his first appearance in first-class cricket in 1949, and was selected for a Test trial in 1950. Last year he did the "hat trick" against Notts and gained his county cap. He is certainly a player to watch.

EAGLE GALLERY
OF FAMOUS SPORTSMEN

No. 67   JOE DAVIS

Joe Davis, undefeated World Snooker champion for twenty years, is one of sport's greatest names. Recently, aged 51, Joe completed his 500th century, a feat that will probably never be equalled. To score a snooker century a player must 'pot' one of twenty-one balls in one of six pockets with every stroke, playing reds and colours in correct order until 100 has been scored.

Joe made his first century in 1927, his 500th in February of this year. Most of his hundreds were made with 'Old Faithful', the cue he bought for 7s 6d in 1929.

PETER MURPHY (Birmingham City) beats his man

Former Spurs player, PETER MURPHY, noted for his speed, craft and accurate marksmanship, has played a big part in Birmingham City's League and Cup success this season, and in the pictures he demonstrates a sleight-of-foot trick that had Tommy Briggs somewhat baffled. 'Got him this time!' Tommy thought to himself as he advanced to the tackle. He was almost certain that Peter would attempt to move the ball outside him. Then he had a moment's doubt. A feint of Peter's foot, and the mere hint of a sway *inside* made Tommy sta shift his weight – just what Peter wanted. At once the quicksilver inside forward ma oblique turn and swept past him on the outside with the ball under close control. Si So it looks in the pictures. But in fact it all happened quick-as-a-wink, the result of Tom split-second's hesitation. And of course it is the result of years of practice on Peter's

RANDY TURPIN'S PET PUNCHES by W. BARRINGTON DALBY No 1

[Pictures by Carl Sutton]

Here you see Randy shadow-boxing, and in the pictures he is setting himself to throw that devastating left hook which has put many of his opponents down for the full count. Notice his beautiful balance and intense concentration as he looks for the opening.

He starts the punch – forward and upward – and then whips it over towards the jaw of his imaginary opponent. Notice particularly how Randy is turning his wrist at the last moment to make sure of landing with the knuckle part of the closed glove.

SPUNKY'S SPORTS QUIZ

What is the length of a Rugby pitch?

Answer: The laws state that the distance between goal-line and goal-line must not exceed 110 yards.

PROFESSOR BRITTAIN EXPLAINS: TIM

ny Questions?

Write to Professor Brittain, c/o EAGLE, if you have any questions or problems you would like him to deal with. He will be on this page from time to time.

P.C. 49'S CHRISTMAS PARTY

All the Gang had got together
  For a wizard Christmas Treat.
Happy laughter shook each rafter at The Club!
Outside was bitter weather –
Driving snow and blinding sleet;
  Inside was Bags of Cheer and Tons of Grub!

Sure, the MULLIGANS were present –
  Och, they're Terrible those Twins!
And they're up to ev'ry mortal kind of trick.
But you can't tell who's the culprit,
For they're like as two new pins
  And you might be blaming PAT instead of MICK.

There were TOBY, MONGATIKI,
  SNORKY, GIGS and BUNNY, too,
With his funny little "physog" all a-shine,
Impatiently awaiting
For a certain Bloke in Blue –
  Their Friend and Founder – P.C. FORTY-NINE.

When at last their Hero entered
  How the Gang began to shout!
They nearly burst his eardrums with the din!
They drank his health thrice over
Till the Ginger Beer ran out,
  Then ev'rybody started tucking in!

How they talked of the Adventures
  They had shared in days gone past
And the perils they had faced beside their Chum.
The pile of grub diminished
And the moments flew too fast
  While they dreamed of New Adventures yet to come.

All too soon the Party ended,
  All too soon the grub was gone,
Then at last The Founder scrambled to his feet.
"Well, Cheerio!" he chortled,
"Time and Crime are marching on,
  And it's time that I got marching on my beat!"

As he stood there, gaily waving
  At the open Clubroom door
He little knew that just across the road
Two evil men were waiting
With a grudge against the Law
  And so begins – "The Case of The Spotted Toad."

CONTINUED

READERS' LETTERS

5/- is paid for each letter published. Readers who want a reply to their letter should enclose a stamped addressed envelope.

You'll See Why, Too

WHEN I saw the photograph of John Bray (*top*), MUG OF THE MONTH in a recent EAGLE, I showed it to my mother and father and told them it was me. I am enclosing a photograph which was taken at school a month ago and you will see why. – David Atkinson, Blackpool.

John Carroll

CONGRATULATIONS, EAGLE, on your really magnificent comic. I have read every one since the first. I have been in hospitals for the last six years on and off. I have had half of my left lung removed and am now going to have half of my right one taken out. But through all that I have never missed my EAGLE. Once more, congratulations and keep up the good work. – John Carroll, Collier Pavilion, Plamount Sanatorium, Newcastle, Co. Dublin.

[Glad you keep so cheerful, John. Best wishes from all of us. – Ed.]

Beats Them All

I AM a regular reader of the EAGLE and I noticed recently a letter from a boy stating that he had kept various animals.

As an animal loving family, we decided to count up the animals we have had, and were astounded to find the total came to 700. Ranging from horses, goats, dogs, cats, wild and domestic rabbits, guinea-pigs, mice, hedgehogs, moles, slow-worms, frogs, toads, newts and cold water fish, poultry; birds comprising budgerigars, canaries, parrots, parrakeets, pigeons, British birds including rooks, jackdaws and a tame little owl, and finally land and water tortoises. Is this a record? – John Bradshaw, Goring-by-Sea.
P.S. – To cap it all I have one brother and four sisters.

[We've had hundreds of letters from readers telling us how many pets they have, but this one caps the lot! – Ed.]

In the very first issue of *Eagle* there is a character called Tommy Walls. He appears as a normal strip and has adventures in the same way as any of the other characters in the comic. But Tommy Walls hides a dark secret. He's not trying to save the world or stop bad men doing nasty things. His only aim is to sell ice cream. This isn't necessarily the first example of subliminal advertising, or even advertorial, but to today's sophisticated audience it appears rather crude. In a world where life was simple, it seems to be taking advantage of naïve young boys who just want to be like their heroes. This type of advertorial appeared throughout the Fifties. It could be a strip as with Tommy Walls (the first few of which were actually drawn by Dan Dare's creator Frank Hampson) or, as here, in story form. Both worked their marketing magic on unsuspecting readers.

READERS' EFFORTS

Why not 'have a go' yourself? Original short stories, poems, drawings or puzzles should be sent to Readers' Efforts, EAGLE, Long Lane, Liverpool 9. A guinea is paid for each effort published.

Stories and poems should be short, please, and do your drawings in Indian ink, on unlined paper. Ask your parent to sign your effort, saying that it is original. If you want it returned, please enclose a stamped and addressed envelope.

← Drawn by T. N. TARLING (*aged 16*), 37 Carlyon Avenue, South Harrow, Middlesex.

Country Cottage. Drawn by C. JONES (*aged 16*), Delfryn, Pemberton, Llanelly, S. Wales.

Another Try!

Written by EILEEN FEARNE (*aged 14*), 35 Leamore Street, Hammersmith, London W.6.

Competitions I have to try
  Although to no avail,
It makes me want to sit and sigh
  To see the way I fail.

Since EAGLE started to appear
  I've always tried my luck,
Sent in puzzles to Bike-a-Week,
  But no luck yet have struck.

There was Competition Corner,
  I've never won that yet,
And then I tried to win myself
  A portable wireless set.

I've tried so hard to win some Trix.
  Please don't call me a ninny,
For I am sending this to you
  To try and win a guinea!

BIRD SILHOUETTES. A puzzle drawn and set by MICHAEL ROSEBLADE (*aged 11*), 4 Rosedene, Christchurch Ave., N.W.6.

The seven silhouettes represent birds found in Great Britain. The birds must be named and the initial letter of each, when put together, spell out an animal. (*Answer: Column 4*).

Drawn by PETER HODKINSON (*aged 13*), 37 Brocklehurst Avenue, Macclesfield, Cheshire.

A coalminer leaving the colliery at the end of the day.

Drawn by BRENDAN LAW (*aged 12*), 10 Randolph Road, London W.9.

Cars

Written by ROBERT ATKINSON (*aged 12*), 12 Arnold Avenue, Birkby, Yorkshire.

Fast cars, slow cars,
Push-along-the-road cars,
Big cars, little cars,
Bulge-out-in-the-middle cars.
Dull cars, bright cars,
Go-all-through-the-night cars.
Loud cars, quiet cars,
Those-that-cause-a-riot cars.
Lend cars, bend cars,
This shall be the end cars.

BIRD SILHOUETTES
Solution to:
1. Pheasant.
2. Oyster Catcher.
3. Lapwing.
4. Eagle.
5. Cormorant.
6. Avocet.
7. Tern.

EAGLE 13 February 1953

BRITISH CARS FOR EXPORT
THE VAUXHALL *VELOX*

Did you know that, on an average, 27,000 British-made cars are exported every month from this country? Their value is £9,000,000.

The new Vauxhall *Velox* is one of these cars and is of outstanding design. It is long, wide and handsome, which has a special appeal for buyers overseas. The model shown here is fitted with left-hand steering. The 2½ litre, 6-cylinder 'square' engine, rated at 23½ h.p. gives a maximum speed of 80 m.p.h. The gearbox is built as a unit with the engine, and acceleration is 0 to 50 m.p.h. through all the gears, using the steering column gear-change lever, in 14 seconds.

The Vauxhall *Wyvern* is a very similar car but has a smaller, 1½ litre engine.

KEY TO PARTS

(1) Cooling radiator and fan. (2) Water pump and thermostat. (3) Air cleaner for carburettor. (4) Zenith carburettor. (5) Overhead valves. (6) Two rear pistons of 6-cylinder 'square' engine, that is, an engine in which the diameter of the piston is equal to the piston stroke. (7) Exhaust pipe. (8) Dynamo for charging battery. (9) Front Lockheed hydraulic brake; two-leading-shoe type. (10) Independent coil-spring front suspension. (11) Worm and ball steering gear. (12) Steering column gear changing connections to gearbox. (13) Single plate clutch. (14) Gearbox with three forward speeds and one reverse; synchromesh on top and second speeds. (15) 12-volt battery for starting, lighting and coil ignition. (16) Ventilation and car heating unit. (17) Ducts to car interior and anti-mist for windscreen. (18) Front universal. (19) Hand-brake lever for mechanically operated rear brakes. (20) Steering column gear-change lever. (21) Push-button door openers. (22) Outside push-button door openers. (23) Propeller shaft to back axle. (24) Propeller shaft recess for allowing up and down movement of the back axle. (25) Upholstery of back seat. (26) Rear universal joint. (27) Hypoid (off-centre) spiral bevel back axle drive and differential casing. (28) Hydraulic brake leads. (29) Leading and trailing shoe type hydraulic rear brakes. (30) Telescopic shock absorbers fixed to rear springs. (31) Petrol tank (11 gallons). (32) Luggage boot. (33) Spare wheel. (34) Exhaust pipe.

L. ASHWELL WOOD

VAUXHA

EAGLE 13 *February 1953*

RADIATOR RECOGNITION

Diagram showing the piston and cylinder of a 'square' engine. The bore and stroke are the same.

LL VELOX

The life of a Universe-saving hero can be tough, so home comforts are always gratefully received. The Automatic Shaving Kit and the hi-tech shower were years ahead of their time. They still are. Occasionally some of the artwork excels even the amazing standards set by the studio, and it is easy to see why so many of the artists worked such long unsociable hours. It seems unnecessary to have such high levels of detail, but it was this specifically which made *Eagle*, and *Dan Dare* and the all-important front-page, stand head and shoulders above the opposition of the time.

UNDER FIRE? YOU'RE TELLING ME, SIR! IT'S A BLOOMING BARRAGE!

WHAT IS IT, SIR? BOMBS OR SHELLS OR WHAT?

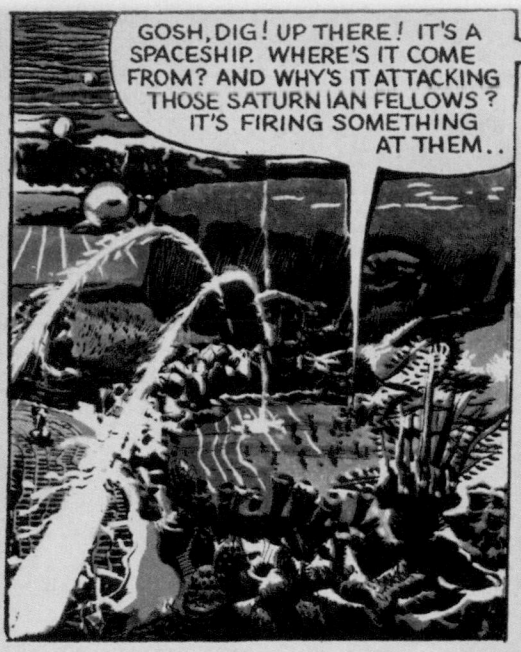

GOSH, DIG! UP THERE! IT'S A SPACESHIP. WHERE'S IT COME FROM? AND WHY'S IT ATTACKING THOSE SATURNIAN FELLOWS? IT'S FIRING SOMETHING AT THEM..

BUT I CAN'T MAKE OUT JUST *WHAT* IT'S FIRING EXACTLY —— THE EXPLOSIONS AREN'T UP TO MUCH, AND . . . .

THERE, SIR — THERE'S A DIRECT HIT — STRAIGHT AHEAD —IT'S A THING LIKE A DART— AND IT'S . .SPINNING . . .

THE PENCIL-LIKE PROJECTILE SPRAYS OUT A HEAVY LIQUID WHICH CATCHES A GROUP OF SATURNIANS...

. . . AND SPINS THEM ROUND HELPLESSLY WITH IT . . .

. . . CONGEALING AS IT MEETS THE AIR. IN A SPLIT SECOND IT SOLIDIFIES INTO A RUBBER-LIKE DISC. ITS CAPTIVES TRAPPED, IT GRADUALLY WOBBLES TO REST.

PHEW— *THEY'RE* WELL AND TRULY STUCK! A DOZEN DISC JOCKEYS *IN* ONE RECORD, EH, DIG? — WONDER WHAT HAPPENS NEXT? . . .

. . . BY THE ROW THEY'RE KICKING UP, *THEY* KNOW ALL RIGHT — AND THEY'RE DEAD SCARED!

OBVIOUSLY THEY'RE **SOME**BODY'S PRISONERS NOW! WE'VE LANDED IN THE MIDDLE OF A WAR — OR THE LOCAL COSH BOYS' CARNIVAL!

OH AYE— *WE WOULD!*

EE— LISTEN — I'M GOING BARMY—SOMEONE'S SHOUTING FOR HELP — *IN ENGLISH!*

BY GEORGE, YES! — IT'S THAT TINY SATURNIAN.

EARTHMEN! HELP! HELP ME, AND I'LL HELP YOU!

CONTINUED

PRIZEWINNERS AT THE CIRCUS

Two thousand EAGLE and GIRL prize-winners were taken to Bertram Mills Circus at Olympia, where they had a wonderful time. Horses, zebras, dogs, elephants, sea-lions and penguins all seemed set to give their best performance and appeared to enjoy the show every bit as much as the onlookers.

During the performance EAGLE readers were first amazed, then delighted, to find that the Mekon himself was performing in the ring.

At the end of the evening, Mr Bernard Mills asked two lucky members, sitting in certain seats, to come down into the ring where he presented them with seven tickets each for next year's Circus at Olympia.

The Auguste whispers a few friendly tips to the Mekon on circus ring procedure.

The Mekon at the Circus! But underneath that grim, green head it's really Paul, EAGLE's postboy!

WHODUNNIT?   Find the vital clue!

Alec, the office-boy, comes back from lunch to find the office ransacked and Miss Potts, the secretary, sitting tied in her chair.

Alec unties Miss Potts and phones the police. "What's happened?" he cries. Before Miss Potts can explain the police arrive.

Miss Potts tells the police inspector that two men held her up and tied her in the chair. Then they started to ransack the office before they found the week's takings.

The inspector seems to be satisfied – but Alec isn't. He tells the inspector something he's spotted which leads to Miss Potts' arrest. Can you spot what gave Miss Potts away?

The Leaf of Life

IN JAPAN there exists a plant which cannot be killed. Even when cut in half it will thrive without warmth or moisture. A leaf of it pressed between the pages of a book can throw out roots and grow. Such a plant was well named 'The Leaf of Life.' – *Ronald Webster, Camelon, Falkirk, Stirling.*

The Mekon's Here!

"HOW'S THIS for a scarer!" It won first prize in the local Coronation Carnival. – *H. Godsland, Easton, Nr. Stamford, Northamptonshire.*

CONKERS ... *a game linking the Elizabethan eras*

The game is as old as the country's horse-chestnut trees – it was mentioned by Shakespeare and played in the villages of Merrie England during the reign of Elizabeth I. Research has shown that the origins of the game are lost in the mists of antiquity; however, the experts say that it is quite likely that the game as we know it differs only slightly from the original game of Conqueror (hence the derivation 'Conkers') played by men in bygone times.

Text books of English folk-lore in the Central Reference Library, indicate that the recognized method of amassing victories, as in the case of a 'fiftyer' becoming a 'sixtyer' on beating a 'tenner', can be traced to the ancient superstitions of primitive warriors, who assumed that the virtues of a defeated enemy's weapon passed into their own when the battle was won.

During the reign of Good Queen Bess, Conkers was already established as a traditional game of English children. In a recent Television production of Shakespeare's *Merrie Wives of Windsor* – the boys in the play were shown playing Conkers. The picture shows a typical old-time game in progress.

Here is twelve-year-old Ian Lyons who recently defeated the pick of England's Conker players to become Television's National Champion. Ian's lapel proudly bears witness to his skill as a Konka player. Ian says, 'It's great fun and more interesting than ordinary Conkers – and most important of all – lets me play my favourite game all the year round!'

This shows the New Elizabethan Konka made of tough cellulose acetate – a material typical of this modern age. The counters and Eagle strung on the whipcord are for scoring, providing actual proof of the owner's prowess.

Here is Ian lining up for a 'strike'. The action is similar to the traditional version, with the difference that great accuracy is required, rather than brute force, to ensure a hit on the nose. Ian is not going to miss this one!

A successful strike! This remarkable stroboscopic action picture taken at 1/10,000 sec. exposure, shows the Konka's cap flying up the cord. Ian is 'keeping his eye on the ball' – a good tip for all would-be champions!

LANCASHIRE HOTPOT

by KENNETH WHEELER

To which Lancashire club will the honours go in this Coronation year Cup Final at Wembley? To famous Bolton Wanderers, six times finalists, three times Cup winners and unbeaten at Wembley; or to gallant Blackpool, three times finalists since the war, but never the winners? Will everybody's favourite, Stanley Matthews, at last capture that elusive winners' medal, or will Nat Lofthouse, the centre forward everyone admires, crown his triumphant season with this additional honour?

Let tomorrow's game decide the better team on the day, and whichever it proves to be you can rest assured that the Cup couldn't go to a finer set of sportsmen.

Now for messages from the rival managers and captains:

England centre forward, NAT LOFTHOUSE, who could prove Bolton's match-winner.

*

Bootle born STAN HANSON is a fine, reliable goalie who joined Bolton in 1935. He is shown winning a duel with Everton's inside left in the Cup semi-final tie.

*

MALCOLM BARRASS, Bolton's international centre half, was born in Blackpool!

JOHNNY WHEELER (Bolton). He is wing half and deputy centre forward.

The Rival Managers

Bill Ridding, who was England's trainer in the World Cup series at Rio, took us into the Bolton dressing room and pointed to a notice hanging on the wall.

Teach me to win when I may, and, if I may not win, then, above all I pray, make me a good loser, we read.

'That is the spirit in which Bolton Wanderers will take the field at Wembley, as they do in all their games', said Bill Ridding. 'But the boys are playing well, they are fit and confident. What's more we've got a match-winner just as outstanding as Blackpool's Stanley Matthews; Nat Lofthouse.

'Perfect timing, balance and co-ordination are his to command as a result of long practice allied to natural ability. You'll note that he has scored in every round so far.

'I must admit to having a personal angle here. As a former centre forward, it was always my ambition to play on the winning side at Wembley, but injury ended my playing days at the age of 24. Now I can only achieve my ambition by remote control and through Nat.

'But football is a team game, and it is on Bolton's splendid harmony and team work this season that I base my confidence that Willie Moir, and not Harry

Johnston, will be first up the steps after the match is over to receive the Cup'.

Next we asked for the views of **Joe Smith,** manager of Blackpool and former international inside forward who scored a winning goal in the first Cup Final ever played at Wembley.

'I've been fortunate enough to play in two Wembley Cup Finals', said Joe Smith, 'and each time I was on the winning side. Strangely enough, my team was Bolton Wanderers!

'There have always been friendly connections, as well as a strong rivalry, between Blackpool and Bolton, but there is no doubt which side I shall be on in this Final.

'Although unbeaten at Wembley as a Bolton player, I've twice seen the team I manage beaten there, and now I want to see Blackpool win the Cup for the first time in history.

'No manager could wish for a finer set of lads than I've got at Bloomfield Road. From star internationals like Stanley Matthews, Stan Mortensen and Harry Johnston – not forgetting Allan Brown – down to the youngest members of the staff – they give a loyalty and service to our club that is without equal.

'I feel that victory can be the only just reward for their fighting spirit'.

The Rival Captains

'I've been a Blackpool player since I was fifteen years old, and there's only one team for me!' said **Harry Johnston,** of Blackpool and England. 'Since I first became skipper I've had one great ambition – to lead the Tangerines to victory at Wembley. Twice I've come near to realizing that ambition; now I'm hoping that it will be a case of third time lucky.

'We have a particular incentive to win this time. We owe it to Allan Brown, who again misses the Final, because he broke his leg in scoring the winning goal in the sixth round at Highbury, and to Stanley Matthews, whose glittering career would be tragically incomplete without the reward of a winners' medal.

'Winning isn't going to be easy because the Trotters are a grand team, but that's the way we want it. We all love a good fight. We'll do

our best, and if that's not good enough then there'll be no bitter feelings down Blackpool way.'

The final word goes to **Willie Moir,** of Bolton Wanderers and Scotland.

'They're cautious folk in Stoneywood, near Aberdeen, where I come from, so you can't expect me to risk a prophecy,' said Willie Moir, 'but this I will say: if we don't win the Cup it won't be for want of trying.

'I'm proud to have been given the honour of leading the Trotters this season, because they are the finest team I've ever known, in every sense. Like Harry Johnston I've been a footballer all my life, and my greatest ambition has always been to be on the winning side at Wembley.

'We can't both win, Harry, but I agree with you – let's make it a good fight, and may the better team win'.

HARRY JOHNSTON, Blackpool Captain.

Harry Johnston [signature]

WILLIE MOIR, the Bolton Captain.

Willie Moir [signature]

(Right) HARRY JOHNSTON, followed by Scottish international goalkeeper GEORGE FARM, leads the Blackpool team on to the field.

(Below). The sturdy Blackpool full-backs, EDDIE SHIMWELL (left) and TOM GARRETT (right).

Hard tackling HUGH KELLY is a hard-playing Scottish international wing half.

ERNIE TAYLOR, born in Sunderland, carves openings for the other Blackpool forwards.

Action plus! Speedy left - winger, BILL PERRY, is a South African. He played in the 1951 Final.

Inside, or centre forward JACKIE MUDIE is another from Scotland. He, too, played in the 1951 Final.

(Right). Making his third attempt to win the only football honour that has escaped him is EAGLE Readers' Favourite Footballer, STANLEY MATTHEWS. With Harry Johnston he shares the hope that it will be a case of third time lucky.

International Bolton forwards are HAROLD HASSALL (left) and BOBBY LANGTON (right).

TROTTERS' TRAINING MACHINE

With England trainer Bill Ridding as their manager the Bolton team are red-hot on training, and bad weather doesn't stop them. They have an indoor running track, and in the dressing room is this special cycling machine. As you move the pedals so the needle moves round the dial in front. Once round the dial represents a cycle ride of ¼ mile.

*

Quicksilver STAN MORTENSEN is the Blackpool shooting-star who could, if he is fully fit, win the Cup for Blackpool. In the pictures on the right (taken by Carl Sutton) Stan is shown making one of his typical full-blooded drives at goal.

THE LAMBRETTA 125 1(d) MOTOR SCOOTER

REDMILL

THE COMPLETE

Motor scooters are not by any means a new type of vehicle. Many were produced after World War I, but they did not gain any great popularity. Today, however, they are firmly established, especially on the Continent. The Lambretta is Italian designed and built.

There are a number of reasons for their demand, notably economy. These small vehicles will do about 130-140 miles to the gallon, a pillion passenger can be carried in comfort and they are as weather proof as an open machine can be. A windscreen and luggage carrier can be fitted and the engine is fully enclosed and reliable.

Our sectional drawing is coloured to show up the machine's various characteristics, the standard colour of the scooter being greenish-grey as shown in the small drawing.

A sidecar for goods or passenger can be fitted.

ENGINE

Capacity: 123 cubic centimetres. Power: 5 h.p. Two-stroke single cylinder, air cooled. Engine, transmission and rear wheel together form a unit, which swings on a strong pivot incorporated in the frame, giving sturdiness and safety. Fan-cooled air directed around cylinder by cowl. Ignition and lighting by flywheel magneto. Unloaded weight: 187 lbs. Saddle height: 30 ins. Wheelbase: 50 ins.

KEY TO PARTS

(1) Torsion bar within transverse tube for rear-springing. (2) Gearbox; 3 speed. (3) Kickstart, not shown, is mounted here. (4) Engine pivot point. (5) Stand. (6) Multi-plate clutch. (7) Silencer. (8) Brake pedal with cable. (9) Foot-rest. This continues by the side of engine for pillion rider's use. (10) Sheet steel body-work. (11) Tool box. (12) Detachable bag. (13) Sprung saddle. (14) Filler cap. (15) Handle for use of pillion rider. (16) Saddle for pillion rider. (17) Spare wheel (extra). (18) Rear light. (19) Twist grip gear-change, combined with (20) Clutch lever. (21) Speedometer. (22) Combined light switch and horn button. (23) Front brake lever. (24) Headlamp. (25) Electric horn. (26-26) Metal panelling, easily detachable. The engine is entirely enclosed. (27) Tyres, 4 by 8 inches. (28) Front suspension by swinging arms and helical springs. (29) Brake arm and cable. Finned brake drums. (30) Fuel tank. Capacity: 1.3 galls. Reserve: ½ pint. Consumption: 140 m.p.g. Range: 190 miles. Lubrication: petroil 5%. (31) Carburettor incorporating a fuel filter. It is fitted on air filter which is not shown. (32) Frame of steel tube. (33) Shaft drive. (34) Wheels are made in two halves that can be taken apart. Therefore no tyre levers are required to fit a new tyre; interchangeable front and rear.

THE COMPLETE MACHINE

MACHINE

From the EDITOR
EAGLE, New St. Square, London, E.C.4.

1 May, 1953

NOTE the date – the first of May! And excitement is really beginning to run high with the Coronation only a month away.

London seems busier, bigger and more bustling than ever. Workmen are still hard at it, fixing stands on the Coronation route and putting up standards to hold decorations. The big stores are vying with one another for the most spectacular window displays to attract our overseas visitors.

Many people from distant lands have arrived already and almost any day you can spot a group of enquiring foreigners around a gesticulating Londoner as he tries, in the language of signs, to tell them which way to go for Trafalgar Square, Piccadilly, Buckingham Palace and so on. Everyone seems to end up looking slightly dazed and rather hazy about which direction to take, but finally smiles break out all round to show there is goodwill in plenty and that spirits are high.

You may like to know who have been appointed to carry the various standards in the Grand Procession in Westminster Abbey at the Coronation on June 2nd. The Union Standard will be carried by Captain J. L. M. Dymoke, the Standard of Wales by Lord Harlech, Ireland by Lord de L'Isle and Dudley, Scotland by Viscount Dudhope and England by the Earl of Derby. Following these will be the Royal Standard carried by Viscount Montgomery of Alamein.

CONGRATULATIONS to *Richard Marston* on winning the MUG's Badge. Nine-year-old Richard, living at 35 Church Road, Westbury - on - Trym, Bristol, had a pretty big responsibility to tackle recently. Just after the family had moved to a new house his father was posted to Egypt for two and a half years and his mother became very ill. No help was available for two days so Richard had to take over. He looked after his younger brother, aged three years, taking care of his mother, doing all the shopping, etc. – and all without any fuss. Even when his mother grew well again Richard still continued to do what he could to help her.

Yours sincerely,

Marcus Morris

...and Home

MY FATHER is a chimney sweep. One day he had to go to a certain address. A lady opened the door to his knock and showed my father the room where the chimney had to be swept. There was a man at an easel, drawing. Who should it be but L. Ashwell-Wood, the man who draws for the centre-page of EAGLE. At that moment he was on a drawing for the EAGLE. – P. D. Ross, Willesden, London, N.W.10.

Whodunnit!

I am an interested reader of 'Whodunnit' in your free supplement.

I have noticed that when the guilty people are trying to prove their 'guilt-lessness' they always hold their forearm out horizontally. I think this proves their guilt. In the Bible, Proverbs Chapter 6, verses 12-13, it says the following: 'A naughty person, a wicked man, walketh with a froward mouth. He winketh with his eyes, he speaketh with his feet, he teacheth with his fingers'. What do you think? – *Reg Mason, Halifax, Yorks.* [*I'm sure the horizontal forearm doesn't prove anyone's guilt, Reg, but I like your quotation from Proverbs. Ed.*]

Lists of prizewinners in EAGLE Competitions can be had on application to: EAGLE Reader Services, Long Lane, Liverpool 9. Please enclose a stamped addressed envelope.

THE RECOGNITION
of H.M. Queen Elizabeth II

When George VI died on 6 February 1952 the accession to the throne by Elizabeth II happened immediately, but it was not until June of the next year that the country was able to celebrate her Coronation. The ceremony on 2 June 1953 allowed an outbreak of joy and merriment. *Eagle* lavished many weeks and pages on the new reign.

With articles on the Royal household, and the state of the Empire in this time of change, the weeks of build-up culminated in a special Coronation Issue. L. Ashwell Wood was given free rein to fill a double-page spread with the Royal Naval Fleet while the route of the official ceremony was laid out in great detail and luxurious colour.

THE NATION

GUILDFORD

Highlight in Guildford's colourful processions and pageants is the scene depicting Queen Elizabeth I's famous speech at Tilbury when danger threatened from the Spanish Armada. Guildford celebrated June 2nd with dancing in the streets. Children received Coronation mugs, old folks got Coronation canisters filled with tea.

LIVERPOOL

This Punch and Judy show has been performing for over 100 years. The family acting the show was in action on this spot before St George's Hall (in background) was started in 1846. This week the show goes on amid Coronation processions and decorations.

Cities planned H.M. Quee 1953. We or unusu

SEDGLEY

The flames of Sedgley Beacon in Staffordshire light the country for miles around to proclaim the Queen's Coronation. The Beacon Tower stands on the highest point of Beacon Hill and dominates the landscape for miles around.

LONDO

PENZANCE

The rocky islet of St Michael's Mount, unique in Britain and teaming with colourful history, is floodlit. There are references to St Michael's Mount in the Domesday Book. The castle's battlements command a view from Land's End to the Lizard.

INVERNESS

Inverness, in its romantic setting of castle and clans, rejoices "wi' a hundred pipers an a' and a'!" A Service in the Parish Church, a military parade and carnival sports for school children are just part of a grand day to celebrate the coronation of a Queen for Scotland.

WOKINGHAM

Celebrations are in traditional manner at Wokingham in Berkshire. In the gay and crowded market place an ox will be roasted on Saturday. Roasting takes almost 12 hours. The ox is basted all the time and the meat is removed as cooked. Who eats it? Probably the old folks of Wokingham. They may be given the succulent ox meat as a treat.

CELEBRATES

Britain have coronation of 2nd of June, most exciting them here.

WARWICK

What more fitting for a country's celebration than a pageant of battles and tournaments, knights in armour, heralds and trumpeters, and all the pomp of the medieval 'Lists'? Staged on the green swards beneath the battlements of Warwick's ancient castle, this pageant has a perfect setting. You can see it in July.

BRISTOL

The beauty of the Avon Gorge prompted Queen Elizabeth I in 1574 to command that she be rowed in a barge down to the mouth of the river and back again. Bristol celebrates our present Queen's coronation by an impressive river pageant portraying the return of Queen Elizabeth I up the river from Avonmouth.

Here in Trafalgar Square, symbolic of all that Britain and the Commonwealth stand for, is the heart of a Nation rejoicing. Fountains play in the floodlit square and the people sing. London is gay with decorations, Coronation balls, bands in the Parks. Visitors are here from all over the world.

PLYMOUTH

In the first Elizabethan era when relations with Spain had become strained, 50 Spanish galleons arrived at Plymouth without dipping their flags in recognition of the Queen. Captain John Hawkins taught them courtesy by taking a shot at their topsails. Just one of the incidents portrayed in Plymouth's Coronation pageant in July.

DURHAM

...ASTER

Doncaster celebrated early with a Coronation Fair – and what better to work off high spirits than sideshows, stalls, maypoles, national dancing and a parade of bicycles through the ages, rounded off with a gay torchlight procession? All the youth organisations took part and helped to swell the community singing.

Boat races on the River Wear add excitement to Durham's celebrations. Services and Parades have been held in the famous cathedral, which you see here, and the restoration of St Cuthbert's Well, situated on the bank of the River Wear, has been taken over by a youth organisation as part of their coronation activities.

THE CORONATION NAVAL REVIEW

Royal Standard

Union Flag

Admiralty

White Ensign

Blue Ensign
(R.N.R.)

Red Ensign
(Merchant Navy)

Admiral

Vice-Admiral

Rear-Admiral

Commodore
(1st class)

Commodore
(2nd class)

Special num-
bered pennants
(1 to 0)

1
2
3
4
5
6
7
8
9
0

THE SOLENT

PORTSMOUTH

SPITHEAD

COWES

RYDE

ISLE OF WIGHT

Map showing the posi-
tion of the Review Fleet
at Spithead.

At 3 p.m. on Monday 15th June H.M. the Queen and Admiral of the Fleet H.R.H. the Duke of Edinburgh, will leave Portsmouth Harbour in H.M.S. *Surprise* to review the fleet at Spithead. In accordance with tradition, the *Surprise* will be led out of the harbour by the Trinity House vessel *Patricia*. As the *Surprise* reaches Spithead, all saluting ships of the Review Fleet will fire a Royal Salute of 21 guns. The Royal procession will then be joined by other vessels including the liners *Orcades*, *Pretoria Castle* and *Strathnavar* with H.M. Government guests on board. The Royal Procession will pass through the lines of ships as indicated by the dotted line on our drawing. The ships will be dressed overall with flags and 'manned', that is to say, the ships' companies will be lined up on the upper decks facing outboard. As Her Majesty passes each ship the ship's company will give three cheers. The *Surprise* will come to anchor ahead of *Glasgow* in line 'E', and at 5.30 p.m. there will be a Fly Past of over 300 naval aircraft. At 10.30 p.m. the ships will be illuminated and a firework display will be given at 11.0 p.m. In this *Eagle* drawing practically the entire Review Fleet of over 200 ships is illustrated, each ship in its correct place. The nine main lines are each seven miles long reaching from Spithead to east of Cowes.

KEY TO LETTERS OF LINES AND SHIPS

Line A: Headed by H.M.S. *Reward*, a fleet tug followed by Landing Craft and fishing vessels. *Line B:* Headed by H.M. Fleet Minesweeper *Rinaldo* followed by Boom Defence vessels and trawlers. *Line C:* Headed by H.M. Fleet Minesweeper *Coquette* followed by minesweepers, four lifeboats and, further along, submarines and motor vessels of the R.N.V.R. *Line D:* Headed by H.M. cruiser *Dido*, followed by H.M. cruiser *Cleopatra*, two fast minelayers and many destroyers and frigates. *Line E:* Headed by H.M. cruiser *Glasgow* followed by other cruisers, destroyers and frigates. *Line F:* Headed by H.M. Battleship *Vanguard* (flagship of the fleet) followed by H.M. Aircraft carrier *Eagle*, eight other carriers, depot ships and submarines. *Line G:* Consists of foreign warships headed by the U.S. cruiser *Baltimore*. *Line H:* Headed by H.M. Aircraft Direction Vessel *Boxer* followed by Surveying ships, dockyard craft, Royal Fleet auxiliaries and Merchant ships. *Line K:* Headed by H.M. Fleet Minesweeper *Pluto* followed by tenders and merchant ships. Lines L and M are representatives of the Merchant Navy. Line N consists of fast patrol boats.

KEY TO NUMBERS

(1) H.M.S. *Surprise*, with Queen Elizabeth and the Duke of Edinburgh on board, forming the Royal Procession headed by the Trinity House vessel *Patricia*. (2) H.M. Government guest liners. (3) Track of the *Surprise* from Portsmouth Harbour. (4) Track of guest liners. (5) Track of the *Surprise*. (6) Return track of guest liners. (7) Return track of the *Surprise*. (8) Position of the *Surprise* for the Fly Past. (9) (10) (11) Areas for anchorage of yachts and other private craft. (12) Stokes Bay. (13) Portsmouth Harbour.

Special Flags used in Naval Signalling

Aeroplane
Ahead
Affirmative
Aircraft Carrier
Astern
Battle Cruiser
Battleship
Black
Blue Affirmative
Blue
Cruiser
Destroyer
Division
Fishery
Negative
Optional
Port
Preparative
Red
Flotilla
Starboard
Sub-Division
Submarine

L. ASHWELL WOOD

EAGLE 1 *January* 1954

THE SILVER EAGLE BADGE

Mugs get a new name.

This week in EAGLE's sister paper, GIRL, we are launching a MUG'S Badge scheme for girls. Their badge will be called the STAR ADVENTURER'S BADGE.

To make the EAGLE scheme of the same type, we are replacing the MUG'S Badge by a SILVER EAGLE BADGE and STAR.

All present holders of the MUG'S Badge may exchange it for a SILVER EAGLE BADGE, if they wish to do so, by returning their MUG'S Badge to:– MUGS, EAGLE Reader Services, Long Lane, Liverpool 9, and enclosing their name and address.

The S.E.B. will be awarded in just the same way as the MUG'S Badge for outstanding examples of courage and service among EAGLE Club Members. Claims should be written by an adult or by friends and addressed to the Editor. *Eaglers* should not send in claims on their own behalf.

We have prepared a new pamphlet called ALL ABOUT THE SILVER EAGLE BADGE AND STAR AD-VENTURER'S BADGE, and we strongly advise you to send in for it. Address your request to SILVER EAGLE BADGE, (Pamphlet), EAGLE Reader Services, Long Lane, Liverpool 9.

When you write, please remember to enclose an envelope addressed to yourself and bearing a 2½d stamp in which we can forward the leaflet to you.

MUGS BECOME SILVER EAGLES

Ever since the early issues of *Eagle*, the editorial team had been awarding the seemingly dubious title of Mug of the Month to various readers for their bravery, courage, and all-round do-gooding-ness. In Issue 35 of Volume 4 (4 December 1953) nine-year-old Barry Ware had the honour of being the last ever recipient of the prize. The fact that he lived in "Hong Kong, China" [sic] indicates just how far *Eagle*'s wing-span reached. According to the report in that week's 'Eagle Club News', Barry had "spent a lot of his young life in hospital. There he has won everybody's affection by his cheerfulness. He is a member of the Hong Kong Wolf Cubs and is well-known everywhere for the courage he shows in spite of a rare bone disease."

To quote from Shakespeare: "Be not afraid of greatness: some are born great, some achieve greatness and some have greatness thrust upon them". – *Twelfth Night*, Act II, Scene V

And so on 1 January 1954 (Issue 1 Volume 5) the world was introduced to the Silver Eagle Badge. In that week's copy of *Eagle*'s sister paper *Girl* the Star Adventurer's Badge was being launched and the dropping of the Mug title was justified by the desire to "make the *Eagle* scheme of the same type", whatever that meant. Whatever the real reason, and given that one of the contemporary definitions of Mug was, "chump: a person who is gullible and easy to take advantage of", we can only guess, it was goodbye to the Mugs.

Having awarded Mug-dom to many people since it was introduced, *Eagle* was careful to make sure they were not forgotten. All Mugs were invited to exchange their Mug's badges for Silver Eagles by returning them to the reader services' offices. A special pamphlet was prepared explaining the new scheme and readers were "strongly" advised to send for it. Remembering of course to enclose an SAE. After all you'd be a mug not to.

THE WAR WITH GERONIMO

After being rescued from an Indian Apache attack by a cavalry troop, Jeff Arnold, Luke and Jim Forsythe resume their journey towards Texas. On arrival at San Domingo, they find the town completely deserted. Jeff and Co decide to spend the night in the town's hotel, but awake next morning to find their horses have been stolen.

STORY BY CHARLES CHILTON
DRAWN BY FRANK HUMPHRIS.

ARE YOU SURE THEY DIDN'T JUST BREAK OUT OF THE STABLES, LUKE?

SURE I'M SURE! I SHUT THE STABLE LAST NIGHT. SOMEBODY OPENED IT!

WELL, WHOEVER IT WAS TOOK THE BRIDLES BUT NOT THE SADDLES!

ONLY A BAREBACK RIDER WOULD DO THAT.

THAT CAN ONLY MEAN ONE THING—*INDIANS*. GET YOUR RIFLES FROM YOUR SADDLE-SCABBARDS. WE'LL GO AFTER 'EM!

So Jeff, Luke and Jim set out across the desert without delay to pursue the horse stealers on foot.

IF WE DON'T FIND THOSE HORSES MIGHTY SOON, WE'RE SUNK. IT'S FIVE DAYS' MARCH TO THE NEXT TOWN.

THESE ARE THEIR TRACKS ALL RIGHT! NO MISTAKIN' THE IMPRINT *THOSE* HORSESHOES MAKE!

AND THE SAND IS STILL SIFTIN' INTO THEM. THOSE TRACKS AIN'T ABOVE TWO HOURS OLD.

WELL, LET'S KEEP GOIN'. WE CAN'T BE FAR BEHIND 'EM!

I SURE HOPE NOT! IF OUR WATER RUNS OUT, WE'RE BUZZARDS' MEAT FOR SURE.

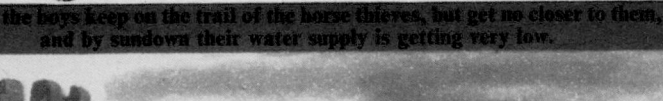

All day the boys keep on the trail of the horse thieves, but get no closer to them, and by sundown their water supply is getting very low.

WE *MUST* FIND WATER SOON, JEFF, OR WE AIN'T GONNA GET HALFWAY ACROSS THIS DESERT.

IF WE'RE TO GET OUR HORSES BACK, WE'VE GOT TO KEEP GOIN'. DON'T DRINK UNLESS YOU *HAVE* TO.

HEY, JEFF—*LOOK!* THAT GLEAM OF SUNLIGHT—THERE'S WATER AHEAD!

YEAH, LOOKS LIKE IT. LET'S HOPE IT AIN'T A MIRAGE.

DRINK YOUR FILL, FELLERS! AND FILL UP YOUR CANTEENS—WE'LL CAMP HERE FOR THE NIGHT.

O-*OH*—THIS IS BETTER THAN THE SWEETEST WINE I EVER TASTED.

CONTINUED

THE BRITISH CAR OF 1953

In this drawing we show the type of car you will see on the exhibition stands at the Motor Show this year. Of no named make, this car has all the salient features of present day practice which have captured the world's markets.

A six-cylinder engine is shown as being the answer for more power and higher speed. The radiator grill is dignified as opposed to the chromium 'mouth organ' shape of American cars. The windscreen is the favoured curved type with no division, as is also the new, large rear window. Shown at bottom of the drawing is the progress in design of British cars over the last 50 years.

50 YEARS OF MOTORING

1903 Wolseley 1906 Austin 1908 Rolls-Royce 1912 Morris 1920 Bentley

THE FAMILY SA

KEY TO SALIENT FEATURES

(1) Radiator air grill. (2) Radiator. (3) Ventilating and car heating unit. (4) Air cleaner for carburettor. (5) 12-volt battery for starter lighting and coil ignition. (6) Overhead valves. (7) Two rear pistons of 23 h.p., six cylinder engine. (8) Distributor head for coil ignition. (9) Dynamo for charging battery. (10) Independent coil spring front suspension. (11) Front hydraulic brake: two leading shoe type. (12) Worm and ball steering gear. (13) Single dry plate clutch. (14) Synchromesh gears with three forward and one reverse. (15) Front needle-roller bearing universal joint. (16) Propeller shaft. (17) All pressed-steel chassis. (18) All pressed-steel welded body. (19) Exhaust silencer. (20) Rear universal joint. (21) Telescopic shock absorber. (22) Hypoid (off-centre) spiral bevel drive and differential casing. (23) Leading and trailing shoe type hydraulic rear brake. This brake is also actuated mechanically by the hand brake lever. (24) Hydraulic Brake piping. (25) Petrol tank. (26) Luggage boot. (27) Spare wheel. (28) Rear suspension semi-elliptic springs. (29) Rear light (each side). (30) Large curved rear window. (31) Push-button door openers. (32) Steering column gear change lever. (33) Fewer instruments with large speed indicator. (34) Curved windscreen without a division.

LASHWELL WOOD

24 Humber   1928 Rover   1933 Standard   1938 Singer   Design 1953

LOON

GREAT ESCAPES

THE COLDITZ STORY

TOLD BY GUY MORGAN·DRAWN BY P.NEVIN.

COLDITZ, A MEDIEVAL FORTRESS ON A 300-FT. CLIFF, FLOODLIT FROM EVERY ANGLE AND WITH GUARDS ALWAYS OUTNUMBERING PRISONERS, WAS GERMANY'S 'BAD-BOYS' CAMP FOR THE HARDENED ESCAPERS OF TWO WORLD WARS. ESCAPE-PROOF IN 1914-18, ITS RECORD WAS SOON BROKEN IN THE LAST WAR.

THESE TOOLS WILL, OF COURSE, BE CONFISCATED, CAPTAIN LAWTON.

THAT'S THE SPOT TO START TUNNELLING— WHERE HE'D LEAST SUSPECT IT— BANG UNDER HIS DESK!

ONE DAY, OBERSTABSFELDWEBEL (R.S.M.) GEPHARDT, CAMP SECURITY OFFICER, HAD CAPTAIN LAWTON INTO HIS OFFICE CONCERNING SOME TOOLS. LAWTON HAD AN IDEA. HE RECKONED THAT THE BEST PLACE TO START TUNNELLING WOULD BE FROM UNDER GEPHARDT'S DESK.

KEYHOLE →

BUT THE DOOR TO THE OFFICE WAS FITTED WITH A SPECIAL UNPICKABLE LOCK, WORKED BY MOVING 8 TINY PISTONS, EACH DIFFERENTLY, WITH ACCURACY OF 1/1000 TH OF AN INCH. A KEY AND KEYHOLE OF THE TYPE IN QUESTION ARE ILLUSTRATED ABOVE. UNDAUNTED, CAPT. VAN DOORNINCK OF THE DUTCH NAVY, USING WATCHMAKING TOOLS, MADE A SPECIAL MICRO-METER GAUGE TO MEASURE EACH PISTON'S MOVEMENT, AND THEN A KEY TO FIT THEM! HIS PATIENCE WAS REWARDED, FOR NOW THEY COULD ENTER THE OFFICE AND START WORK.

LOCKING THEMSELVES IN AT NIGHT, THEY TUNNELLED UNDER THE FLOOR OF GEPHARDT'S ROOM AND THROUGH AN 18-INCH WALL INTO A STORE-ROOM WHERE POLISH P.O.Ws WERE OFTEN BROUGHT FROM THE TOWN TO FETCH STORES.

ONE NIGHT, WHILE THEY WERE AT WORK, THERE WAS AN ALARM AND A GENERAL SEARCH WAS MADE BY THE GUARDS. LUCKILY, THEY DIDN'T THINK IT NECESSARY TO LOOK IN THE SECURITY OFFICER'S ROOM!

NO NEED TO SEARCH IN THERE—THE DOOR HAS A SPECIAL LOCK.

OBERSTABSFELDWEBEL

ONE MORNING, WEARING HOME-MADE POLISH UNIFORMS, FIVE BRITISH OFFICERS, LED BY VAN DOORNINCK IN THE UNIFORM OF A GERMAN N.C.O., MARCHED OUT OF THE CAMP FROM THE STORE-ROOM, CARRYING CIVILIAN CLOTHES WITH THEM IN THE BOXES! FOUR WERE RE-CAPTURED, BUT VAN DOORNINCK AND F/LT. BILL FOWLER REACHED SWITZERLAND SAFELY SIX DAYS LATER.

IT ISN'T TRUE !

That Camels Store Water In Their Humps

AS POLAR BEARS BELONG TO THE ARCTIC, SO CAMELS BELONG TO THE DESERT: TO THE SUN-SCORCHED PLAINS OF WATERLESS SAND WHERE WELLS MAY BE HUNDREDS OF MILES APART, WHERE, WITHOUT WAR-NING, BLINDING SANDSTORMS THREATEN DEATH.

EVEN TODAY, WITH AIR FREIGHTING AND CATERPILLAR-TRACKED VEHICLES, THE CAMEL CARAVAN IS STILL USED TO TRANSPORT MERCHANDISE ACROSS THE DESERT. IT IS OFTEN THOUGHT THAT THE HUMP OF THE CAMEL IS A SORT OF RESERVOIR OF WATER.

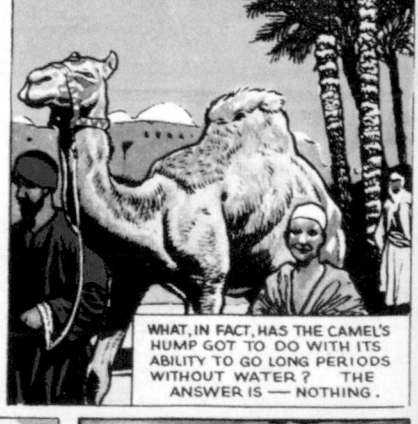

WHAT, IN FACT, HAS THE CAMEL'S HUMP GOT TO DO WITH ITS ABILITY TO GO LONG PERIODS WITHOUT WATER ? THE ANSWER IS — NOTHING.

FABULOUS STORIES HAVE BEEN TOLD ABOUT THE CAMEL'S ABILITY TO LIVE WITHOUT WATER. IN FACT THE LONGEST RECORD WITHOUT WATER IN WHICH THE CAMEL HAS SURVIVED IS TEN DAYS; THIS WAS A SOMALI CAMEL, A STRAIN NOTED FOR ITS HARDINESS. BUT IN A TERRIBLE MARCH FROM SUEZ TO ABU KLEA IN EGYPT IT WAS REPORTED THAT ALL CAMELS WITHOUT WATER FOR SIX DAYS DIED.

IF THE HUMP WAS CONNECTED WITH WATER STORAGE, THE BACTRIAN CAMEL WHICH INHABITS MONGOLIA AND TURK-ESTAN AND WHICH HAS TWO HUMPS, SHOULD BE ABLE TO LAST MUCH LONGER WITHOUT WATER THAN THE SINGLE-HUMPED VARIETY. BUT THIS IS CERTAINLY NOT THE CASE.

THE CAMEL'S HUMP IS, IN FACT, JUST A HUGE LUMP OF FAT. WHEN FOOD IS SHORT IT PRO-VIDES A MASS OF EMERGENCY NOURISHMENT. BUT, WHEN THE CAMEL IS GOING TO BE OUT FOR MORE THAN THREE DAYS, IT CARRIES ITS RESERVE OF WATER IN TWO PANNIER BAGS: CERTAINLY NOT IN THE HUMP!

CIRCUS prizewinners

The 24 winners of our Circus Competition were brought to London to spend the day at Bertram Mills Circus, Olympia.

Their day started with a visit 'behind the scenes' of the circus where they were introduced to the various artists. Two of the *Eaglers*, Barry Hope and Kenneth Young, helped Freddy Knie to rehearse his horses for the afternoon performance. Then they had lunch with Mr Cyril Mills, our Editor and other personalities. In the afternoon, they had ringside seats at the circus and how they enjoyed themselves. After a huge tea, they were seen on to their trains for home. All voted it was a truly wonderful day.

Eagler Barry Hope takes over the Ringmaster's job!

Here's an odd sleeping partner for Eagler Kenneth Young!

EAGLE 26 March 1954

MACDONALD HASTINGS EAGLE SPECIAL INVESTIGATOR

I AM A MAGICIANS APPRENTICE

1. Tommy Cooper, the crazy magician, has invited me to join his act. "I hope something happens," he says.

2. "Let's try this one for a start, shall we?" Tommy suggests. "It'd be wonderful – wouldn't it? – wonderful if something came out of it at your first attempt."

3. "Oh dear, I do hope it's going to work. Are you feeling as nervous as I am? The suspense is awful, isn't it? All right, one to be ready..."

4. Oh, it's worked all right. Two enormous snakes jump out of the tin at me. Tommy dances with glee at his success.

5. "Now we'll try something more difficult," he says. I watch him as he drops a china egg into a black bag, and makes it disappear.

6. Tommy blows into the bag to prove that the egg has vanished. But when he tries to bring it back

7. ... He can't do it. He hunts among my clothes, searching agitatedly for the missing egg.

8. "Ah," he says, "I know what's happened." But, while he's looking the other way, I find the egg.

9. "You've found it!" says Tommy. "In the bag? I never put it there. This is magic."

READERS' LETTERS

School play has big success

AT MY SCHOOL we had a concert. It was called "The Charcoal Burner's Son". I was a soldier in the army (the middle one at the bottom). We had two programme sellers and they got a guinea. It was a great success. After the play our teachers were so pleased they filmed it– Terry Bisgrove, Walton, Somerset.

Dan Dare Dentist

I WAS very interested to see the picture of the Mobile Dental Unit in EAGLE. I received treatment at one last year. It was identical with the one shown in the picture, and the dentist called it his spaceship. The dentist was very nice and called his mouth wash syringe his space pistol. – J. Stevenson (aged 9), Hythe, Kent.

Our Police Dogs are wonderful

MY DAD AND I read the story about "Rap", the Police Dog, in EAGLE.

This week, my dad was at the Training School for Police Dogs with his dog, Bruce, when he was told to go and lay a track for Rap to follow. He very soon found my dad hiding in a tree – Kenneth Kendall, Blackheath, London.

Wrong way round dog

EVERY NIGHT, when my dog goes to bed, she jumps into her box, and instead of putting her head on the soft padding, she puts it at the other end of the box, which is just bare wood. Then, my mother has to say: 'Not that way, the other way round.' Immediately, she jumps out of her box, and gets back the right way round – C. Fox, Lee, London, S.E.12.

10. "Now I'll show you a trick," says Tommy, "which always works. It's one of my favourites. I put a rope round your neck."

11. "Hold my watch while I get together the rest of the props. Whatever you do, don't move. If you do, the trick won't work."

12. "Feeling all right? This is going to be good. Really good. We'll just balance the pail on your head to finish you off."

13. And this is how Tommy got his own back on me. He picked up a soda-water syphon and squirted the jet straight in my face!

EAGLE 19 *February* 1954

YOUR LETTERS TO MAC HASTINGS

Here is the letter which wins the first
Special Investigator Jack-knife

I think that Eaglers would appreciate Mac's articles a lot more if they knew about the work that goes into them. Why not tell us? He could write an article showing us how he gets in touch with his 'victims' and how he obtains the permission that is sometimes needed. I am sure that many difficulties arise. Just once, I'd like to hear not about the trouble that Mac gets into learning something new every week, but the trouble he gets into putting the article together to amuse us.

PETER RUTLAND, Burton-on-Trent.

You've got the right idea, Peter. The hardest part of the job is arranging the very special adventures that Eaglers want to hear about. And your Special Investigator couldn't do it without the help of the Editor, the photographers, and the whole staff of EAGLE. Special
Investigator is a team job. Before very long, we will take you behind the scenes and show you how one of his adventures is organized, from the moment when Mr Marcus Morris first approves the idea until 'Mr Printer' finally puts it on the giant presses at Liverpool.

— and here are some of the other letters which Mac received.

Scotland Yard Caught Napping

In Special Investigator's Murder Case, it would appear that the ballistic evidence went astray. The evidence states that a .45 Automatic Pistol was found and, that the micro-examination of the bullet compared exactly with the markings on the bullet fired from the pistol.

My reasons for pointing this out are: (1) An automatic pistol ejects its spent cartridge cases; (2) An empty case was found in the outer office; (3) The bullet found in the body and the empty case found in the adjoining office *(shown in the photograph)* are, incidentally, *Revolver* ammunition. In which case, no empty case would have been found, as the *revolver does not eject.* The revolver cartridge (as shown) has a flat-round base with a protruding rim, but the automatic pistol cartridge has a recessed rim to enable the 'claw' mechanism of the extractor to operate on the recoil.

TONY WEBB, Sandiway, Cheshire.

Your reasoning, my dear Holmes, is conclusive. We congratulate you, and many other Eaglers who wrote to us, on a magnificent piece of detective work. Superintendent Percy Law, of Scotland Yard, says he made a deliberate mistake to test you out. But he'll know better next time!

E.S.I. Caught Napping

In 'Murder', Macdonald Hastings says: "Before I knew who did it, I was shot through the *heart.*" But the photograph shows blood on his shirt below the right shoulder blade. If, therefore, Mac's statement is true, I must say that his heart is in a funny place.

BRIAN WITCOMBE, Canvey Island, Essex.

The wound below the right shoulder blade was supposed to show not where the bullet went in but where it came out, as it would. You are right, Brian, because E.S.I. made the mistake of saying that the bullet was recovered from his body.

Think again, Raymond

I have been following up Eagle Special Investigator and find it very educational. But why not let Macdonald Hastings go through the sound barrier in a 'Hawker Hunter'?

RAYMOND FITZSIMMONDS, Dagenham, Essex.

No, Raymond. That suggestion isn't good enough to win a jack-knife. A Hawker Hunter is a single-seater plane. Nobody could possibly fly alone through the sound barrier, not even Special Investigator, without years of specialized training.

Your Mistake, John

I am very keen on fishing and wish to draw notice to a mistake which was in the story 'I Go Fishing with Dick Walker' by Macdonald Hastings. EAGLE stated that the British record for a perch is 5 lbs. 15 ozs. 3 drms. There were at least three perch heavier than that. (1) 8 lbs. caught in the Wiltshire Avon; (2) 9 lbs. 3 ozs. caught in Serpentine in Hyde Park; (3) 10 lbs. caught in Lake Bala in Wales.

JOHN MERCER, Thornliebank, Glasgow.

The official British record for a perch caught on rod and line is 5 lbs. 15 ozs. as stated in 'EAGLE'. People may have caught perch of the weights John Mercer mentions, but the evidence of weight has been insufficient for official acceptance.

Eagle Reader's Monster

Having read Dick Walker's article on fishing this morning, I went out and caught a 14 lb. pike at Rackenhayes near Newton Abbot. It is the biggest fish caught there this season. Has any other EAGLE reader caught a bigger one?

MICHAEL WINTER, Newton Abbot, S. Devon.

Wot, No Salmon?

In the table of British records compared with Dick Walker's best there was no mention of salmon. I also missed Macdonald Hastings' usual happy-go-lucky, try-my-hand-at-anything paragraph or two.

WILLIAM VINCENT, Brecon, Brecknock.

So far, Dick Walker hasn't fished for salmon. Mac is an experienced angler and has caught a salmon of over 32 lbs.

Suicide Mission

I think it would be a good idea if Macdonald Hastings would try to drive a naval motor torpedo boat. It would be more than interesting for certain readers who are interested in that sort of thing, for he tried to, and did, drive a Centurion tank, so let him please try the navy on the water.

MICHAEL MELOY, Kings Norton, Birmingham 30.

Well, Michael, we'll ask the Royal Navy what they've got to say about your idea.

More Thrills and Spills

My only regret is that some of the things Mac does now seem very tame compared with the adventures in the Eagle Special Investigator book. For instance, he's going fishing with Dick Walker, and becoming a Zoo keeper, instead of riding the Cresta, being a knife-thrower's target and driving a Centurion tank.

KEVIN MICHAEL PELHAM, Morden Park, Surrey.

E.S.I. writes: So you want to kill me, too, eh, Kevin? Don't give up hope. There are plenty of assignments ahead of me quite as exciting as the ones in the book. But, apart from that, I hope you don't judge adventure by the amount of danger in it. I think that catching a fish with Dick Walker is quite as exciting as riding the Cresta. And, by the way, if you imagine that being a keeper at the Zoo is 'tame', you wouldn't think that if you'd been inside the cage with a cheetah and had to manage an elephant.

Bird or Animal?

In 'I Become a Keeper at the Zoo', Macdonald Hastings referred to the Kiwi as that strange *bird* from New Zealand. Then, in the next paragraph, he referred to the Kiwi as an *animal* who normally sleeps in the daytime. Does this happen to be a misprint?

MAURICE BUARD, St. Saviours, Jersey, C.I.

A bird is an animal, Maurice. Come to that, so are you.

(Next week: I am a Crack Shot's Target.)

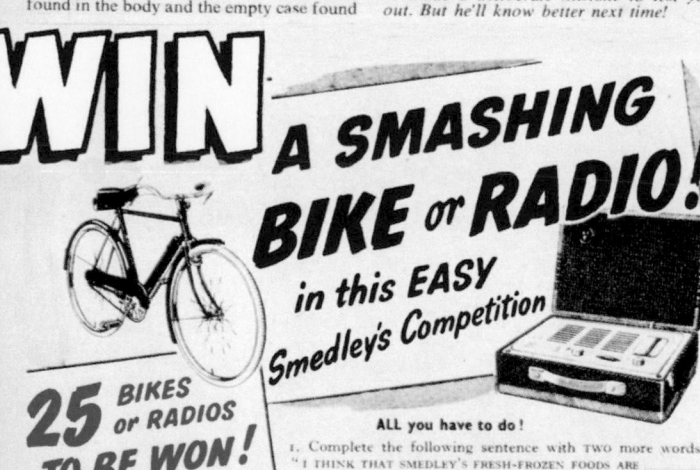

PHOSPHATES FROM A CORAL ISLAND
IN THE PACIFIC OCEAN

When the Queen and the Duke of Edinburgh cross the Pacific Ocean in the Royal Ship *Gothic* (see ... pass many coral islands. Some of these islands contain phosphates, which are needed for agricultur... shown here, millions of tons of natural phosphate rock have been discovered. It is easy to quarry, but ... presented a great problem. The island is surrounded by a great coral reef which extends 400 feet ou... came to the rescue and, as shown here, an ingenious system of conveyors and great swinging cantile... the edge of the reef, enable ships to be loaded at the rate of 1,000 tons an hour at all states of the ti... buoys, but must keep steam up so that they can make out to sea in the event of a sudden gale.

KEY TO OPERATIONS

(1) Main conveyor from drying plant. This conveyor comes right through the inland forest. (2) Travelling carriage which tips off the phosphate rock at any desired point. (3) Phosphate in storage bin. (4) Storage bin, capable of holding 12,000 tons of phosphate rock, awaiting shipment. (5) Special doors through which the phosphate rock drops to the conveyor below when required. (6) Conveyor belt. (7) Conveyor to hopper. (8) Jetty with light railway for conveyor parts, etc. (9) Compensating hopper which divides the phosphate rock on to two conveyors. (10) Weighing machines. (11) Conveyor motor house. (12) Conveyor to cantilever arm. (13) Lattice structure for securing cantilever arm during a gale. (14) Position of cantilever arm when secured. (15) Swinging cantilever arm with conveyor inside. (16) Telescopic conveyor extension and delivery spout to ship's hold. (17) Control box. The operate... arm can watch the loading and is in control of ... ments. (18) Securing structure for cantilever ... Conveyor to cantilever arm. (20) Phosphate r... from one conveyor on to another above the pi... cantilever arm. (21) Motor house and 30 h.... motor for swinging the arm. (22) Concrete ... Rack and pinion gear for swinging the arm. (... terbalance weight. (25) Phosphate rocks dr... telescopic conveyor. (26) Adjustable telescopi... or and delivery spout. This enables the cor... tioning over the ship's holds. (27) One o... mooring buoys with deep anchorage. (28) Le... tide. There is a heavy undercurrent here. (29) ... and steel foundations for piers. (30) Coral re... ing 400 feet out to sea. (31) Abrupt drop to 180...

How the phosphate rock is excavated. First the trees are felled (A) and then piled up to wither with the coarse grass (B). They are then burnt (C). The overburden or top soil is removed (D). The phosphate rock is then dug out by native labour, loaded into light railway trucks and taken to a drying plant (E). Phosphate rock deposit (F). Coral rock (G).

PHOSPHATES F

All plants need phosphate to develop their root system and stimulate growth.

Vegetable lacking in phosphate in the soil and one which is well supplied.

The plants draw phosphate from the soil. Domestic animals obtain phosphates which they need for bone structure from the plants. Animal bones used to be burnt, leaving ash of calcium phosphate which was returned to the soil. Later it was discovered that certain rocks contained calcium phosphate and nowadays nearly all the superphosphate used in agriculture is manufactured from this.

L. ASHWELL WOOD

OR THE WORLD

HULLO, *VALIANT*! ENEMY FIGHTERS ATTACKING — OPEN FIRE WITH ALL GUNS!

AMPHIBIOUS OPERATIONS with DAN DARE!

DAN DARE *SPACE COMPASS

Your navigation will be all the more accurate when you use this Space Compass, that has been adjusted for Earth* use to point to the Magnetic North.

Price 2/6d.

*In Outer Space it points to Extra-Terrestial North

DAN DARE WATER JEEP

For coming in on the surf, and for manoeuvring round the lido, there is nothing more exciting – or more fun – than the Dan Dare Water Jeep. Daddy will only be too pleased to see that you have this wonderful toy that will help you learn to swim and protect you while doing so.

Price 10/-.

DAN DARE COSMIC RAY GUN WITH TRI-BEAM

RED . . . . . . Paralyses
GREEN . . . . Neutralises
WHITE . . . . Penetrises*

For marine or mainland signalling, and for interplanetary warfare, you – like Dan Dare – will want this amazing gun. It is modelled on the type used by him for his adventures. Secret compartments for concealing MESSAGES and MICROFILM.

Price 19/11d. *Penetrates blackest black.

Get these 3 pieces of DAN DARE equipment at your nearest SPACE STORE (IT MAY BE DISGUISED AS A TOY SHOP)

If you cannot find them near you, write to Captain Planetos, Cascelloid, Abbey Lane, Leicester.

Celebrity endorsements were all the rage in the post-war period. David Nixon was, in his time, the most famous magician in the country. In spite, or maybe because, of being tonsorially challenged he became the face of Arvin Shavers.

"Just my line"

"Just my line"

says DAVID NIXON famous T.V. Star

"Perhaps it's because I'm fond of vanishing tricks that I like the Arvin Shaver. It certainly makes my whiskers do the disappearing act. I just plug in and in a minute or so I get a close, smooth refreshing shave, and a comfortable feeling of being well-groomed."

The Arvin Consort is a high-quality shaver at a specially low price. Self-aligning shears, self-sharpening cutting head. A.C. only. 12 months guarantee. Only 75/-. Other models: De-Luxe, £5.5.5, '33', £8.19.9, in real hide case. Send for free illustrated leaflet E16.

ARVIN ELECTRIC SHAVERS

First—and still the foremost all British electric shaver

ARVIN ELECTRIC LTD. FERNBROOK AVENUE, SOUTHEND-ON-SEA, ESSEX

CONTINUING —

THE ARIZONA KID

Jeff Arnold chases the Arizona Kid as far as Sulphur Springs, and learns that the young Bandit has travelled on to Big Bend. After sending a telegram to Luke and Jim at Benson, telling them to follow him, Jeff rides to Big Bend. When he hears that the Kid has been seen heading towards Camp Apache, Jeff at once resumes the chase.

STORY BY CHARLES CHILTON: DRAWN BY FRANK HUMPHRIS.

In the Marshal's office at Camp Apache.

YES, HE'S HERE — RODE IN TWO DAYS AGO. ARE YOU GOIN' TO TRY TO ARREST HIM?

THAT'S WHY I CAME, AND THERE AIN'T ANY "TRY" ABOUT IT — I'M GOIN' TO DO IT!

BUT THAT KID'S DYNAMITE, JEFF! HE'S THE SLICKEST SHOT I'VE EVER SEEN.

I KNOW, BUT I AIM TO GET HIM FIRST — AND I'LL TAKE HIM ALIVE!

DON'T RISK IT, JEFF. I KNOW YOU'RE THE ONE MAN THAT MIGHT BEAT HIM TO THE DRAW — BUT YOU'LL HAVE TO KILL HIM TO DO IT!

I'VE GOT IT ALL FIGURED OUT, MARSHAL. HE WEARS TWO GUNS AND FAVOURS THE CROSS DRAW. BUT IN A GUN-FIGHT WITH ME, HE'LL USE *ONE HAND* ONLY — HIS SLICKEST!

IF HE DRAWS HIS LEFT GUN WITH HIS RIGHT HAND, HIS WEAPON WILL BE CLEAR OF HIS BODY FOR JUST A FRACTION OF A SECOND. THAT'S MY CHANCE TO SHOOT THE GUN FROM HIS HAND — *BUT IT'S A MIGHTY SLIM ONE!*

JEFF, WATCH OUT — HE'S GUNNING FOR YOU!

HUH?

THE KID! HE KNOWS YOU'RE HERE AND SAYS HE AIN'T SCARED. IF YOU WANT HIM, GO AND GET HIM. HE'S AIMING TO SHOOT IT OUT — SWEARS YOU'LL NEVER TAKE HIM ALIVE!

WHERE IS HE?

HE'LL BE COMING ALONG THE MAIN STREET IN A COUPLE OF MINUTES.

So, after loosening his gun in its holster, Jeff steps out into the street to meet the Kid.

WELL, I AIN'T GOT ANY CHOICE BUT TO GO OUT AND MEET HIM!

GOLDARN IT, THE TEXAN DOESN'T STAND A CHANCE AGAINST THE KID — HE'S GREASED LIGHTNING!

ARNOLD AIN'T EVER LOST A GUN-FIGHT YET!

I'VE COME TO TAKE YOU IN, KID — AND TO TAKE YOU ALIVE!

NOBODY'S TAKING ME ANY PLACE — UNLESS THEY CARRY ME, FEET FIRST!

I DON'T WANT TO HAVE TO HURT YOU, KID — THERE'S NO NEED FOR ANY GUNPLAY!

WHAT'S UP — ARE YOU YELLOW? WHY DON'T YOU *DRAW?*

I GIVE YOU TILL I COUNT THREE — THEN START SHOOTING!

CONTIN—

Early in 1956 Eagle came up with the idea of a sticker book. Famous Men of Today featured each week two well known faces to be cut out and stuck into a separately sold album. Looking at it today many of the faces are difficult to place but occasionally both are recognisable, even now. It is interesting to compare and contrast the randomly chosen couple's places in history. The two here, Eamonn Andrews and Laurence Olivier, undoubtedly hold a place in many people's heads and hearts, but there are probably not many situations where they are seen as a pair.

FAMOUS MEN

FAMOUS MEN OF TODAY

Here are two more photographs for your 'FAMOUS MEN OF TODAY' Album. Decide whose pictures these are, and stick them into the appropriate spaces in your Album.

for choice!

COFFEE CREAM !   TURKISH DELIGHT !

GOOSEBERRY CREAM !   CARAMEL !

PRALINE PÂTÉ !   NOUGAT ! !

6 different chocolates on every

Caley Tray MILK

CALEY

for choice!

EAGLE 5 March 1954

Three of these mobile dental clinics, combining a dental surgery and laboratory, on wheels, have been brought into service by the Kent County Council for use in areas where village schools are remote from the usual services in towns.

The clinics cater for children of all ages and, in addition, for nursing mothers, who receive dental services free of charge.

A detachable 'mechanical horse' (or prime mover), which is a 28 h.p. Austin 3-5 ton articulated short chassis, moves all three clinics about the county in turn, from village to village.

Each clinic is fitted with the finest modern equipment and consists of a waiting room for six people, reached by portable steps on the nearside of the vehicle, a surgery and a combined recovery room and laboratory. They have their own X-ray apparatus and facilities for the development of X-ray films and for a technician to make dental appliances.

Advice is given on the correct way to clean teeth and gums after eating sweets and sticky foods, and why you should – 'Clean them twice a day and so prevent decay'.

THE DENTIST CO

EAGLE 5 *March* 1954

A MOBILE DENTAL CLINIC
(FOR VILLAGE SCHOOLS)

KEY TO CLINIC

(1) 28 h.p. Austin (the prime mover). (2) Spare wheel. (3) Articulated chassis. The clinic is jacked up and left at a school whilst the prime mover goes off to move another one. (4) Wardrobe. (5) Waiting Room. (6) Entrance door (with portable steps from ground). (7) Drug cupboard. (8) Electrical control cabinet. (9) Electric light and double insulated skin which surrounds the whole vehicle. (10) Electric drill. (11) Dental unit with warm water syringes, cuspidor, switches and instrument table with Bunsen gas burner. (12) Adjustable dental chair. (13) Electric sterilizer. (14) Instrument cupboard (cut away). (15) Fresh water tanks. These are used when main water supply is not available for connection. (16) Calor gas cylinder for water heating. (17) Air compressor for forcing water from tanks. (18) Water pipes. (19) Wash basin with hot and cold water. (20) Nitro-oxygen anæsthetic machine. (21) Adjustable arms of X-ray machine enabling it to be moved to any position. (22) X-ray machine. (23) Fire-extinguisher. (24) Dark room lamp, used when developing X-ray films. (25) Developing time clock. (26) Cylinders of fixer and developer. (27) Dental lathe. (28) Sink. (29) Dental and X-ray accessory storage. (30) Work bench. (Folds upwards when recovery couch is in use.) (31) Recovery or rest couch. (32) Rear doors. (33) Plugged-in electric cable from grid system. The whole clinic is electrically operated and, as most villages are now on the grid system of electricity supply, the clinic may be plugged in. In case electricity supply is not available, a portable petrol-driven motor generator is carried.

L ASHWRL WOOD

MES TO VISIT

ITALIAN "DIRETTISSIMA" ROUTES ARE SPECIALLY DESIGNED FOR HIGH-SPEED TRAVEL AND THE MOST DIRECT COURSE POSSIBLE IS TAKEN. THEY INCORPORATE THE MAXIMUM NUMBER OF STRAIGHT STRETCHES AND CURVES OF LARGE RADIUS. MANY TUNNELS AND BRIDGES WERE NECESSARY IN ORDER TO KEEP GRADIENTS TO THE MINIMUM. THE CARME TO TUNNEL, ON THE BOLOGNA-FLORENCE ROUTE, SHOWN HERE (BEFORE OVERHEAD ELECTRIFICATION WAS INSTALLED) IS A TYPICAL EXAMPLE.

A STREAMLINED ELECTRIC 3-CAR "RAPIDO" OF THE ITALIAN STATE RAILWAYS. THESE TRAINS ARE CAPABLE OF VERY HIGH SPEEDS. IN JUNE, 1939, AN ITALIAN 3-CAR ELECTRIC TRAIN AVERAGED 102 M.P.H. FROM FLORENCE TO MILAN, A DISTANCE OF 195¾ MILES. (BELOW) ANOTHER ITALIAN ELECTRIC STREAMLINER, WHICH HAS IDENTICAL ENDS. THE DRIVER SITS IN THE DOME OF THE FRONT CAR AND PASSENGERS USE THE FRONT END BELOW AS A GLASS-ENCLOSED LOUNGE. IT IS SHOWN CROSSING A TYPICAL ITALIAN VIADUCT ON A "DIRETTISSIMA" ROUTE.

A "DIRETTISSIMA" IS BUILT WITHOUT FEAR OF NATURAL OBSTACLES THROUGH WHICH IT HAS TO PASS, AND ON THE BOLOGNA-FLORENCE ROUTE THIS NECESSITATED THE BORING OF THE GREAT APENNINE TUNNEL, 11 MILES-879 YARDS LONG — THE SECOND LONGEST IN THE WORLD. IT IS OFTEN CONSIDERED TO BE THE GREATEST EXAMPLE OF TUNNEL CONSTRUCTION IN EXISTENCE, FOR IT IS BUILT FOR A DOUBLE TRACK, WHEREAS THE SIMPLON (WORLD'S LONGEST) HAS SINGLE TRACK TUNNELS. THE APENNINE COST THE LIVES OF 97 MEN, SUCH WERE THE TREMENDOUS DANGERS AND DIFFICULTIES THAT HAD TO BE OVERCOME DURING ITS CONSTRUCTION. A TRAIN IS SHOWN HERE EMERGING FROM THE STRIKING NORTHERN PORTAL.

AT THE POINT WHERE THE SALTASH BRIDGE STANDS, THE RIVER IS 1,100 FT. WIDE. EACH MAIN SPAN IS 455 FT. IN LENGTH, WITH LONG VIADUCT APPROACHES. THE DECK OF THE BRIDGE IS SUSPENDED FROM ARCH-SHAPED, HOLLOW WROUGHT-IRON TUBES, OVAL IN SHAPE, 16¾ FT. BROAD AND 12¼ FT. HIGH. THESE TUBES CARRY THE WHOLE WEIGHT OF THE GREAT BRIDGE AND ARE A TYPICAL EXAMPLE OF THE INGENIOUS IDEAS THOUGHT OUT BY BRUNEL.

THE BRITANNIA TUBULAR BRIDGE ACROSS THE MENAI STRAITS, BETWEEN NORTH WALES AND ANGLESEY, WAS 100 YEARS OLD IN 1950. IT IS THE WORK OF ANOTHER OF BRITAIN'S FINEST ENGINEERS—ROBERT STEPHENSON. THE CENTRE TOWER STANDS ON BRITANNIA ISLAND, FROM WHICH THE BRIDGE GETS ITS NAME. EACH OF THE RECTANGULAR TUBES WHICH CARRY THE TRAINS IS 1,510 FT. LONG AND WEIGHS 4,680 TONS.

THE BRITANNIA BRIDGE HAS A VERY PLEASING APPEARANCE, THE STONE-WORK BEING CARRIED OUT IN ANGLE-SEY MARBLE. BOTH ENDS ARE GUARDED BY PAIRS OF MASSIVE LIONS CARVED OUT OF LIMESTONE (ONE CAN BE SEEN IN THE DRAWING). THE BRIDGE IS ON THE ROUTE OF ONE OF BRITAIN'S MOST FAMOUS TRAINS—"THE IRISH MAIL". THIS IS THE OLDEST NAME TRAIN IN THE WORLD, HAVING BEEN INAUGURATED WELL OVER A CENTURY AGO! ONE OF TODAY'S "IRISH MAILS" IS SHOWN HERE, IN CHARGE OF A "ROYAL SCOT" 4-6-0 LOCOMOTIVE, JUST LEAVING THE BRIDGE.

THE ROYAL ALBERT BRIDGE, SPANNING THE TAMAR AT SALTASH, LINKS DEVONSHIRE AND CORNWALL. TO-DAY, IT STANDS AS A MONUMENT TO ONE OF BRITAIN'S GREATEST ENGINEERS OF ALL TIME — ISAMBARD KINGDOM BRUNEL. IT WAS, IN FACT, HIS LAST AND PROBABLY FINEST FEAT OF RAILWAY ENGINEERING. THE BRIDGE WAS OPENED ON MAY 3RD, 1859 AND BRUNEL DIED A FEW MONTHS LATER IN THE SAME YEAR. IT IS ON THE PLYMOUTH-PENZANCE ROUTE AND CARRIES THE TRACK 110 FT. ABOVE THE WATERS OF THE TAMAR. OUR VIEW IS ONE LOOKING ALONG THE DECK OF THE BRIDGE.

FOR 14 MILES ACROSS THE ROMNEY MARSHES, IN KENT, RUNS THE ROMNEY, HYTHE AND DYMCHURCH RAILWAY—THE WORLD'S SMALLEST PUBLIC RAILWAY! IT ACTUALLY FILLS A TRANSPORTATION NEED IN THIS AREA AND THE TRAINS OPERATE TO TIMETABLES, JUST LIKE A FULL-SIZED LINE! THE GAUGE OF THE LINE IS 15 INS. AND THE POWERFUL MINIATURE LOCOS ARE BUILT TO A SCALE OF 4 INS. TO THE FOOT. ENGINE NO. 10 "DR. SYN", SHOWN HERE, ATTRACTS CONSIDERABLE ATTENTION, BEING MODELLED ON THE CANADIAN PACIFIC STYLE. A SIMILAR ENGINE, NO. 9, BEARS THE NAME "WINSTON CHURCHILL".

THE R.H. AND D.R. PLAYED ITS PART DURING THE 2ND. WORLD WAR. A SPECIAL ARMOURED TRAIN WAS CONSTRUCTED DURING THE INVASION THREAT OF 1940. ENGINE NO. 5 "HERCULES" WAS COUPLED BETWEEN TWO BOGIE-MOUNTED TRUCKS, THE WHOLE FORMING AN ANTI-AIRCRAFT UNIT WHICH REGULARLY PATROLLED THE MARSHES AND SAW PLENTY OF ACTION.

THERE ARE A NUMBER OF WELL-BUILT BRIDGES ON THE LINE CARRYING ROADWAYS OVER THE TRACKS. LOCO NO. 2 "NORTHERN CHIEF" IS SHOWN HERE THUNDERING OUT FROM BENEATH ONE OF THEM, THE ARCHES OF WHICH HAVE A HEAD CLEARANCE OF ONLY 6 FT!

"THE BLUECOASTER LIMITED", EQUIPPED WITH LUXURIOUS PULLMAN COACHES, IS THE 'CRACK' TRAIN OF THE R.H. AND D.R. HERE IT IS SEEN CROSSING THE DUKE OF YORK'S BRIDGE. THIS BRIDGE IS NAMED AFTER THE LATE KING GEORGE VI WHO, WHEN DUKE OF YORK, DROVE A TRAIN ACROSS. 57 FT. LONG AND 12 FT. 10 INS. WIDE, IT SPANS A CANAL AND INCORPORATES 7 TONS OF STEEL-WORK.

ONE OF THE STRANGEST RAILWAYS EVER BUILT WAS THE FLORIDA EAST COAST KEY WEST EXTENSION. THE FLORIDA KEYS—A CHAIN OF SMALL ISLANDS—REACH OUT INTO THE MEXICAN GULF, TERMINATING IN KEY WEST, 114 MILES FROM THE MAINLAND. THE RAILWAY USED THE KEYS AS PART OF ITS ROUTE, BRIDGING THE STRETCHES OF SEA BETWEEN THE ISLETS. THE HAVANA SPECIAL IS SHOWN HERE CROSSING THE LONG KEY VIADUCT, A CONCRETE ARCHED STRUCTURE 2½ MILES LONG.

THIS MAP SHOWS THE RAILWAY LINKING MIAMI WITH KEY WEST, AN AMERICAN NAVAL BASE. BEFORE LEAVING THE MAINLAND, THE LINE CROSSES A COUNTRY OF BOG AND SWAMP KNOWN AS THE EVER-GLADES. AMONGST THE ISLETS EXCELLENT BOATING AND FISHING ARE ENJOYED IN FLORIDA'S WARM CLIMATE.

FLORIDA — MIAMI — LARKIN — ROCKDALE — HOMESTEAD — EVERGLADE — JEWFISH — KEY LARGO — ROCKHARBOUR — PLANTATION KEY — INDIAN KEY — ATLANTIC OCEAN

GULF OF MEXICO — ROCKLAND KEY — Florida Bay — KEY WEST — PINE KEY — KNIGHTS KEY — LONG KEY

A TRAIN CROSSING KNIGHT'S KEY BRIDGE (7 MILES LONG) EXPOSED TO THE FULL FORCE OF THE GALES AND TROPICAL STORMS THAT SWEEP THIS REGION. COMPLETED IN 1912, THE RAILWAY RANKED AS ONE OF THE GREATEST ACHIEVE-MENTS IN RAILWAY ENGINEERING. IN 1935, ANOTHER HURRICANE WASHED THE TRACKS AWAY IN MANY PLACES. IT WAS DECIDED THAT TO REPAIR THE LINE WOULD COST TOO MUCH, AND SO THE CAREER OF THE RAILWAY ENDED. THE CAUSEWAY WAS RESTORED AND IS NOW USED AS A ROADWAY.

WHEN THE LINE WAS BEING BUILT (WORK COMMENCED IN 1905), THE WORK-MEN EMPLOYED WERE HOUSED IN A NUMBER OF SCOWS CONVERTED INTO FLOATING CAMPS. A HURRICANE HIT THE WORKINGS IN 1906 AND MANY HOUSE-BOATS WERE TORN LOOSE FROM THEIR MOORINGS AND SHATTERED AGAINST THE KEYS. OVER 70 MEN WERE LOST IN THE DISASTER.

DRAWN BY BACKHOUSE

FISH LIVE IN ALMOST ANY WATER, FRESH OR SALT. THEIR GILLS TAKE OXYGEN FROM THE WATER, BUT SOME KINDS, LIKE THE AFRICAN LUNG-FISH, CAN LIVE IN A HOLE IN THE MUD AFTER THE LAKES HAVE DRIED UP. MOST FISH LAY GREAT NUMBERS OF EGGS. SOME, LIKE THE DOGFISH, HAVE LIVING YOUNG. FISH ARE AT THE SAME TEMPERATURE AS THE WATER AROUND THEM.

THIS WHALE SHARK IS THE BIGGEST KIND OF FISH, REACHING FIFTY FEET IN LENGTH AND WEIGHING MORE THAN AN ELEPHANT. AS IN ALL SHARKS AND DOGFISH, ITS SKELETON IS MADE OF HARD GRISTLE AND NOT OF PROPER BONE. THE SKIN IS TOUGH AND ROUGH. THIS HUGE FISH FEEDS ON SHRIMPS.

THIS VERY BEAUTIFUL NEON FISH COMES FROM SOUTH AMERICA AND IS ONE OF THE SMALLEST KINDS. IT IS VERY POPULAR IN TROPICAL AQUARIA.

THE PLAICE IS KNOWN AS A FLATFISH BECAUSE IT HAS BECOME VERY BROAD AND FLAT. THESE FISH LIVE ON THE BOTTOM OF RATHER SHALLOW WATER AND THEIR UPPER SURFACE GENERALLY HAS THE SAME COLOUR AND PATTERN AS THEIR SURROUNDING

ALTHOUGH THE EEL MAY LOOK LIKE A SNAKE, IT IS A TRUE FISH. IT SPENDS MOST OF ITS LIFE IN FRESH WATER, BUT GOES TO SEA TO LAY ITS EGGS.

THE ATLANTIC SALMON IS THE FINEST RIVER FISH, BUT IT GOES TO SEA WHEN ONLY A FEW INCHES LONG AND COMES BACK TO LAY ITS EGGS. WHEN IT RETURNS TO THE RIVERS, IT DOES NOT FEED.

THE PIKE IS THE BIGGEST BRITISH FRESHWATER FI IT IS SOMETIMES CALLED A "RIVER WOLF" FROM HABIT OF EATING OTHER FISH. IT SPENDS AL ITS LIFE IN RIVERS AND LAKES

READERS' LETTERS

Pictures on the sky

RECENTLY I went to Switzerland and I saw a rocket-shaped object that was invented by a Swiss engineer to project pictures on the sky at night. I enclose a snap of it being taken out of the garage to be tested. – *Leslie R. Burke, Cricklewood, N.W.2.*

GEORGE CANSDALE VISIT

GEORGE CANSDALE paid a visit to our School recently and brought with him two pets, a bushbaby, and a small python; he allowed us to pass the python round, while the bushbaby jumped from shoulder to shoulder. Afterwards, he gave a very interesting lecture on natural history in the Gold Coast. – *J. N. Kirkman, Bolton, Lancs.*

UMBRELLA DOG

MY GRANDMA's dog was taken ill. As it was raining the day it was taken to the vet, it was carried under an umbrella. In a week's time there was the dog by the door, barking to go out, with an umbrella at his feet which was taken from the stand. He wanted to go for a walk in the rain. – *Kenneth Davies, Swansea, Glam.*

COOL ANYWAY

WHILE I was in Africa, I went out to call for my two-year-old brother to come in for his dinner. At last I found him, and where do you think he was? He was hidden in a big bucket with the water tap running on him. – *Julie Atkinson, Batley, Yorks.*

5/- is paid for each letter published. Readers who want a reply should enclose a stamped, addressed envelope.

George Cansdale was superintendent at London Zoo from the late Forties to the early Fifties and was a regular contributor to various comics and television programmes. His nature page in *Eagle* was generally accompanied by a drawing of him cuddling a monkey. George was responsible for introducing a tortoise on the BBC's *Blue Peter*. The ancient reptile was named George in his honour and died aged 83. Coincidentally Cansdale was 83 when he died in August 1993.

Another of *Eagle's* occasional series on random subjects, this one covered vehicles such as the Mercedes-Benz Whale, a car built specifically to gain the land-speed record; and the Roadable from 1946 – a car to which wings and propeller could be added to turn it into a plane. On the sea, there was the Lakatoi, a craft from New Guinea, which was two canoes stuck together. And so it went.

Can you spot an engine-spotter?

ODDITIES OF LAND, SEA AND AIR   AIR

1954 THE FLYING BEDSTEAD IS POWERED BY TWO ROLLS-ROYCE NENE JET ENGINES, HORIZONTALLY OPPOSED AT EITHER END OF THE FRAME. THE JETS ARE DUCTED THROUGH 90° SO THAT BOTH ENGINES DISCHARGE VERTICALLY DOWN. THERE ARE FOUR COMPRESSED AIR JETS AT EACH CORNER, SO TO SPEAK, TO PROVIDE STABILITY. FLIGHTS OF TEN MINUTES DURATION, AT A HEIGHT OF UP TO 25 FEET, HAVE BEEN ACHIEVED.

1948 THIS IS THE CIERVA AIR HORSE, AT THAT TIME THE BIGGEST HELICOPTER IN THE WORLD. IT HAD THREE ROTORS WITH THREE BLADES EACH, SPACE FOR 24 PEOPLE OR THREE TONS OF CARGO, AND A ROLLS-ROYCE MERLIN ENGINE OF 1,640 H.P. DROVE IT. WHAT WITH FLYING BEDSTEADS, HORSES, ETC., THE OLD SAYING THAT "PIGS MIGHT FLY" STANDS A GOOD CHANCE OF COMING TO PASS.

You write to the Editor

Trishaw. The enclosed photograph shows one on a bridge in Singapore with my mother, brother and myself standing nearby. – *Trevor Nightingale, Dumbarton, Scotland.*

RICKSHAW'S DESCENDANT

WHILE my brother and I both enjoy reading the EAGLE and have done so since No. 1, we feel that you have slipped up over Rickshaws in Singapore. *No! No!* sir, not even for Storm Nelson and his crew! We know, as we have spent several years there and only returned to U.K. last year. The means of transport now used is the Rickshaw's descendant, the

THE MEKON IS HERE!

THE MEKON is now terrorizing our back garden, but luckily he is only in snow.

I spent all of last weekend making him. I had to make his body a bit thicker because his head toppled off a couple of times, one of them narrowly missing me. – *Clive Wilcocks, Farnham Common, Bucks.*

The EAGLE Brush

Concluding...

WEIGHT LIFTING WITHOUT WEIGHTS

By AL MURRAY
(the famous National Coach)

Al Murray demonstrates the Single-legged exercise

VERTICAL JUMP

CHAIR DIPS

CHAIR DIPS

More exciting news about EAGLE CLUB

WONDERFUL CHEAP HOLIDAYS

Are you coming?

In co-operation with the Youth Hostels Association EAGLE Club has organized some thrilling, cheap-but-good holidays for EAGLE Club members who are twelve and over. Details of walking and cycling tours are given below.

Study the places and dates carefully and see which one you want to join.

'THE CLIMBERS' Walking Tour of North Wales

In North Wales the hostels are full of climbers – some quite famous! Many "Everest" expeditions have trained above the slopes that you will scramble over. The most spectacular feat will be the attempt to climb Snowdon.

- **Assembly Point : CHESTER**

Tour D2 Aug 14th to 21st
Tour E2 Aug 21st to 28th
Tour F2 Aug 28th to Sept 4th

Inclusive cost from Assembly Point £3. 8. 0.

The 'PENNINE WALKERS' Tour

For those with an urge to climb some of the highest peaks in Britain – and to explore the remains of former underground rivers.

- **Assembly Point : LEEDS**

Tour B1 July 31st to Aug 7th
Tour D1 Aug 14th to 21st
Tour F1 Aug 28th to Sept 4th

Inclusive cost from Assembly Point £3. 6. 0.

The 'WATER RATS' Cycling Tour of the Fens

For cyclists who also like swimming and messing about with boats this tour takes in Cambridge, Ely, Newmarket and Saffron Walden.

- **Assembly Point : CAMBRIDGE**

Tour A2 July 24th to 31st
Tour B2 July 31st to Aug 7th

Inclusive cost from Assembly Point £3. 3. 0.

The 'WEST RIDERS' Cycling Tour of the Yorkshire Dales

Castles, Caves, Swimming and Scrambling.

- **Assembly Point : BRADFORD**

Tour A1 July 24th to 31st
Tour C1 Aug 7th to 14th
Tour E1 Aug 21st to 28th

Inclusive cost from Assembly Point £3. 5. 6.

The 'TOPLINERS' Walking tour of the Lakelands

This tour takes you through some of Britain's finest mountain scenery: crags to climb, lakes to bathe in. It's a good stretch to the top, so bring your best pair of legs with you.

- **Assembly point : KENDAL**

Tour C3 Aug 7th to 14th

Inclusive cost from Assembly Point £3. 5. 6.

WHAT YOU HAVE TO DO

Discuss these holiday tours with your parents. You can assure them that you will be well looked after. There will be ten in each party in charge of an experienced Youth Hostels Association adult leader. You must arrange your own transport to and from the Assembly Point (where you meet), so choose a town convenient to you. If you are coming, fill in the Holiday Application form on page 11 as directed.

FURTHER ANNOUNCEMENTS WILL BE MADE NEXT WEEK ABOUT TOURS STARTING FROM LONDON, BIRMINGHAM and TYNESIDE

CRICKET

By arrangement with the M.C.C. and County Cricket Clubs, EAGLE Club members, on presenting a valid EAGLE Club card, will be allowed free admission after 4.30 p.m. to the county cricket grounds as listed in last week's EAGLE. ADDITIONAL: The same privileges will extend to the following County Cricket Clubs. Please add them to your list in last week's EAGLE and keep for reference.

SURREY C.C.C.
Free admission to the Oval Cricket Ground on dates to be announced in EAGLE.

WORCESTERSHIRE C.C.C.
Worcester and Kidderminster. (Excluding Bank Holidays and Benefit matches).

A further arrangement has been made with the M.C.C. regarding free admission to Minor County Championship Matches. We shall announce the matches and grounds concerned on EAGLE Club Page in the issue before the week in which the various fixtures take place.

Please Note

New Membership cards. If you are already a member of EAGLE Club you should send your card (or name and address and birthday date if you have lost your card) to EAGLE Club, Eagle Reader Services Long Lane, Liverpool 9. Please enclose a stamped and addressed envelope (2½d stamp).

You will receive a new membership card which will be valid until April 1st, 1955. You cannot take part in these new Club activities until you have your new card. *If you want to join now.* If you are not yet a member, fill in the coupon on page 11 as directed. You require a postal order for 1/6 to join the Club.

Please Note

THE EDITOR IS PRESIDENT OF THE CLUB: THESE FAMOUS MEN ARE YOUR VICE-PRESIDENTS.

| Neville Duke | Stirling Moss | Denis Compton | Stanley Matthews | Godfrey Evans | Trevor Bailey | Leonard Cheshire V.C. |

OUR VITAL

Pure water is one of the vital necessities of life. For the maintenance of health and cleanliness it is indispensable.

In this drawing we see how a modern city or town gets a supply of pure water, from the storage reservoir to your kitchen tap. All the various items are grouped together for convenience of illustration, but this would not be the case in actual practice. Some would be a considerable distance apart and also the piping arrangements would be much more complicated.

The storage reservoir would be filled either by water pumped from a river, as in London, or from a dammed-up valley or artificial lake miles away, the method used in the Manchester and Birmingham supply system.

SEQUENCE OF OPERATIONS.

(1) Large storage reservoir. (2) Outlets and valves at various levels. (3) Metering house where the flow is measured. (4) Outlet main or conduit. (5) Pumping house. (6) Water meter. The flow of water is constantly measured at different stages. (7) Chemical mixing house. (8) Settling tank. Here the chemicals take impurities to the bottom of the tank. (9) Screens. (10) Pumps forcing water to the primary filters. (11) Primary or quick filters. The water passes downwards through a layer of sand and graded shingle. (12) Water collects at bottom of channel. (13) Water meters and valves. (14) Water passes to the secondary or slow filters. (15) Slow filter beds. (16) The water slowly filters down through a layer of fine sand and various grades of gravel, which remove further impurities. (17) Sterilizing house. Here the filtered water is treated with one part per million of chlorine; that is, one gallon of chlorine to one million gallons of water. (18) Pumping house. (19) Water meter. (20) Water inlet to service reservoir. (21) Service reservoir. Here sterilization is completed and the pure water is stored ready for use. (22) Air vents. (23) Bottling house for water samples. A check on the purity of water is maintained at all times and samples sent to the laboratories for testing. (24) Pure water outlet. (25) Main pumping station. Here the pure water is pumped into the street mains and may also be pumped to other service reservoirs. (26) Final metering. (27) Street mains. These may be up to 48 inches in diameter. (28) Side street main of 6 inches diameter. Even smaller pipes lead off to the houses. (29) Main supply to distant service reservoir. (30) Service reservoir on high ground. (31) The pressure to supply mains is, in this case, maintained by gravity.

WATER SUP

ER SUPPLY

Your house supply.

A. 6 inch main supply.
B. Half-inch house supply.
C. Water authorities stop-cock.
D. Your outside stop-cock.
E. Your inside stop-cock.
F. House supply cistern.

Finally, pure water comes to your tap.

PLY

CHRISTMAS SPORTS QUIZ

TEST YOUR WITS AGAINST THE EXPERTS. PUZZLES FOR YOUR CHRISTMAS PARTY

OUR sports experts have set a Quiz to puzzle you and your friends at your Christmas Party. There are ten puzzles in all. Who can find the most correct answers? Solutions are printed at the foot of this column.

③ HANDS

Trying to reach a hot drive made by Johnny Leach (right), Jimmy Smith dropped his bat but, by quick thinking, was able to return the ball with the palm of his hand. What should the umpire have done?

(a) allowed play to continue
(b) awarded the point to Johnny Leach
or (c) called a 'let'.

④ A SOCCER HA! HA! QUIZ

Here are ten soccer posers containing the names of players, teams and places. See if you can fill in the missing letters. The answers look funny now – and if you don't finish them, they'll keep laughing right back at you!

1. Famous Scottish stadium, noted for its 'Roar'. **HA - - - - -**
2. Known as 'The Haddocks'. **- HA - - - -**
3. Their proper name? We call them 'Wolves'. **- - - - HA - - - - -**
4. This brilliant ball artist plays for Sunderland and England. **- HA -**
5. Wolves' inside forward who played for England in the last World Cup series. **- - - - HA -**
6. 'Long John', who plays centre-half or centre-forward for Leeds United and Wales. **- HA - - - -**
7. They play at Craven Cottage. **- HA - - - -**
8. Wolves' 'Mighty Atom' who has played for England on both wings. **HA - - - -**
9. Preston's full back who skippered Scotland in the World Cup. **- - HA -**
10. This Fulham favourite has won both Junior and Senior caps for England. **HA - - - -**

① SEASONABLE SIGNPOSTS

Ever heard of these places? They are all in England, and you may have come across them when out for a hike, or a training spin.
Can you say where they are?

⑤ FIND THE LINK

LEN **HARVEY** & B.B. **FITZSIMMONS**
HEAVYWEIGHT CHAMPION OF BRITAIN 1933 & 1938 — HEAVYWEIGHT CHAMPION OF THE WORLD 1897-1899

What is the interesting common link between these two great heavyweight boxers? Is it that both –
(a) won medals in the Olympic Games?
(b) were the same height and weight?
or (c) came from Helston, in Cornwall?

⑥ WHICH SPORT?

Mel Barnett, pictured above, is a champion sportsman. At which sport?
(a) Weight lifting   (c) Swimming
(b) Wrestling   *or* (d) Boxing

② SPOT THE CAR

The sports car pictured (right) was first raced at Charterhall in 1952, since when it has won many victories, including the Goodwood International 9-hour race, the British Empire Trophy and the Ulster T.T. races. Is it a –
(a) Jaguar XK 140?
(b) Aston Martin DB3S?
(c) Frazer-Nash *Sebring*?
or (d) Swallow Doretti?

⑦ HE'S ALSO

Gordon Bradley, the well-known professional tennis player (pictured here) is also a famous –
(a) Olympic swimmer (b) Marathon Runner (c) Test cricketer *or* (d) Cup Final goalkeeper. Which?

⑧ WHAT'S MY TEAM?

They call them the 'Throstles', and this is their badge. Who are they?

⑩ TEST THE GOALIE

In this drawing, the goalie is trying to catch the ball. Does he save, or does he miss?
To find the answer, put a small slip of card along the line A-B, holding it upright. Keeping your right eye on the goalie, and your left on the ball, move your face towards the picture – and see what happens!
Well, were you right? It's good fun this. Try drawing your own pictures in this manner, and ask your pals to test *your* goalie.

⑨ WHO IS IT?

The rider on the left of this exciting [pic]ture (the other is Geoff Mardon, on inside) was the first Englishman ever to [win] the World Speedway Championship. Is [it]
(a) Jack Parker?   (c) Tommy Price?
(b) Ronnie Moore?   (d) Split Waterma[n]

PROFESSOR **PUFF** and his dog **WUFF**

43-44, SHOE LANE, LONDON, E.C.4.

From the Editor to you—

25th February, 1955

I HOPE many of you will be able to take advantage of the Easter Holiday Tours which we have been able to arrange for you in co-operation with the Youth Hostels Association. You can assure your parents that you will be very well looked after and that each group is in charge of a responsible leader. We are planning bigger and better Summer holidays for you, too, so keep watching EAGLE Club announcements for more news.

I PAID a flying visit to Stockholm the other day for the launching of the Swedish edition of EAGLE, which is now being published there under the title of FALKEN. It looks just like an English EAGLE – except that, as you might expect, it has been translated into Swedish! It was fun to meet Swedish enthusiasts of Dan Dare and P.C. 49, and I hope that later on we shall be able to put English and Swedish readers in touch with each other. Meanwhile, we wish FALKEN the best of luck – may it fly high.

ALTHOUGH only 11, Howard Williams, of 18 By-Pass Road, East Ham, London E.6, has shown, during his mother's illness, initiative, common sense, and helpfulness which would do credit to a much older boy. We are pleased to award him the Silver Eagle Badge.

Yours sincerely,

Marcus Morris

★ EAGLE ACROSS THE SEA ★

EAGLE is now published in Sweden under the title FALKEN. Here you see our Editor, Marcus Morris, sharing the first copy with a Swedish reader. We may have news about Swedish readers to interest you later on

Five years after hitting the door mats of homes all over the UK, the *Eagle* landed in Sweden. For this foreign market the name was translated to *Falken*. Dan Dare became Dan Djärv, PC 49 was Konstapel 49 and Jeff Arnold was Jeff Arnold.

Eagle Special Investigator is warned

SIMBA!
(Lion!)

SIMBA!
(Lion!)

IN SEARCH OF THE LITTLE YELLOW MEN
(8)

TREKKING through the thirsty Kalahari in sweltering heat, EAGLE's African expedition have pitched camp in lion country. Read on from here the exciting real-life adventure of MACDONALD HASTINGS, your own special correspondent.

Fun in the shower at the end of a mission

STORM NELSON — SEA ADVENTURER

STORY BY EDWARD TRICE: DRAWN BY BELLAVITIS.

BEGINNING TODAY

THE QUEST OF THE GOLDEN QUEEN

"NELSON. S.Y. 'SILVER SPRAY'. IF UNENGAGED. MEET ME VENICE. URGENT. DON KENYON".

Storm Nelson and the crew of his Silver Fleet – Spanner, Bash, Jonah McCann and Kerfuffle – are homeward bound from Singapore, when Storm receives a signal from an old friend.

WONDER WHAT OLD DON'S UP TO IN ITALY?

I EXPECT SOMEONE'S ASKED LLOYDS FOR A FIRE - INSURANCE ON VESUVIUS.

AYE – AND HE WANTS US TAE PUT IT OOT.

DON'T BE SILLY – THAT'S AT NAPLES. NOT VENICE.

And so the Silver Fleet sails into the Venetian Lagoon bound on a thrilling new adventure . . .

AND LATER . . .

HULLO, STORM! HOW'S TRICKS?

HULLO, DON! HOW'S LLOYDS?

DON'T SAY YOU BROUGHT ME ALL THIS WAY JUST TO TAKE ME SIGHTSEEING?

HOLD YOUR HORSES! I'M GOING TO SHOW YOU A SIGHT THAT'S *WORTH* SEEING.

CARVED IN SOLID GOLD – *THE QUEEN OF BUCINTORO!*

PARDON MY IGNORANCE, BUT WHAT'S THE BUCINTORO?

THE QUEEN IS THE LAST OF THREE FAMOUS PIECES FROM THE SHIP – AND IT'S INSURED AT LLOYDS FOR HALF A MILLION POUNDS.

TOO BAD FOR LLOYDS IF IT GOT PINCHED!

Kenyon explains that the Bucintoro was a ship of fantastic richness used in a ceremony of olden days for the symbolic wedding of Venice with the sea.

THE OTHER TWO – THE ANGEL GABRIEL AND THE LION OF ST. MARK – *WERE* STOLEN. AND IT'S MY HUNCH THAT THE QUEEN IS GOING TO BE, BUT I DON'T KNOW BY WHOM.

AH, MR KENYON! KEEPING AN EYE ON THINGS?

SEÑOR DIEGO, THE FAMOUS ART COLLECTOR – COMMANDER NELSON A FRIEND OF MINE.

DELIGHTED TO MAKE YOUR ACQUAINTANCE, COMMANDER. I SAW YOUR YACHT COME IN. YOU MUST VISIT ME ON MINE. WE'RE LYING OFF THE LIDO.

I'LL BE GLAD TO.

THE STATUE'S ONLY ON EXHIBITION. I WANT YOUR HELP IN ESCORTING IT SAFELY BACK TO ITS OWNER.

ECCOLI CHE VENGONO! THEY ARE COMING NOW!

It looks like an ambush! Will Storm and Don fall into a trap?

CONTINUED

Registered at the G.P.O. for transmission by Magazine post to Canada (including Newfoundland). Eagle Magazine with which is incorporated The Merry-Go-Round, printed in Great Britain by Eric Bemrose Ltd., Long Lane, Liverpool 9, for the Proprietors and Publishers, Hulton Press Ltd., 43/44 Shoe Lane, London, E.C.4. Sole agents for Australia and New Zealand, Gordon & Gotch (A/sia) Ltd.; South Africa, Central News Agency Ltd.; Sole agents for Israel, Pales Press Co. Ltd. Subscription Rate: Inland and abroad, 12 months 26/-, 6 months 13/-. Postage for single copies: 1½d.; Canada 1d. You can have Eagle sent to any address in this country or Overseas for one year for 26/-, and to Canada at a special rate of 23/10½. To readers in U.S.A. or Canada, we will mail copies each week for

The 1,000 m.p.h. atomic-jet: Long-distance airliners would be pilotless and guided by radar and advanced electronics.
For internal routes, rocket-jets would be used in vertical rising convertiplanes (as shown on the left).
At the airport, sound-muffled take-off runs would be a feature and passengers would arrive by overhead monorail from the congested cities.
Trans-World Airlines, who have recently sponsored a similar interest in 'Aviation 30 years from now', celebrate their 30 years of service this year.

KEY TO PARTS: (1) Control tower radar-scanners. (2) Central control tower. (3) Underground subway and lifts.   KEY TO CONVERTI-PLANE (Left): (4) Convertiplane rising vertically. Passengers in gyroscopic-mounted seats. (5) Rocket-jet power unit. (6) Rockets attached to tail controls for converting to level flight. (7) Firing pit. (8) Firing control, and loading and mooring tower (lowered). (9) Underground passenger subway.   KEY TO ATOMIC-JET LINER (Centre): (10) Jet tail pipes inclined downwards into sound mufflers for take-off. (11) Atomic reactor and jet engines in shielded compartment against radiation. (12) Downward jets for vertical lift. (13) Swept back adjustable wings retracted. (14) Passengers' cabin. Seats lowered during acceleration at take-off. (15) Sleeping cabins. (16) Radar and electronic control apparatus. (17) Launching guide cradle. (18) Aircraft transporter. (19) Sound muffler and take-off run.   KEY TO OTHER FEATURES: (20) Convertiplane with loading and mooring tower raised. (21) Convertiplane in level flight. (22) Swept back adjustable wings extended for take-off. (23) Downward jets giving con-tinuous vertical lift. (24) Aircraft transporter. (25) Take-off run, with sliding doors closed ready for landing. (26) Underground maintenance hangars and lifts. (27) Radar scanners and aerials for guided control. (28) Observation lounge (1985 would also be the age of new glass – bendable and unbreakable). (29) Restaurant. (30) Underground subway to central control tower. (31) Passengers' entrance and exit ramp, to and from aircraft, with moving stairs. (32) Main aircraft control room, with pilot and co-pilot at the guiding controls and radar screens showing all air-craft movements. (33) Three-D cinema projecting moving cloud shapes and weather conditions. (34) Customs' Room. (35) Overhead monorail direct to airport.

THE FUTURE

30 YEARS FROM NOW
A FUTURE COMMERCIAL AIRPORT

In this exclusive EAGLE feature, we endeavour to portray what a commercial airport might look like in 1985 – when Eagle will be 35 years old! This drawing is based on developments now pending and predictions of leading aeronautical scientists.

CITY AIRPORT

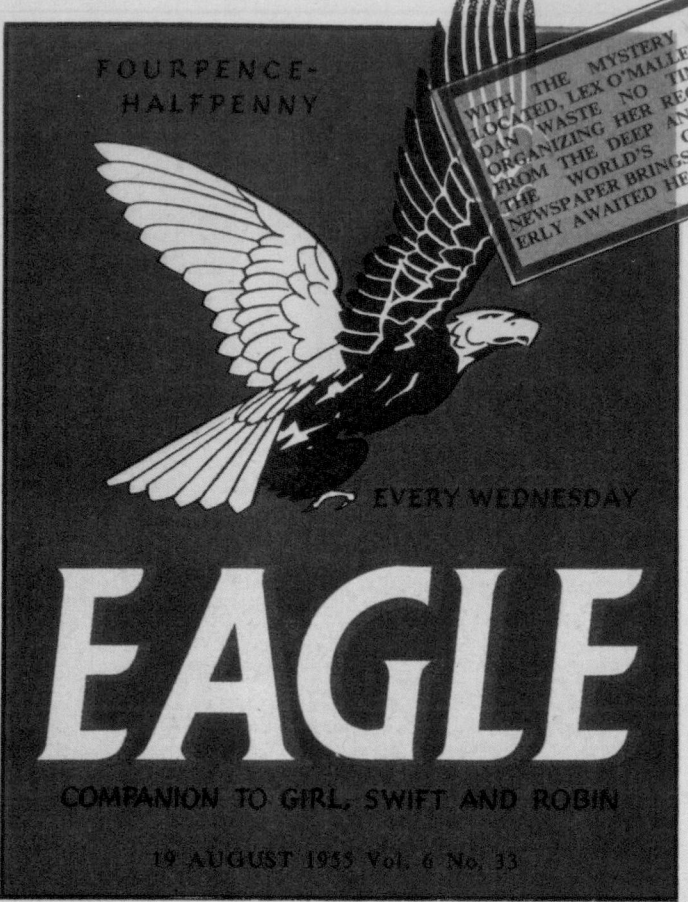

FOURPENCE-HALFPENNY

EVERY WEDNESDAY

EAGLE

COMPANION TO GIRL, SWIFT AND ROBIN

19 AUGUST 1955 Vol. 6 No. 33

WITH THE MYSTERY SHIP LOCATED, LEX O'MALLEY AND DAN WASTE NO TIME IN ORGANIZING HER RECOVERY FROM THE DEEP AND SOON THE WORLD'S GREATEST NEWSPAPER BRINGS THE EAGERLY AWAITED HEADLINE . . .

ONE PENNY EUROPE : TEN CENTS PANAMERICA : FOUR ANNAS ASIA : ONE SUT PANAFRIC

DAILY WORLD POST

SIMULTANEOUSLY IN LONDON, NEW YORK, SAN FRANCISCO, TOKIO, DELHI, BAKU, ROME, BULAWAYO, SYDNEY, MARSVILLE AND MEKONTA

LONDON

SUBSCRIBER'S ROCKET MAIL COPY
ATLANTIC EDITION
DATE AS POSTMARK.

THE HULTON PAPER

JUST RELEASED: THIS OFFICIAL SPACEFLEET PHOTOGRAPH IS FROM A TELE-FILM AUTO-RECORDED ON AN OBSERVER SCREEN. IT SHOWS THE MYSTERY SHIP A MOMENT BEFORE IT EXPLODED AND CRASHED INTO THE PACIFIC.

MYSTERY SHIP IS RAISED – OFFICIAL

SALVAGE FEAT MAY SOLVE SPACE RIDDLE

TOKIO, Tuesday.

THE salvage fleet assembled by R.N. and U.S.N. Units of the U.N. Naval Service has succeeded in raising the wreck of the mystery Intruder from the Tuscarora Deep. Working under conditions of strictest secrecy, experts from many nations teamed together under the leadership of Commander Lex O'Malley, R.N., to achieve the almost impossible – the raising of a wreck of considerable size from a depth of six miles.

Novel and daring methods must have been employed to lift the ship from the ledge of Basalt on which it was found by Commander O'Malley, and Colonel Dan Dare of the Space Fleet. The wreck is being towed to Yokohama, where it will be disassembled by Space Fleet Experts and Rocketed to H.Q. for investigation.

DARE HAS SUPER-OPTIC SPEED THEORY

Space-Ace Colonel Dan Dare is reported to have advanced the theory that the strange ship which broke through Earth defences last week had achieved a speed faster than light! Professor Sigmund Sax, Director of Space Research Council, commented:– "Ridiculous! Dare should stick to flying and leave such matters to those better qualified to deal with them!" But the S.R.C. spokesman must face the fact that the man in the street is gravely concerned at the Council's failure to produce any explanation as to why the Solar Observation Corps completely failed to plot the course of the intruder prior to its sudden appearance on Space Fleet's Astroscope screens.

COMMENT

The anxiety felt by most people at the sudden appearance of an unknown Spaceship, and its apparent ability to penetrate unseen through Earth defences, will be relieved to some extent by this morning's news.

Prompt action by the Royal Navy has more than justified "World Post's" successful campaign to keep that incomparable service in being at the time of the Universal Disarmament Convention.

Now that the ship has been raised, the Interplanetary Space Fleet has the opportunity to recover public esteem by answering 3 questions. HOW did the ship get through? WHERE did it come from – and WHY?

'LUCKY' LEX O'MALLEY DOES IT AGAIN

Commander Lex O'Malley, R.N., the colourful and unorthodox Irish submarine explorer, has earned new fame by his successful direction of the salvage operation. Author of two books on submarine exploration, the black-bearded Commander probably has more experience of the abyssal depths of the world's oceans than any other living man.

SALVAGED FOOD CAPSULES COULD SAVE 'MAN FROM NOWHERE' TOKIO, Late

Reported that Canisters of what appear to be some kind of food or vitamin capsules are being sent by special Rocket to London.

Discovered in the wreck when experts boarded her, it is hoped that they may help in the fight for the life of the "Man from Nowhere".

Three more survivors

Questioned by our correspondent on the spot, Sir Hubert Guest revealed a further three survivors were rescued from the ship's pressurized cabin. All have common racial characteristics with the "Man from Nowhere" found in Brazil's Mato Grosso shortly after the intruder crashed. The survivors are being rushed to London for interrogation.

'HIGHLY INTELLIGENT' SAYS HEMMING INSTITUTE

"Cranial form and brain structure indicate he is a creature of highest intelligence," said Sir Alan Cope, noted Anthropologist, after examining "The Man from Nowhere" at the Hemming Institute yesterday. A 3D model of the Stranger's head prepared by the Institute is shown at right.

SPORTS NEWS

Heli-Tennis 'Battle of the Century' opens

Lhasa was thronged today with excited crowds making their way to the Potala stadium for the long-awaited clash between the celebrated Frau Keller, the twin rotor "Menace from Mulhausen", and Pat Pulukovoski (Brooklyn Navy Yard) who favours the lighter "pulse jet" rig.

FRAU KELLER   PAT PULUKOSOWKI
CARTOONS BY

One of the best benefits of joining the Eagle Club was free entry to sporting events, more specifically football and cricket matches. While the football freebies seemed to be limited to the lower leagues, cricket was much more generous. All the 17 major counties (Durham wasn't admitted till 1991) offered an open door policy to anyone carrying the yellow Eagle Club card.

After a short time though, it would appear that too many youngsters were taking advantage of the scheme and so it was limited to entry after 4.30 p.m. Even so, in a world where there is no such thing as a free lunch it must have been fabulous to stroll through the gates of Lord's, flash your yellow card, and sit down to watch Fred Trueman steaming in and hurling them down at Denis Compton. All for free, nothing, gratis, thanks to your friends at *Eagle*.

You write to the Editor

SPACESHIP DESIGNER

I AM enclosing a photograph of a supersonic spaceship which I have designed and made all myself. You can see the ramp and spaceship, which are painted with aluminium paint and look very realistic. – *John Malby, Grimley, Worcester.*

LUCKY CHAP

I HAVE some good news for you. I am living in a nice new house now. The council man came to tell my mummy and daddy on my daddy's birthday that we had a new house, and that my daddy had to go for the keys. It's smashing. I have a bedroom of my own now, and I can see fields and trees for miles, too. There is a big field at the bottom of our back garden where I can fly my kite and play football with my friends. – *Bryan Baker, Seaham, Co. Durham.*

BREAD FOR BAIT

ONCE when I was fishing in Wiltshire for trout, I got a bite; my bait was bread. I called to my father who was fishing nearby. He came and helped me play it. At last we got it in and it weighed 5 lb. 1 oz. We took it home. Now the fish is in a glass case in the dining room. – *Christopher Rawlence, Nr. Lingsfield, Surrey.*

5/- is paid for each letter published. Readers who want a reply should enclose a stamped, addressed envelope.

EAGLE CLUB NEWS

CRICKET FREE VIEWING !

Look! Here are the County XIs you will be able to see in action –

Derbyshire	**Northamptonshire**
Essex	**Nottinghamshire**
Gloucestershire	**Somerset**
Hampshire	**Surrey**
Kent	**Sussex**
Lancashire	**Warwickshire**
Leicestershire	**Worcestershire**
M.C.C. and Middlesex	**Yorkshire**

and all Minor County Matches, too !

WITH the Cricket Season just around the corner, we can now announce wonderful FREE VIEWING FACILITIES which have been arranged especially for EAGLE by the M.C.C. and the Management Committees of County Cricket Clubs. By using your YELLOW Club Card, you will be able to follow the fortunes of your favourite Cricket XIs throughout the whole of the Cricket Season.

You will be allowed into these Matches at certain times during the day, so you must watch EAGLE every week for announcements about the times of viewing and the Matches to be played.

Your cricketing Vice-Presidents are:
Denis Compton * Trevor Bailey * Godfrey Evans

It may be YOUR turn for a Birthday Gift this week !

IF YOUR birthdate appears in the list below and you are an EAGLE Club Member, you are entitled to a FREE birthday gift! Choose it from the following list: stamp album, jigsaw puzzle, stationery folder, adventure book, ball-point pen or propelling pencil.

Then state the gift of your choice clearly on a post-card, giving us your name, address and Club Number and also the date you were born, and post it to Birthday Present (108) EAGLE Club, Long Lane, Liverpool 9. Your post-card must reach us by Thursday, April 28th. Though the same birthdate may appear more than once, no Member may claim more than one gift.

OCT 17 1945
DEC 20 1944
JAN 29 1942
MAY 7 1943
JULY 20 1945
DEC 8 1946

2 more Circus Visits

HERE'S another FREE offer for Circus tickets for lucky Club Members living in or near **NEWPORT** and **CARDIFF**. We have twenty tickets for the Bertram Mills Circus visiting each of these towns on the following dates :–

Newport – **Monday, May 2nd at 4.45 p.m.**
Cardiff – **Monday, May 9th at 4.45 p.m.**

Write to EAGLE Circus Visits, Long Lane, Liverpool 9. The first 20 letters opened for each town will be the lucky ones. State your name, address, age, Club Number, and which show you prefer to see.

To join EAGLE CLUB, fill in this form

Please enrol me as a Member of the EAGLE Club

I ENCLOSE A P.O. VALUE 1/6d.   BLOCK CAPITALS, PLEASE

NAME...

ADDRESS ....

....

Date of Birth : Day.............. Month.............. Year............

Post form with order for 1/6 to EAGLE Reader Services, Long Lane, Liverpool 9. P.O. should be made out to Hulton Press Ltd., and crossed '&/Co'.

Address this label to yourself in BLOCK LETTERS

NAME...

ADDRESS ....

EM

EAGLE SPORTS NEWS

● INFORMATION
● INSTRUCTION

Team of the year – 1955
★ CHELSEA ★

Goalie McIntosh (Sheffield Wednesday) collects a high ball, challenged by Chelsea skipper Roy Bentley. By winning this match, Chelsea made certain of the Div. I title.

THE BIG KICK-OFF

"We believe in YOUTH at Chelsea"

says TED DRAKE

(interviewed by Kenneth Wheeler)

(Manager of the Year 1955)
TED DRAKE

AS a player, Ted Drake gained every major honour; but none of his individual achievements mean as much to him as the success gained by Chelsea, the team he manages, in their Jubilee season of 1954-55.

Every Chelsea team won something! They brought no less than nine trophies to Stamford Bridge, including those for the First Division, London Combination and Metropolitan League Championships.

What was the secret of Chelsea's success? "Team spirit, and 100 per cent effort by everyone," says Ted Drake. "We're one big happy family at the Bridge, and we've learned to put the team first in all that we think and do.

"The youngest boy who sweeps the terraces is just as important to us as the longest-serving player. We want him to feel that he belongs, to learn from his seniors and strive for a place in the team. The training that he gets is of a kind that I hope my three sons may one day enjoy. Edward, he's 14, Robert (12), and Graham (9) all want to follow in my footsteps and become cricketer - footballers when they grow up, and I hope that they will show the necessary ability.

"As a matter of fact," Ted Drake continued, "the success of our youngsters last season pleased me more than anything. Conducted by our Chairman, Mr Mears, who is also Chairman of the English Selection Committee, they visited Amsterdam last Easter to compete with the best Youth teams of Europe for the Z.S.G.O. Cup, which I'm proud to say they won.

"I'll give you an example of what it can mean to join Chelsea," said Ted Drake. "One morning last season I motored across London to discuss the future of a promising 15-year-old player who had just left school. I wanted to give him a job, and after a chat with his parents I was able to satisfy them about his prospects.

"Less than one hour later, this youngster was on the field at Stamford Bridge, wearing Chelsea colours and playing in a trial game as inside partner to Roy Bentley.

"That, surely, must be a world record in sport for any 15-year-old. And to cap it all, Roy Bentley took the boy to lunch and offered him all the help he could give.

"The boy's name – Peter Brabrook. He played in two big matches for us last year – and I'm convinced that he is going to make a big name for himself in soccer."

"LUCKY CHELSEA"

DURING their close-season tour of Spain and Portugal, the English team were sitting in the hotel lounge. "I think I'll skip tea," Roy Bentley told Nat Lofthouse. "I want to cut down on my eating before the big match." But Roy was persuaded to stay. If he had himself forgotten that it was his 31st birthday, the other England players hadn't ! Presently the chef carried in a large birthday cake, baked in Roy's honour. "We've put a special message on it, instead of the usual greetings," said Trainer Jimmy Trotter. Roy read the message, piped on top of the cake with icing sugar. "LUCKY CHELSEA" it said.

How the game has changed… Chelsea 1955 – 'We believe in youth.'
Chelsea 2007 – still believe in youth, but other clubs'

43-44, SHOE LANE,
LONDON, E.C.4.

From the Editor to you –

19th August, 1955

ON page 15 you will see the first announcement of our National Table Tennis Tournament for 1955/1956, and I hope as many of you as possible will take part.

This Table Tennis Tournament is not for experts only – it's for all of you who would like to have a try, so don't be bashful about joining in. Even if you aren't a very good player, you will learn a lot about Table Tennis and have a chance to meet some of the experts, who are eager to show you how to improve your play.

NOW for a word about that 'newspaper look' on EAGLE's front page (and it's for one week only!). You'll see an advertisement for a *Junior Helirig*, but please remember that *The Daily World Post* is a paper of the future and that the *Junior Helirig* hasn't been invented yet – so don't send in for one, please! Your enthusiastic letters about our present Dan Dare story show very clearly that "The Man from Nowhere" has captured your imagination! There's even more excitement to come.

Yours sincerely,

Marcus Morris

SPOTTERS' CORNER

THE A.E.C. REGAL Mk. IV coaches used by British European Airways are a familiar sight on the roads between Waterloo Air Terminal and London Airport. There are 50 of them, and they are the biggest single-deckers in the country, with seats for 37 passengers, and a luggage compartment under the raised rear half-deck big enough to hold up to three suitcases for each person. Between them, they carry about 1½ million passengers each year.

Although specially designed, after careful study of the requirements by B.E.A. engineers and the London Transport Executive, the coaches use many of the same components and fittings as standard L.T. vehicles. Their bodies were built by Park Royal, and they have six-cylinder underfloor Diesel engines. They are painted in the standard B.E.A. colours with two shades of grey, white flash line and dark red trim.

WATCH FOR the "1½-deck" appearance resulting from the unstepped roof, which is unusual for a half-deck coach, and the insignia. Overall Length: 30 ft. Width: 8 ft. Unladen Weight: 8 tons, 3 cwt.

SUBMARINE ESCAPE — LATEST METHODS

New methods have recently been developed by which submariners have a much greater chance of escape should their craft be unable to surface. Amongst them is the "free-ascent" technique, which may be used up to depths of 300 ft. Another is the one-man escape chamber (A) which, following tests in the submarine *Solent*, is likely to be fitted in all new craft. The great advantages of this are speed of operations and the fact that a whole compartment does not have to be flooded, as with the use of the Twill escape trunk (see AA), which is now standard. In the compartments containing the latter is an air-supply manifold with individual leads, so that men may receive fresh air while awaiting their turn to come up. Drawing B shows a submarine bell in operation. These have proved most successful with the U.S. Navy, but can only be used if the submarine is on an even keel. H.M.S. *Kingfisher*, recently converted into a rescue ship, carries one of these. It weighs 10 tons, has a crew of 2 and can bring up 7 others each trip. BB shows the bell being lowered from the rescue ship, which has to be very carefully moored, for the former has to fit on to a special flange on the submarine's deck. Unfortunately this flange – for structural reasons – cannot be fitted to our existing vessels. C shows one of the two marker-buoys by which a submarine reveals her position. The forward one is red and yellow, the after one all yellow. Each has a flag and a flashing light which is surrounded by cat's eye reflectors. D illustrates the "free-ascent" technique, in which submariners have now been trained. No breathing apparatus is worn, only goggles and nose clip. Initially the lungs are under pressure, but during the ascent the air in them expands as water pressure decreases. Each man is therefore trained to keep his mouth open then, so that excess air may be slowly expelled. The immersion suits are not needed for the ascent, but to provide warmth and buoyancy when on the surface. Inflatable, they have electric heating.

In drawing E, the dotted lines show the extent of the working space in a submarine. It is planned that new ones shall have two escape compartments, each large enough to take the whole crew and protected by a very strong bulkhead. In each, there will be a one-man escape chamber (A) and fittings for a rescue bell (B).

KEY TO NUMBERS
(Submarine Escape)

1. Escape hatch.
2. One-man escape chamber.
3. Entrance.
4. Observation window.
5. Handle for raising floor (if required).
6. Drain to bilges.
7. Air under pressure.
8. Housing for hatch controls.
9. Escape hatch.
10. Flange on deck, to fit base of bell.
11. Lifting gear, also air and electric leads.
12. Compressed-air motor for winding gear.
13. Upper hatch.
14. Lower hatch lid.
15. Tackle for raising lower hatch.
16. Water ballast tanks.
17. Flange for bell.
18. Marker-buoy cable.
19. "Iron man" observation chamber.
20. Recompression chamber.
21. Immersion suit, pressed close to body by water pressure.
22. Red electric light.
23. Immersion suit inflated (note peculiar quilted effect).
24. Buoyancy stole.
25-25. Large escape compartments.
26-26. Specially strengthened bulkheads.

LAURENCE DUNN

THE D

EPTHS

BREAKING THE SPACE BARRIER

Earth satellites that will circle the upper atmosphere of the earth at 18,000 m.p.h. will be in being by 1957, that is official. This will be a step nearer the realm of Dan Dare, the pioneer of spaceships and interplanetary travel.

America will send up these "basketballs" by means of multi-stage rockets to a height of about 250 miles. They will weigh 110 pounds and have a diameter of 19½ inches, twice the size of footballs, circling the earth every 90 minutes.

The object will be to find out about the upper atmosphere, the mysterious cosmic rays, the ultra-violet rays, etc., and automatically radio these recordings back to earth. After a short time, the satellite would be slowed down by the rarefied air. It would then spiral towards the earth and vaporize when it hit the heavier lower atmosphere. In this exclusive Eagle feature, "Operation Basketball" is made clear.

KEY TO MULTI-STAGE ROCKET: (1) Turbine of first stage rocket. (2) Fuel tanks, empty. (3) The spent first stage rocket falls away at about 80 miles altitude. (4) Attachment bolts automatically sheared. (5) Second stage rocket; sheared at about 160 miles' altitude. (6) Venture of second stage turbine. (7) Combustion chambers. (8) Turbine and pumps. (9) Liquid oxygen tanks. (10) Alcohol tank. (11) Double skin and cooling coils against frictional heat. (12) Third stage rocket; this will finally reach an altitude of 250 miles. (13) Shearing bolts. (14) Third stage turbine. (15) Fuel tanks. (16) The satellite mounted in a ring. (17) Instruments for recording information on the way up. (18) The satellite is launched by explosive blast at about 250 miles altitude, when it then orbits the earth.

KEY TO THE EARTH'S ATMOSPHERIC BELT

A. Mount Everest, 29,003 feet.
B. The Troposphere (next to earth) and the Tropopause.
C. The Stratosphere.
D. Ordinary wireless waves are bent to earth by the Heaviside layer. Beam wireless waves are bent by the Appleton layer at about 170 miles' altitude.
E. The Ionosphere.
F. Limit of visible meteors.
G. Streamers of Aurora from here upwards.
H. The light of sky disappears into inky darkness beyond.
J. Satellite launched by rocket into outer space outside the atmospheric belt.
K. Outer space.
L. Electrons colliding with atoms of the upper atmosphere, resulting in cosmic rays.

HEIGHT IN MILES

L ASHWELL WOOD

THE HE

KEY TO REVOLVING SATELLITE: (19) Gamma ray recorder. (20) Antenna. (21) Sun's rays. (22) Sun ray collecting-rings. (23) Ultra-violet ray recorder. (23A) Electron recorder. (24) Alpha ray (X-ray) recorder. (25) Axis about which the satellite revolves. (26) Solar power turbines. (27) Magnetized tape recorder for radio transmitter. (28) Recording drum and gears. (29) Automatic radio transmitter and radar reflector. (30) Battery in protective wrapping. (31) Cosmic ray recorder. (32) Aurora recorder. (33) Short wave radio beams to earth. **KEY TO INSET LEFT:** (34) Satellite orbiting the earth at 18,000 m.p.h. (35) What keeps it up? The satellite's speed will tend to take it straight out into space, but gravity will be pulling it back to earth at the same time. The effect of these two opposing forces is to make the satellite travel in an orbit. (36) Upper atmosphere. (37) Short wave radio beams from satellite are picked up near the North Pole by aircraft. (38) Aircraft relays the radio information to earth. (39) Earth's gravitation pull. (40) Spent satellite spirals to earth and is vaporized by the heavy lower atmosphere.

IGHTS

Announcing our

EAGLE PAINTING COMPETITION

Below we give you details of a Nation-wide Competition open to all readers of EAGLE, as well as our companion papers GIRL and SWIFT

WE announce today the opening of our National Painting Competition and Exhibition, in which every reader of EAGLE, GIRL and SWIFT can enter, free.

Prizes worth £1,000 will be awarded. The boy whose entry shows most promise will visit Rome, with one parent, and other prizes will include gramophones, bicycles, art equipment, cameras and radio sets!

Your drawing or painting can be of any sub-ject that appeals to you, and you can colour it with paints or crayons, use charcoal or oils, or make pencil drawings – just as you wish. You are allowed to send in as many entries as you like, but a coupon cut from EAGLE must be sent with each one. Your entry can be any size, but you must remember to paste a very small paint-ing or drawing on to a backing at least eight inches by ten.

Very distinguished art experts will judge your entries – **Professor Robin Darwin, C.B.E.,** Prin-cipal of the Royal College of Art, **Lady Ogilvie,** well-known educationalist, **James Laver, C.B.E.,** famous art critic and curator at the Victoria and Albert Museum, and the distinguished artist, **Lynton Lamb, F.S.I.A.** They will look for imagination and the promise your work shows, as well as the quality of your actual drawing.

As entries will be judged in four age-groups, everyone has a chance in this competition.

When the paintings are chosen, they will form a collection which will be shown at Hulton House, in Fleet Street, London.

HURRY up with your entries, EAGLE readers. The closing date for our competition is April 23rd, 1956, but we shall be pleased to see your drawings and paintings as soon as you have finished them.

👁 SPOTTERS' CORNER 👁

THE VOLKSWAGEN MICROBUS has become popular all over the world because of its combination of high per-formance and low running costs. It could hardly be described as handsome, but it offers as much comfort as the average 'station wagon' type of car and is far more roomy, having been designed from the start to carry as great a load as possible within its small dimensions.

Powered by the standard 36 b.h.p. Volks-wagen air-cooled four-cylinder engine, mounted at the rear of the chassis, the *Microbus* cruises safely at 50 m.p.h. and has an average fuel consumption of 30 miles to the gallon. It carries eight per-sons and about 16 average-size suitcases, which can be loaded through the top-hinged rear door while passengers are entering the double side-doors. The interior is air-conditioned by a heater and adjustable roof-mounted ventilation system. The *de luxe* version has additional wrap-round rear windows, a sunshine roof and other refinements.

WATCH FOR the large Volkswagen badge on the snub nose, and the absence of any kind of radiator grille.

● Overall Length: 13 ft. 9 ins.　Width: 5 ft. 8 ins.　Loaded Weight: 36¼ cwt. ●

✳ Read these rules carefully with your parents

1. Paintings may be done in any colour medium. They may be of any subject, but must be original and not copied from other pictures or paint-ings. Entries may be of any size, but paintings or drawings measuring less than 8″ x 10″ must be mounted on a sheet of paper, canvas or cardboard not less than 8″ x 10″.

2. The coupon on this page must be filled in by you and signed by a par-ent, guardian or teacher in the place marked. It must then be glued firmly to the back of your painting before the painting is sent to us.

3. You may send in as many entries as you like, but each one must be accompanied by a coupon cut from EAGLE. These coupons will be appear-ing each week.

4. All entries should be sent to: EAGLE Art Council, EAGLE Reader Services, Long Lane, Aintree, Liver-pool 9. Final closing date of the competition is April 23rd, 1956, but we would welcome entries as soon as possible.

5. Paintings must be carefully packed. They should be sent in flat, unframed and without glass. We accept no responsibility for those lost or damaged in transit.

6. Each parcel must contain stamps for return postage and a self-addressed label if you want your painting returned. Those paintings chosen for exhibition or reproduc-tion will become the property of EAGLE for the period required.

7. The competition is open to all EAGLE readers in four different age-groups: (a) nine and under; (b) ten and eleven; (c) twelve and thirteen; (d) fourteen, fifteen and sixteen. These age groups apply as at 23rd April, 1956.

8. The decision of the Editor is final and we regret that no correspondence can be entered into regarding any of the entries submitted.

A visit to Rome for the Winner!

Start painting today!

COUPON E 1　　USE BLOCK LETTERS TO FILL THIS IN, PLEASE.

This painting is the original work of:

See page 139 for the winners

SCHOOL ....

TITLE OF PAINTING ....

Signature of parent, teacher or guardian ....

(*Cross out those which do not apply.)

P.C. 49 by ALAN STRANKS JOHN WORSLEY — THE CASE OF THE NEW MEMBER

CONTINUED :
P.C. 49 AND THE BOYS'CLUB GANG ARE TRAPPED AT THE BOTTOM OF A STEEP CLIFF BY "NUMBER ONE" AND MYSTICO, TWO CROOKS WHO HAVE STOLEN SECRET PAPERS AND LEFT MICK MULLIGAN TO DROWN IN A NEARBY CAVE. AS NIGHT FALLS, P.C. 49 AND HIS YOUNG CHUMS PREPARE FOR ACTION . . .

YOU CHAPS HAVE PUT ME IN A STICKY SPOT. THOSE CROOKS ARE ARMED — AND I'VE GOT TO KEEP YOU UNDER COVER.

TIDE'S RISING FAST — WE'LL DROWN IF WE STAY HERE!

I'VE GOT TO FIND MICK! HE'S IN DANGER — I CAN FEEL IT IN MY BONES.

IT'LL BE PITCH DARK IN A FEW MINUTES.

NOT SO, O ELMER! SEE THAT FLASHING LIGHT?

THAT'LL BE LAMPREY LIGHT-HOUSE. IF WE COULD GET A SIGNAL TO THE KEEPERS...

T-TOO MUCH T-TALK! "OVER THE T-TOP", SAY I!

P.C. 49 by ALAN STRANKS JOHN WORSLEY — THE CASE OF THE SQUARE RING

MY LORDS — EAGLERS — AND GENTLEMEN!
THIS IS A THIRTEEN-ROUND SERIAL, FEATURING P.C. 49, THE BOYS' CLUB GANG AND A NUMBER OF NEW FACES — SOME GOOD AND SOME NOT SO GOOD! PERMIT ME TO INTRODUCE . . .

ON MY RIGHT . . .

ON MY LEFT . . .

P.C. 49

TOBY

KID GLOVER (KNOWN WELTERWEIGHT)

KAYO KILLIGAN (REIGNING WELTER CHAMPION)

PAT

MICK

MAXIE MONKS (KAYO'S MANAGER)

GUMMY GULLETT (DEUCE'S STOODGE)

TIKI

GIGS

DOC WILDE (KID'S TRAINER)

DEUCE SPADE (A CROOKED GAMBLER)

SECONDS AWAY! ROUND ONE!

BUNNY

EVERY WEDNESDAY

4½d

EAGLE

COMPANION TO GIRL, SWIFT AND ROBIN

24 FEBRUARY 1956 Vol. 7 No. 8

DAN DARE
PILOT OF THE FUTURE
in ROGUE PLANET

I'VE LOST COUNT OF HOW LONG IT IS SINCE I'VE EATEN. LOOK AT ME — FAIR FADING AWAY!

WE MUST GET SOME GRUB FROM SOMEWHERE! WHAT ABOUT THAT FRUIT YOUNG "STRIPEY" IS GUZZLING?

THE STORY SO FAR: On *Cryptos*, Dan Dare, Lex O'Malley, Digby and their Crypt friend Lero have defeated a group of invaders from the rogue planet *Phantos* and released the prisoners whom the Phant guards were carrying away to slavery. Dan and Lero maroon the guards on a 'geyser-bouncer' — an island suspended above the Wilderness of Wex by gases — and then hurry back through the jungle to rejoin the others. Meanwhile, Lex and Digby are waiting with "Stripey" in a captured Phant wagon.

IT'S *POISON!* I TRIED SOME ONCE AND IT MADE ME SICK AS A DOG.

THOSE PHANTS LOOKED A FIT LOT. MAYBE THEY CARRY RATIONS IN THOSE LOCKERS ASTERN...

...THIS LOOKS LIKE THE GRUB-CACHE! CAPSULES—SAME TYPE AS THE CRYPTS EAT, BUT A DIFFERENT COLOUR.

GUESS I'D BETTER BE THE GUINEA-PIG ON THIS LOT...

PAST THE TEETH, OVER THE GUMS, LOOK OUT, STOMACH, HERE IT COMES!

I WISH YOU HADN'T DONE THAT, SIR. IT MIGHT BE MEDICAL KIT — OR DEADLY POISON!

TIME WILL TELL DIG! IT TASTES SWEETISH...

TWENTY MINUTES LATER...

HOW DO YOU FEEL NOW, SIR?

GRRRRRRR!

THAT'S A NICE WAY TO TALK! I WAS ONLY...

?

LOOK OUT, "STRIPEY" — HE'S WRECKING THE JOINT!

The story of 'The Rogue Planet' hinges on the accidental discovery by Lex O'Malley of nutritional tablets which turn whoever consumes them into aggressive monsters. There are also tablets which can make a whole race into passive beings. In this tale the Crypts eat only yellow pills, while the Phants, the warrior race, live on purple pills. Fact being at least as strange as fiction, at around the same time this story was coming out, the American Army was experimenting on its own soldiers with various drugs, most notably lysergic acid diethylamide (LSD), to make the ultimate soldier.

Members of the studio producing the strips each week were continually used as models for the drawings. In this panel from 13 April 1956, Dan does a very passable impersonation of Digby to help Stripey understand his message.

EAGLE 16 March 1950

WELL, I'M JIGGERED !

The Maharajah's Elephant. That's the Maharajah's private riding elephant, one of the fifty elephants he owns, giving the salute. This elephant's name is Ranga. And that fellow riding the other elephant over the way . . . ?

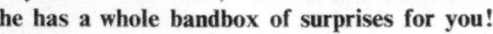

Last week, E.S.I. had a private audience with the Maharajah of Mysore. This week, he has a whole bandbox of surprises for you!

EAGLE EXCLUSIVE
Macdonald Hastings
IN INDIA

Why, it's E.S.I. up to his tricks again!

The Maharajah's Garage. Have you ever clapped eyes on such a super lock-up? I haven't. It's where the Maharajah of Mysore keeps his 14 private cars; not counting station-wagons, lorries, safari cars, *and* his 1921 vintage green Rolls-Royce. He's got a fleet of Rolls-Royces, Bentleys, Austins and Delahayes. Every car is decorated with the Maharajah's crest; and every car has its own chauffeur in the Maharajah's livery.

The Palace Guard. The Guard turned out specially so that you could have this picture. The bugler sounds the salute whenever the Maharajah leaves or enters.

A Hindu family very kindly asked me to their house so that I could sample a real Indian curry.

After working through about twenty dishes, I felt just as if my inside had caught alight.

They offered me butter-milk and seed-cake to 'tame' the curry. But it didn't help very much.

Made with vegetables, because strict Hindus don't eat meat, the curry was far too hot for me.

In the end, I just pushed my handkerchief into my mouth until I had cooled down somewhat.

This is the Maharajah's Sacred Horse, Jaya Raghara II, which is never ridden. He is a pure-bred Khalthewar. With the Sacred Elephant and the Sacred Bullock, he attends the Maharajah's processions. You might well ask why that cow is wandering in the streets. The reason is that, in India, cows are sacred. They are allowed to wander where they like and do what they like. Between you and me, they are an awful nuisance!

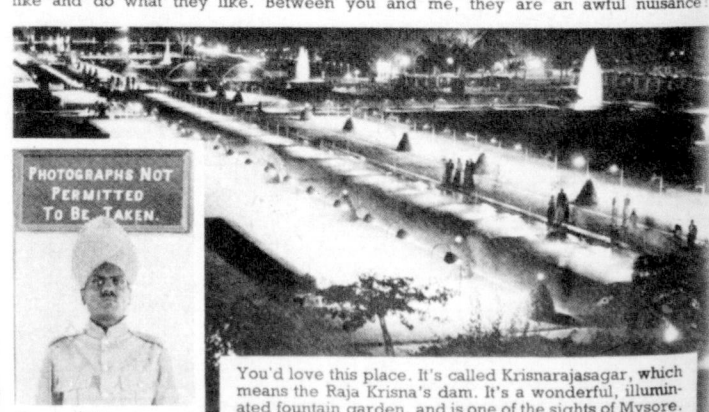

PHOTOGRAPHS NOT PERMITTED TO BE TAKEN.

Trust E.S.I. to get round that one!

You'd love this place. It's called Krisnarajasagar, which means the Raja Krisna's dam. It's a wonderful, illuminated fountain garden, and is one of the sights of Mysore.

He wants to be a CIVIL ENGINEER

He wants to be a CIVIL ENGINEER

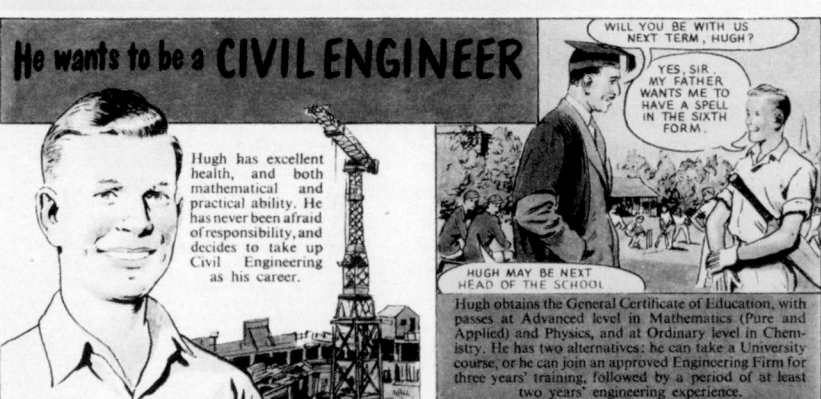

Hugh has excellent health, and both mathematical and practical ability. He has never been afraid of responsibility, and decides to take up Civil Engineering as his career.

WILL YOU BE WITH US NEXT TERM, HUGH?

YES, SIR. MY FATHER WANTS ME TO HAVE A SPELL IN THE SIXTH FORM.

HUGH MAY BE NEXT HEAD OF THE SCHOOL

Hugh obtains the General Certificate of Education, with passes at Advanced level in Mathematics (Pure and Applied) and Physics, and at Ordinary level in Chemistry. He has two alternatives: he can take a University course, or he can join an approved Engineering Firm for three years' training, followed by a period of at least two years' engineering experience.

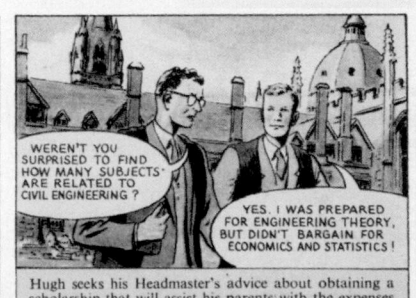

WEREN'T YOU SURPRISED TO FIND HOW MANY SUBJECTS ARE RELATED TO CIVIL ENGINEERING?

YES. I WAS PREPARED FOR ENGINEERING THEORY, BUT DIDN'T BARGAIN FOR ECONOMICS AND STATISTICS!

Hugh seeks his Headmaster's advice about obtaining a scholarship that will assist his parents with the expenses of a University education, and at 18 he starts his 3-year course, during which he enrols as a Student member of the Institution of Civil Engineers. He does well at the University, and is awarded the degree of Bachelor of Science (Eng.). He then obtains two years' training under agreement with an approved engineer.

YOU SEE THE PROBLEM WE HAVE HERE. THE SITE WILL NEED EXTENSIVE DRAINING.

IT'S WORTH IT, THOUGH. THE TOWN BADLY NEEDS A NEW SUBURB.

At 23, Hugh does his National Service. The time is usefully spent, as he increases his experience in a technical unit. On his return to his firm, part of his time is spent in the field on surveying and construction work. He earns about £600 p.a. and can become an Associate Member of the Institution of Civil Engineers.

THIS WILL SOON BE A GREAT AIRPORT.

YES, AND A VITAL LINK WITH AUSTRALIA AND THE EAST.

The title Civil Engineering denotes design and constructional work of all kinds. Some of it is prosaic, such as providing essential services. Some has a more romantic appeal, such as building railways, bridges, harbours and airports. There are many openings for civil engineers in places overseas, and salaries obtainable for service abroad are higher by about 60%.

THE FIRST OF THE 'BREEDER' POWER STATIONS, BUILDING A NEW ERA OF PROSPERITY.

IN A FEW YEARS THERE'LL BE OTHERS ALL OVER THE COUNTRY.

Hugh has made a fine reputation for himself, and always has sufficient work to keep him fully employed. Conditions and requirements vary with every job he undertakes, and he enjoys meeting each fresh challenge as it comes.

WATER-TA

Three of these full-scale water tanks form a new appearance on the landscape at the Royal Aircraft Establishment at Farnborough.

Under new regulations, cabin-pressurized civil aircraft have to be submitted to water-tank tests to determine their safe metal-fatigue life. In this drawing, we show one of the new Bristol *Britannia* turbo-prop airliners undergoing this test. The almost complete air-frame, except for the tailplane, is contained in a metal tank which holds some 300,000 gallons of water.

Water pressure is increased inside the pressurized portion of the fuselage to represent the air conditions when flying at great heights.

The wings, protruding from the sides of the tank, are subjected to up and down stresses by a system of hydraulic jacks.

Three stages of testing are continued for the equivalent of 20,000 flying hours, and all stresses are carefully recorded by scientific instruments in the control room.

KEY TO THE MEANS AND METHOD

(1) Control and pump rooms. (2) Dividing wall, and rear tank section for testing smaller components. (3) Tank filled to 300,000 gallon capacity. (4) Inlet and outlet water-grilles. (5) Water-pressure pipe to inside fuselage. (6) Fin stub protrudes above water with air-escape vent-pipes. (7) Tail support and load carrier. (8) Rear pressurized fuselage bulkhead. (9) Rear fuselage load weights. (10) Fuselage outer skin. (11) Water pressure is increased inside the pressurized section of the fuselage to represent high-flying conditions. (12) Water-pressure pipe. (13) Non-pressurized section under floor. (14) Front fuselage lever-loading system. (15) Front fuselage load (or ballast) weights. These represent a fully-loaded aircraft. (16) Front pressurized fuselage bulkhead. (17) Nose-wheel opening; non-pressurized. (18) Inlet and outlet water-grille. (19) Nose-wheel mounting. (20) Load carrier. (21) Rubber sealing strip of starboard wing root. (22) Inner starboard engine load weight. (23) Main-wheel mounting. (24) Outer starboard engine load weight. (25) Fore and aft stabilizer. (26) Inner

wing hydraulic jacks. (27) Hydraulic pipe-line from control room. (28) Outer wing loading system. (29) Outer wing hydraulic jacks; these jacks vibrate the wings up and down to represent air gusts and load in flight. (30) Vibration recorder. (31) Port wing. (32) Water reservoir tank. (33) Inlet and outlet mains to control room, and pumps for filling and emptying the tank.

The three testing cycles of three minutes each: **(A)** Tank filled to equal pressure — ground-level conditions. **(B)** Equal water pressure. Hydraulic jacks vibrate wings — 'take off' and 'climb' conditions. **(C)** Water pressure increased in fuselage. Wings still vibrated — high-flying conditions. The three cycles are then reversed — descent and landing conditions.

L. ASHWELL WO

PROVES ONCE AGAIN WHY HE I

STING THE BRITANNIA

OD
HE KING OF THE CUTAWAY

EAGLE 27 July 1956

Our Painting Competition

Here is a selection from the best paintings in our recent National Painting Competition. Throughout, the standard was very high indeed and gained the admiration of the judges. See Editor's letter for full list of winners.

GROWING SHADOWS *by Paul Scholey*

MARKET *by Douglas John Boyd (aged 16)*

IN HARBOUR *by Malcolm Dunnett*

43-44, SHOE LANE, LONDON, E.C.4.

From the Editor to you—

15th June, 1956

FROM time to time you may have heard of boys or girls being hurt because they have picked up an explosive object in the fields or on the beaches; usually a relic of the last war.

Although clearing of wartime training and defence areas has been carried out very thoroughly, there is just a remote possibility of a buried missile being ploughed up to the surface or of an unexploded mine being washed up by the sea. The War Office have asked me to pass on these words of advice to you: –

Do not touch any strange metal object. Tell the police.

Do not enter a firing range or a training area. They are clearly marked by fencing and warning notices.

There is no need, of course, to go around the fields and beaches on tiptoe, fearing the worst and waiting for a great big bang! The chance of meeting with an explosive object is very remote indeed. BUT – if you *should* chance to see something that looks odd, remember – don't touch it, however exciting it looks.

Yours sincerely.

Marcus James

You write to the Editor

ROBERT'S PUP

I HAVE a one-month-old puppy named Satish. Every time I tap her nose she snaps at me, and she loves to crawl under the food cabinet. But when I call out "Ho, Ha, Ho, Ha, Ho," she rocks her head from side to side and then crawls out. Here is a photograph of me holding Satish, when she was a fortnight old, with my sister Shirley. – *Robert Pringle, Tripoli.* ED. – *Robert, you forgot to give us your full address. Would you kindly send it to us in order that we may send you your prize?*

5/- is paid for each letter published. Readers who want a reply should enclose a stamped, addressed envelope.

CRICKET CLUB

LAST November, a few of my friends and myself decided to form a 'Colts' Cricket Club and, with the help of an M.C.C. Youth Coach, we grew in membership, until now we have 25 members. Last week Mr Fred Titmus, the Middlesex and England cricketer, very kindly accepted the offer of being Club President. He also said that he would try to come to our trial match.

Later I had the honour of being photographed with Mr Titmus. – *Brian Collins, Enfield, Middlesex.*

WE'RE IN THE ARMY NOW!

I AM a reader of the EAGLE and have just joined the Army. In the Education Centre here, they have pinned the centre pages of the EAGLE showing the working parts of lorries, ships, etc. It is an excellent way of teaching drivers, and mechanics, how to strip and repair machines. – *23470087 C. R. James, Aldershot, Hampshire.*

EAGLE 27 July 1956

INDUSTRIAL LANDSCAPE *by John Braben (aged 11)*

TRAFALGAR SQUARE
by Frank Elsey (aged) 15

THE CRESCENT *by Jeremy David Annett (aged 14)*

A special letter from the Editor

43-44, SHOE LANE,
LONDON, E.C.4.

27th July, 1956

THE picture shows just a fraction of the best paintings from which the judges, headed by Sir William Richardson, President of the Royal Academy, chose the top prizewinners in our National Painting Competition. The finalists were: – *Groups 14, 15, 16:* Douglas Boyd of Weybridge; Jeremy Annett of London; Charles Prosser of Harrogate. *Group 12 and 13:* Paul Scholey of Retford, Notts; Christopher Tilley of Launceston, Cornwall. *Group 10 and 11:* John Stevens of Ewell, Surrey; and Martin Lange of Margate.

Douglas Boyd and Jeremy Annett win the trip to Italy. I shall tell you more about that later.

I feel extremely proud of the tremendous show your paintings made and congratulate not only the winners but every one who tried.

Yours sincerely,

Marcus Morris

You write to the Editor

WELSH RABBIT

I WOULD like to tell you how I got my tame rabbit, which I caught at Landulas, Wales. Whilst on the mountain called Leaping Maria, I saw this black and white creature hiding in a cave. I crept along to the rabbit and picked him up. He didn't struggle or bite, and now he is my pet. Every day, while I am at school, he sleeps between my dog's paws. – *Stanley Thompson, Ardwick, Manchester* 12.

MARTIAN HASTINGS

WOULD IT not be a good idea if Mr Macdonald Hastings carried out an investigation into flying saucers? I am very interested in this subject, and I am sure many other EAGLE readers are, too.

If I get this printed, I will put the 5/- towards a flying-saucer book. – *D. Daniels, Hove* 3.

[*I think it's rather early days for any such expeditions, and Mr Hastings is still very busy with so much to explore on terra firma. But I wish you good reading with your book! – Ed.*]

LISTEN TO THIS

I HAVE just made my fifth and smallest crystal receiving set – in a *match-box*. On reading that Miss Grace Kelly had been given one in a lipstick-holder, I thought I would make one: but as Mother could not part with her lipstick-holder, I had to use a match-box instead.

This was most successful and the reception was very clear. – *David Marks, St. Leonards-on-Sea, Sussex.*

[*What patience and skill you must have used, David. Congratulations on your success.–Ed.*]

> 5/- is paid for each letter published. Readers who want a reply should enclose a stamped, addressed envelope.

He wants to be a CHEF

At 15, Harry has had a good general education. He is interested in food, and has creative ability. When he leaves school, he wants to be a Chef.

> WHY WOULDN'T YOU SERVE STEAK AND KIDNEY PUDDING FOR THE FIRST COURSE OF A MEAL, WITH 'PLUM DUFF' TO FOLLOW?
> TOO STODGY.
> TOO MANY CARBO-HYDRATES, SIR.

Harry starts a full-time, two year, Hotel Cook's course at a Technical College. In addition to the theory and practice of cookery, he will learn menu planning, food values, kitchen planning and equipment, accounts, English and French. As Harry is under 18, the cost is low.

> WHAT A WONDERFUL SPOT FOR A HOTEL.
> I HOPE THE KITCHENS ARE AS NICE AS THE REST OF IT.

At the end of his course, Harry passes the City and Guilds of London Institute examinations. He shows such promise that he is given the opportunity to spend a year abroad, under the Student Exchange Scheme sponsored by the British Hotels and Restaurants Association. This gives him experience of Continental methods and customs, besides improving his knowledge of a foreign language.

> YOU HAVE THAT KNIFE AT TOO SHARP AN ANGLE, HARRY, THICK SLICES ARE NOT APPETIZING.
> CARVING IS QUITE AN ART, ISN'T IT?

After his National Service, during which he gains experience of large-scale cooking, Harry joins the kitchen staff of a big hotel, where he works in each section as a 'commis chef'. He starts work in the larder which, being cool, is the least tiring. Under the 'chef garde manger' he prepares meat, poultry, fish, salads and cold dishes. Later he prepares egg dishes, vegetables and soups under the 'chef entremetier', and cooks fish for the 'chef poissonier'. He earns about £10 a week.

> THIS DECORATION LOOKS NICE.
> GARNISHING IMPROVES A GOOD DISH, BUT CAN'T REDEEM A BAD ONE!

When Harry moves on to the section of the 'chef rôtisseur', he cooks joints, poultry and game. He makes and decorates cakes and sweets under the 'chef pâtissier', and lastly, under the 'chef saucier' he prepares entrées, grills and hot sauces. He earns about £14 a week, and now has enough confidence to take charge of any of the sections when the 'chef de partie' is off duty.

> THIS WON'T DO, WAITER. THE HELPING IS TOO SMALL.
> I'LL TAKE IT BACK.

Harry has a good head for business, and is promoted to 'sous chef' at a salary of about £1,000 per annum. He looks forward to rising to the top of the tree, and eventually becoming a 'chef de cuisine'. His work is exacting and tiring, since it entails long hours (as in any responsible job), but he thoroughly enjoys exercising his creative abilities in his chosen art.

EAGLE SPECIAL INVESTIGATOR holds an enquiry

CALLING ALL FLYING SAUCERS!

DO YOU BELIEVE IN THEM?

Is there really any life on other planets? Do Flying Saucers actually exist? Reader Daniels suggested that MACDONALD HASTINGS should investigate. This is the second instalment of E.S.I.'s report...

HERE'S a strange story which made news thirty-nine years before Kenneth Arnold, an American air-man, reported sighting a flight of strange objects in the sky which he described as 'flying saucers'.

Nobody had heard of flying saucers when this incident happened. Nobody was searching the sky in search of unusual objects.

Flying itself was still in its infancy. In the spring of 1909, the skies over East Anglia were invaded 'by some strange friend or potential enemy; none knows which'. It was described at the time as a mysterious airship (because gas-filled airships were then very much in the public eye), but it was unlike any airship that anybody had seen before.

It was sighted in many parts of East Anglia, including Ipswich, Lowestoft, Peterborough, Southend, King's Lynn, Saxmundham, Ely and Lincoln, the stories of all the eye-witnesses supporting each other in a remarkable manner.

"I was in the garden," said Mr J. A. Smith, a local worthy, "when my daughter called me that a strange object was in the sky. I got hold of my glasses just as the postman and a constable came up, and what we seemed to see were two distinct objects, the upper like a huge grub, while the other, much lower down, was distinguishable by an exceptionally bright gleam, of the searchlight description. It passed out of sight in a quarter of an hour, so its pace and engine-power must have been extraordinary."

Press reporters hunted the lonely places of East Anglia for the airship's secret base. Everybody who saw it in the air agreed that it moved at a remarkable pace, far faster than any airship known at that time; and that it was 'a monarch of the air'. It was widely believed to be a 'secret weapon'.

In fact, they talked about it just as people talk about 'flying saucers' now.

People who are satisfied that the Earth is watched by visitors from other planets would probably describe it as a mother ship, one of the luminous, cigar-shaped craft which are supposed to carry 'flying saucers' inside them – like aircraft carriers.

Of course, you have always got to watch out, especially in considering the evidence of something as fantastic as a spaceship from another planet, not to twist the evidence to help yourself to believe what you want to believe. The story I have told you isn't evidence; it's just another queer story in a very queer business which has been going on for a very, very long time.

The Hindu myths are full of stories of flying saucers, which they call 'Vimanas'.

An Egyptian record of 1500 B.C. talks about 'circles of fire coming from the sky'; the Bible has its 'fiery chariots'; and the ancient Romans recorded 'ships in the sky'.

In 1953, a thirteenth century manuscript was discovered at Ampleforth Abbey, in Yorkshire, describing what seems to have been a saucer passing over in 1290 A.D.

'When Henry the Abbott was about to say grace, John, one of the brethren, came in and said there was a great portent outside. Then they all ran out and Lo! a large round silver thing like a disk flew slowly over them and excited the greatest terror.'

But, to my mind, the most startling thing happened on the slopes of the Old Man, Lake Coniston, on 15th February, 1954. Two boys, Stephen Darbishire (13 years old) and his cousin Adrian (8 years old) took a snapshot of a flying saucer in the air. The picture which they took showed a saucer at an angle of 25 degrees to its vertical axis. It was compared with other photographs taken by a man named Adamski in the Californian Desert. The two objects were so similar that, either the man in California and the two English schoolboys must have got together to produce a fake, which wants some believing, or they both saw a flying object in the

1290 A.D. "Lo! a large round silver thing like a disk flew slowly over them and excited the greatest terror"

air for which, so far, we cannot account.

So, even if flying saucers don't exist, there's no argument that Earth people have been seeing – or imagining they've been seeing – something extremely strange, and very like them, for thousands of years.

The historical facts (and the full record is as long as the London Telephone Directory) have been passed to me by Councillor Patrick Murray, of Edinburgh, who has made a study of 'flying saucers' and filed all the evidence he can collect on them. He himself is convinced that, within a long lifetime, the facts will be scientifically established.

He wants to be a POSTMAN

YOU CAN GET TO THE TOP OF THE TREE IN THE POST OFFICE, IF YOU ARE CAPABLE.

I MEAN TO WORK HARD, SIR

At 15, Pat is healthy, over 4 ft. 10 ins. tall and of British Nationality. He sees his Youth Employment Officer, who arranges for a Post Office interview. Pat is given a medical examination and a short aptitude test.

He is issued with free uniform and protective clothing, and receives a daily meal-voucher. Pat is employed on the delivery of telegrams by foot, pedal-cycle and then motor-cycle. He attends College one day a week during office hours.

Pat, who does normal National Service, earns about £3 15s. 0d. p.w. at 15, rising to £8 15s. 0d. at 24. He works a 48-hour week and has 2 weeks' holiday. There are many sports facilities available.

PLEASE SEND A COPY OF THAT MEMO ABOUT TELE-COMMUNICATIONS TO ALL LOCAL OFFICES.

Pat is given many opportunities to compete for higher Post Office and Civil Service jobs, and looks forward to becoming a Head Postmaster.

Spaceships

Vampire

HULTON'S
BOYS AND GIRLS EXHIBITION
at OLYMPIA, LONDON

Giant Puppets

Film Making

OUR grand exhibition is in full swing, and boys and girls from near and far are flocking to Olympia with their friends to see the amazing galaxy of entertainment awaiting them. Remember, it is open every day from 9 a.m. to 9 p.m. until 8th September. Admission: 1/6d. Make up YOUR party and go along NOW! Don't forget that you have only got until Saturday next to see all the wonderful exhibits.

Just to give you an idea of the things in store: models of cars, railways, naval equipment; working chemical and other models; press-button exhibits; a rifle range – and many other things, including the Personal Appearance of Famous People! You pay at the door, so please don't send in for tickets to EAGLE.

MOUSE TOWN

Model Trains

HURRY – YOU'VE ONLY GOT TILL SATURDAY!

Wear your EAGLE Club badge – there is a special Club Room for Members only.

Cadet Class Yacht

Make your own jig-saw

Power Station 2,000 A.D.

THE AVENUE OF THE FU[TURE]

AT THE HULTON'S BOYS AND GIRLS EXHIBITION, OLYMP[IA]

The Treen Space Fighter Fleet

The Hovering Space Helicopter

The Moon and Earth Mural

X 34

This is how the great National Hall at Olympia, London, will look on the occasion of the Hulton's Boys and Girls Exhibition from Tuesday, 28th August, to Saturday, 8th September. The scene is dominated by the Space Satellite Station in the centre and the Space Rocket Fleet on the right. To the left are the Treen ships and hovering helicopters. Viewing can be made from the galleries at either end of the Hall.

The exhibition is crammed full of things to interest every EAGLE reader, including a super model railway, a midget submarine of the Royal Navy, which you will be able to go inside, and a real Vampire jet. You can take part in treasure hunts and competitions, speak to famous personalities and enjoy all the Fun of the Fair.

There is a special competition on page 5 for EAGLE Club members, with ten wonderful prizes of a visit to the Hulton's Boys and Girls Exhibition and a trip to France. Why not enter?

THE FUTURE OF

F10

The Space Flagship

The Saturn Mural

X38

X39

X 36

The Space Rocket Fleet

X37

pace Satellite Station.
magnetic cranes move
down on the left. The
space ship launching
may be seen in front.

Avenue
nce

ASHWELL
WOO

THE WORLD

SILVER EAGLER OF THE YEAR

John Wilson

PICKING the Silver Eagler of the Year has been especially difficult this year. We have had many outstanding claims come in — some for single acts of courage, some for exceptional initiative, some for magnificent records of social service, some for that quieter kind of courage which overcomes the setbacks of illness, disability or accident. But, in the end, we were in no doubt that the special honour of Silver Eagler of the Year for 1956 should be accorded to John Wilson, aged 12, of Muirkirk, Ayrshire.

One of a family of seven, John has undertaken, during the last six years, the heavy extra burdens arising from the fact that his father, unfortunately, has poor health. Recently his mother also became ill. Refusing to be discouraged by this extra setback, John redoubled his efforts, answering any demand upon him that the critical situation called for. Heavily pressed in this way, some boys would have thought that here was an excuse for going easy on their school work. Not John. His school record is as splendid as his record at home. John's claim is strongly supported by a county councillor, a doctor, John's head-teacher, and his minister. We think that John lives up to the high standards we expect of a Silver Eagler of the Year.

✶ ✶ ✶ ✶ ✶ ✶ ✶ ✶ ✶ ✶ ✶ ✶ ✶ ✶ ✶ ✶ ✶ ✶

In addition to the awards already published, the following boys established a claim for a Silver Eagle Badge during the course of 1956.

Melvyn Jones

Peter Richardson

Michael Beck

Peter Goodall

MELVYN JONES
of East Croydon. For his kindness to animals.

JOHN HATCH
of Wokingham, Bucks. For promptness and initiative in an emergency.

MICHAEL HORNE
of Baughurst, Hants. For outstanding service to his Church.

MARTIN REDMAN
of Edgeworth, Lancs. For courage in overcoming a physical disability.

DAVID SHARPE
of Gt. Malvern, Worcs. For courage and fortitude in facing sickness.

PETER GOODALL
of West Molesey, Surrey. For social service.

LEONARD THWAITES
of Dunscroft, Doncaster. For promptness and initiative in an emergency.

RAYMOND BUNYAN
of Luton, Beds. For a high standard of unselfishness and service at home.

PETER RICHARDSON
of Lancing, Sussex. For determination and courage in facing sickness.

HECTOR NEWNHAM
of Milton, Clackmannanshire. For grit and determination in facing illness.

MICHAEL BECK
of Boscombe, Hants. For determination and courage in facing illness.

Hector Newnham

Raymond Bunyan

Leonard Thwaites   Michael Horne   Martin Redman

John Hatch   David Sharpe

★ ✰ ★ ✰ ★ ✰ ★ ✰ ★ ✰ ★ ✰ ★ ✰ ★ ✰ ★ ✰ ★ ✰ ★

★ A Note to Parents . . .

. . . and also to teachers, clergymen, doctors, youth leaders and others in a position to recognize exceptional qualities in young people. We invite you to let us know about members of the EAGLE Club who deserve consideration for the Silver Eagle Badge. If you have a boy in mind who has a record which you think justifies a claim, please write to us at EAGLE Reader Service, Long Lane, Aintree, Liverpool 9, enclosing a stamped and addressed envelope, and we shall be very glad to forward to you the special booklet describing the Silver Eagle Award in full detail.

EAGLE MOON PROPHECY COMES TRUE

WHEN the first announcement was made of the successful launching of the Russian Satellite, readers of EAGLE might well have said "Well? What's new about that? *We* knew it was going to happen, two years ago!"

For in September, 1955, EAGLE told its readers that "Earth satellites that will reach the upper atmosphere will be in being by 1957." This statement accompanied a centre-spread cut-open illustration which showed the now familiar 3-stage rocket, used to carry the satellite on the first stage of its journey – to that position where it was left to fend for itself and to make history with its first encirclement of the earth.

But some will remember that this subject was introduced still earlier – in fictional form – six years ago, when admirers of Dan Dare followed his adventures with the Red Moon, an imaginary 'rogue' planet. Only in one way has our prediction gone astray – for it has been Russia, not America, that has started this new era in the exploration of outer space. Since then, as we all know, a second, much larger satellite has been launched into a similar orbit. This weighed half a ton. It carries instruments and a husky dog, whose health has been continuously recorded and signalled to earth.

At first there was some difference of opinion as to the height attained by the first satellite, but it was later accepted that it at first reached a height of 560 miles above the surface of the earth. A fortnight later, after it had made some 200 circuits of the earth and was still travelling at approximately 18,000 m.p.h., its orbit varied in height, from 100 miles in the Northern Hemisphere to 615 miles down South. At the same time the spent rocket was some 10,000 miles ahead, but travelling on a slightly more easterly course.

Some surprise has been expressed at the "Red Moon's" orbit, for it is far more polar that equatorial. If it had been the latter, as that of the proposed American satellite, it would have gained initial impulse from the spin of the earth. As it is however, scientists in the British Isles have the benefit of being able to observe the satellite as it passes directly over us, and for this work the new giant radio telescope at Jodrell Bank was hurriedly pressed into service. In the first excitement, the "death" of the satellite was expected any day, and a temporary break in the reception of its signals was regarded as the beginning of the end. However, the United States Space Satellite Project have now announced that, by their calculations, the satellite may circle the earth for at least a year.

It may well be that by the time you read this, a third satellite will have been sent up, or even an attempt made to reach the moon.

What exciting times we live in!

The two orbits, Russian and proposed American. In this schematic diagram the earth is not to scale. Its polar diameter is 7,900 miles.

The satellite was launched by an Inter-Continental Ballistic Missile of three-stage type, probably on the lines of the 70ft. U.S. VANGUARD (left). The diagram above explains how, at dawn and dusk, it is possible to see the rocket with the naked eye. The satellite is only above the horizon for about 20 minutes at a time. Scientists have been surprised, however, to receive signals when it has been well below the horizon. Thanks to reflection these have been received for as long as 35 minutes. If or when its batteries fail, our only means of communication will be by means of radio telescopes, such as Jodrell Bank. Below is the probable launching sequence.

EAGLE-GIRL ADVENTURE TOURS 1957

Happy Holidays for Club Members

The way to a HAPPY HOLIDAY

Now is the time to start planning the most exciting holiday you've ever had. Blue skies and sun are just around the corner, and this year you really can enjoy the holiday you've been dreaming about during the Winter months. The 1957 EAGLE Holiday brochure is your key to adventure.

Join a sunshine EAGLE Tour, in co-operation with the English, Welsh and Scottish Youth Hostels Associations, and have an adventurous holiday in your own countryside – whether by hill, moor, loch or sea. If you have already seen a lot of Britain, why not visit a foreign country with other Club Members.

If you apply NOW, we will send you a fully descriptive brochure, which has been specially prepared to give you *all* the information you will wish to have about these fascinating holidays. Every EAGLE Club Member is eligible if he is twelve years of age and still under seventeen. The cost of each tour is £4.10.0., although there are a few exceptions depending on your choice. Write today to : EAGLE SUMMER HOLIDAYS, Long Lane, Aintree, Liverpool 9, stating your Club Number and enclosing a stamped, self-addressed LABEL.

The list below gives you a preview of the wonderful holiday news contained in the brochure.

CYCLING

South Coast & Downs Garden of England – Yorkshire Dales – The Welsh Border – New Forest & Hampshire – Devon – Dorset – Exmoor – Lakeland North Yorkshire Moors & Coast – The Fenland West of the Wye – The Ridgeways – The Chilterns The Thames Valley – The Wye Valley

EUROPEAN HOLIDAYS

Sailing in Holland
Walking by the Rhine

WALKING

The Pilgrims' Way Yorkshire Dales – Wye Valley – North Yorkshire Moors & Coast – Isle of Man – Isle of Wight – Gower Peninsula – Dorset – Devon – Exmoor Lakeland – High Peak – Mendips – Cotswolds Snowdonia – Highlands

SPECIAL EVENTS

Sailing at Maldon Walking and Riding in Wales – Canoeing on the Thames or Wye – Fishing in Wiltshire – Sub-Aqua Expedition

161/166, FLEET STREET,
LONDON, E.C.4.

From the Editor to you–

18th January, 1957

I HAVE just received a letter from one of our readers in Hungary. I cannot give you his name for obvious reasons, but here are some extracts from his letter : –

> "The guns thundered night and day, and tanks rushed through the streets. We children built barricades before the tanks. When they fired, we lay down behind the barricades.

> "Unfortunately, our fine capital is today, in certain parts of the town, a heap of ruins. We are thankful to the English people who helped us and invited many Hungarian refugees to Great Britain."

I know you will join with me in sending our heartfelt sympathy to the children of Hungary.

Yours sincerely,

Marcus Morris

It's getting near the Great Day!

Keep watching EAGLE to find out all about

The Thrill of A LIFETIME

More exciting news about **EAGLE CLUB**

Are *you* coming?

He wants to be an **AIR STEWARD**

From the Editor to you—

27th December, 1957.

YOUR favourite artist, Frank Hampson, has drawn, especially for you, a Christmas picture which you see on page 15. I would like to tell you something about it.

IN the first instance the picture is a straightforward one, looking through the entrance of the Inn, across the courtyard to the stable. Camel drivers camped in the courtyard and guests from the accommodation on the upper floors are being told of the birth of Christ by the shepherds. A passing Roman officer and Imperial Official look curiously and suspiciously at the scene. Listening to the shepherd in the foreground is a Pharisee with the beginnings of opposition on his face.

But the picture can also be viewed as a brief allegory of the earthly life of Christ. It starts with the stable in the background, comes forward with the preaching of The Word (the bringing of the light) in the middle distance, then forward again to the dark archway and the figures of civil, military and religious authority which ended it. But finally, triumphantly, right up in the foreground is the aged Peter representing the Church carrying the Word forward and on.

I WISH you all, wherever you may be, a very happy Christmas.

Yours sincerely,

Marcus Morris

He wants to be an **AIR STEWARD**

Alfred has a good general education and excellent health. He always keeps himself neat and clean, likes meeting new people, and has a very tactful and pleasant manner of dealing with them.

CUTLERY SHOULD BE LAID IN THE ORDER OF USE. YOU HAVE SOUP BEFORE FISH, ALFRED, NOT AFTER IT.

On leaving school, Alfred starts a two-year Hotel and Catering Training Course at a Technical College. No fees are payable under 18, and grants are available for boys who need help. During the Course, Alfred takes nationally recognized examinations, including Waiting & Restaurant Service.

After National Service, Alfred applies to B.O.A.C., at 21. He starts in the Cabin Services Training Unit, and learns how to 'brief' travellers; how to deal with Health and Immigration procedures, and ships' documents; and about food preparation.

YOU WOULD NEVER OFFER BEEF TO AN INDIAN PASSENGER — HIS RELIGION FORBIDS HIM TO EAT IT.

While under training, Alfred earns £7.13.0. per week and, when he is posted to a ship, he gets £2.0.0. p.w. extra flying pay, plus 15/- a day overseas allowance, with free uniform. Alfred makes his first flight as one of a team of two or three stewards, and helps to prepare food in the galley.

LOOK ALIVE, ALF! WE'RE GETTING BEHIND SCHEDULE.

ALL RIGHT— IT'S JUST READY...

MAY I PAY FOR MY CIGARETTES IN LIRA, STEWARD?

CERTAINLY, SIR!

He is promoted to Bar Steward. In addition to serving passengers in other ways, Alfred has to keep his wits about him, as he deals with many currencies during long journeys. He earns from £8.1.6. to £9.6.6. per week, with £2.0.0. flying pay, and 15/- per day when overseas.

WELL, THAT WAS A NICE, UNEVENTFUL TRIP —CONGRATULATIONS!

THANK YOU, SIR.

Alfred eventually attains his ambition, becoming Chief Steward on an airline, and thoroughly enjoys his life of change and variety, both in the people he meets and the places he visits. He earns a basic salary of £11.4.6. per week, with a flying allowance of £2.10.0. p.w., plus 15/- per day overseas pay. He takes a personal pride in promoting the comfort of travellers in his care.

EAGLE 3 May 1957

Eagle SPORTS news

CUP FINAL SPECIAL

CAN ASTON VILLA STOP THE MIGHTY BABES?

(from left to right)
Back Row: W. Foulkes, E. Colman, W. Whelan, R. Wood, M. Jones, D. Edwards.
Front Row: J. Berry, D. Viollet, R. Byrne (capt.), T. Taylor, D. Pegg

(from left to right)
Back Row: P. Aldis, P. McParland, S. Lynn, N. Sims, S. Crowther, J. Dugdale. Front Row: L. Smith, J. Sewell, J. Dixon (capt.), P. Saward, R. Chapman

MANCHESTER UNITED can't lose! or so they say.

Matt Busby's mighty 'Babes' (average age 23) have already earned the title *Team of the Year*, and have been chasing, all the season, soccer's 'impossible' Triple Crown to prove themselves *The Best Team of All-Time*. Despite the tremendous strain involved in this quest, meaning, as it has done, the playing of a key match every week, United go to Wembley as the hottest favourites in Cup history. They have swept through to the Final with five straight wins, and no club so far has had a look-in against them.

Is there, then, no hope for United's fit, fast and spirited Midland opponents? Of course there is hope – and more! The records are strewn with the names of 'unbeatable' teams who came a cropper in the final test, and Johnny Dixon and Co. have all the stamp of giant-killers about them.

Whichever way the honours go this, the 76th Cup Final, has all the makings of a really thrilling soccer duel.

How they got to Wembley

MANCHESTER UNITED		ASTON VILLA	
v. Hartlepools (a)	4-3	v. Luton Town (a)	2-2
v. Wrexham (a)	5-0	- replay - (h)	2-0
v. Everton (h)	1-0	v. Middlesbrough (a)	3-2
v. Bournemouth (a)	2-1	v. Bristol City (h)	2-1
v. Birmingham		v. Burnley (a)	1-1
(Hillsborough)	2-0	- replay - (h)	2-0
		v. West Bromwich Albion (Molyneux)	2-2
		-replay- (Birm'gham)	1-0

In Issue 18 of Volume 8 (3 May 1957), the sports page celebrated the achievement of Manchester United's Busby Babes in reaching the FA Cup final, having already secured the league title. The team, led by Duncan Edwards, lost the game 2–1 to Aston Villa and thus missed out on the Double. It was the league title that led to United entering the European Cup for season 1957–58. As football followers around the world know, that campaign was to end in tragedy. Returning from a match against Red Star Belgrade the team's plane crashed as it attempted to take off from a snow-stricken Munich airport. Eight of the Babes lost their lives as a result. Against all odds United reached the Cup final again in 1958, this time losing to Bolton.

THE R

Most people think of ice c
origin is lost in the mists
tradition, was the first in th
ionery'; not ice cream as w
and milk, sweetened and s
Today, the mamfacture of

KE TO TH
(1) MIXING VAT. (2)Here the
– are mixed and heard. (3) t
the-mix, under high ¡essure, t¹
fat into particles, maing the
(purification by heat:The ten
15 seconds, and tht imme
LABORATORY. Consnt tests
This has a capacity of1,600 g
(8) Temperature reerder. (9
of the mix from the orage vat
frozen ice-cream pip¡o extru
ice cream is pushed at in ri⁷
conveyor band. (13)?ARDEN
through this tunnel we the tem
stainless-steel convey band. (
30 m.p.h. cold-air tst, with

L. ASHWELL
L. WOOD

THE ROMANCE

ANCE OF ICE CREAM

...ention, but in fact its
... Great, according to
...enjoy 'frozen confect-
...ourse, but fruit juices
...ded by frozen snow,
...st standard of quality

is a highly scientific process, and definite rules are laid down for ice cream by Government Regulations. Good ice cream requires milk solids, fats, sugar and flavouring; in this feature, we show the process of manufacture of the familiar Lyons Maid Choc Ices In this ultra-modern plant, nearly everything is made of stainless steel; the highest standard of hygiene is maintained throughout, the ice cream never being touched by human hands.

...ATIONS
...fats, sugar and flavourings
...n throughout). This forces
...pertures and breaks up the
...hout. (4) PASTEURIZING
...d to 176 F, held there for
...(5) Control panel. (6)
...y, etc. (7) STORAGE VAT.
...t at between 35 and 40 F,
...NG. Here the temperature
...out 15 or 18 F. (10) Semi-
...UDING (to push out). The
...f nozzles. (12) Ribbons on
...cream ribbons move slowly
...ther 27 F. (14) Continuous
...turn band. (17) Circulating
...below freezing point. (18)

Cold air return. (19) Plain freezing coils. (20) Finned freezing coils. The used return air passes through these pipes, and the temperature is again reduced to 70 F below freezing point. (21) Circulating fan. (22) Conveyor band driving roller. (23) CUTTING. The now firm ribbons are cut across into bars of equal length. (24) Wire-mesh conveyor. (25) CHOCOLATE ENROBING. Here the bars are coated with chocolate, actually passing through a curtain of warm liquid chocolate. (26) The surplus chocolate is used to coat the underside of the bars. (27) CHOCOLATE COOLING. Here the chocolate coating is set. (28) Cooling plates. (29) Conveyor belt. (30) WRAPPING MACHINE. Here the bars are automatically wrapped. (31) Packed into cartons. (32) Cartons closed and sealed. (33) Carton conveyor belt to cold-store. (34) COLD-STORE. The cartons are received and packed. (35) Millions of Choc-Ices are held in cold store, prior to despatch. The men working here have to wear 'Arctic' clothing. (36) Insulated cold-store outer door. (37) From the cold-store, the cartons are taken on platforms called 'pallets' to the loading-bays. (38) Giant refrigerated lorry, capable of carrying 150,000 portions of ice cream. These are delivered to depots all over the country. From the cold-storage at the depots, they are delivered by van, as required, to the shops.

OF ICE CREAM

Many of the adverts in *Eagle* involved competitions. The prizes ran the whole gamut of possibilities from bikes to radios. Actually, those were almost the only prizes ever on offer. In one year alone in the middle of the decade it would have been possible to enter 36 different competitions to win a bicycle.

FREE!
'Cars
OF THE
future'

Now! There's a thrilling 'Car of the Future' picture to cut out, on the back of Shredded Wheat packets! You'll find a Helicopter Taxi, a Rocket-Powered Racer and many other exciting cars. Be *the first* to collect the whole series!

An exciting series of cards for Shredded Wheaters to cut out and collect!

NOW ON PACKETS OF
WELGAR SHREDDED WHEAT
REGISTERED TRADE MARK

A PRODUCT OF NABISCO FOODS LIMITED

Convertible
Here's just one of Shredded Wheat's fabulous 'Cars of the Future'. When rain falls, the drops complete an electric circuit in the special "Rain Guard" and the roof closes automatically!

The Greatest EAGLE News Yet!

IT has been our ambition that one day we might be able to present to EAGLE readers the life story of the most famous man in the world—

SIR WINSTON CHURCHILL

We are proud to announce that in our issue No. 40, dated 4th October, we are to begin the epic story of this great man. The many exciting incidents in Sir Winston's adventurous life will be recorded faithfully in pictures to bring you a magnificent story of heroic endeavour and achievement.

This news will cause a heavy demand for EAGLE, and readers are advised to place a firm order now with their local newsagents. The coupon below will ensure that *your* copy is reserved.

Your EAGLE of 4th October will carry other new and exciting stories as well, which will make fine winter reading.

Make sure *YOU* are a regular EAGLE reader

Sir Winston Churchill gives the Victory sign on the steps of 10 Downing Street

Eagle had numerous historic serials covering the lives of famous men and women, but their most trumpeted was 'The Happy Warrior' which charted the many ups and downs in the career of Winston Churchill. It was drawn by Frank Bellamy who was soon to take over from Frank Hampson on 'Dan Dare'.

SUPER BICYCLES AND BOOKS TO BE WON! SEE PAGE 11

EAGLE

EVERY WEDNESDAY

4½d

COMPANION TO GIRL, SWIFT AND ROBIN

6 SEPTEMBER 1957 Vol. 8 No. 36

DAN DARE
PILOT OF THE FUTURE
in REIGN OF THE ROBOTS

THE STORY SO FAR
Earth is in the grip of the Mekon, who is trying to force Dan to help him conquer the universe. Dan and Co. know that their only chance is to find and destroy the power station of the Elektrobots, mechanical monsters controlled by the Mekon's voice vibrations. Dan escapes in the Mekon's ship and evades pursuit by a Treen squadron. As he bores deeper into uncharted space, Dan sees . . .

JUMPING JETS! I MUST HAVE STRUCK THE GRAVE-YARD OF EVERY SHIP THAT EVER WENT OFF-BEAM SINCE SPACEFLIGHT BEGAN...

FRANK HAMPSON PRODUCTION

The Mekon's proud boast that 'no human brain can defeat' the mind reading vidi-sphere, was easily proven wrong by Digby's willpower, and his sheer love of foo

FISH AND CHIPS!

WITH LASHINGS OF SALT AND VINEGAR!

HE STILL THINKS OF FOOD...INCREASE THE POWER.

TURKEY AND TRIMMINGS— AH! THAT'S GOOD, WHAT'S THERE FOR AFTERS, CHRISTMAS PUD?

THE MYSTERY OF THE LOCH NESS MONSTER! SEE PAGE 4

In this cover from the classic adventure 'Reign of the Robots', one of London's icons, Big Ben, fills the background. It was this use of familiar buildings and places which made Dan Dare seem so real to the reader. By keeping the stories grounded in everyday reality, the reader was continually challenged to remember what was real and what was not.

It had long been a dream of Frank Hampson to draw the life of Jesus. In the story, scripted by Marcus Morris, Hampson poured his all onto the pages, displaying all his trademark style and eye for detail. It was to be his last great contribution to the comic he had helped create.

THE BIRT...

And they came with...
and Joseph, and the ...

And when they had s...
abroad the saying which ...
this child.

And all they that he...
things which were tol...

F JESUS

and found Mary,
ing in a manger.
they made known
d them concerning

wondered at those
by the shepherds.

2, vs. 16, 17 and 18

The HAPPY WARRIOR

The true life story of
SIR WINSTON CHURCHILL

OPERATION OVERLORD

Under this code name, the Allied invasion of France had been fixed for 5th June, 1944. While the Germans fortify the Atlantic Wall on the French coast, the Allied armies gather in Southern England. Churchill tells King George VI that he plans to watch invasion operations from the cruiser *Belfast*. The King, fired by this idea, says he would like to go too.

TOLD BY CLIFFORD MAKINS
DRAWN BY FRANK BELLAMY

MAP ROOM, ADMIRALTY.

ADMIRAL RAMSAY, HIS MAJESTY WOULD VERY MUCH LIKE TO BE WITH ME ON THE *BELFAST* ON D-DAY.

HIS MAJESTY? I COULDN'T POSSIBLY SUPPORT SUCH AN IDEA! THE RISK IS TOO GREAT.

AH, WINSTON, IF THE RISK IS TOO GREAT FOR ME, THEN IT IS TOO GREAT FOR YOU.

BUT, SIR, I AM GOING AS MINISTER OF DEFENCE, IN THE EXERCISE OF MY DUTY!

But the King agreed to stay at home, and soon afterwards persuaded Churchill to do likewise. And now D-Day, 5th June, was close at hand – but the weather forecast was gloomy.

H.Q. GENERAL EISENHOWER, SUPREME COMMANDER ALLIED EXPEDITIONARY FORCES, EARLY MORNING JUNE 4th, 1944.

IN FOUR HOURS' TIME, WE CAN EXPECT RISING WINDS AND THICK, LOW CLOUDS.

WE SHOULDN'T CHANCE A LANDING UNDER THOSE CONDITIONS.

AIR OPERATIONS WILL BE SEVERELY CURTAILED.

AT THIS STAGE, DELAY MIGHT BE FATAL. I THINK WE SHOULD GO!

NO, NO! I THINK WE MUST WAIT— THE ATTACK MUST BE POSTPONED. WE MUST HOPE AND PRAY THAT THE WEATHER WILL IMPROVE IN THE NEXT TWENTY-FOUR HOURS.

WELL, THERE IT IS – THE WEATHER'S STILL NOT GOOD, BUT IT HAS IMPROVED A LITTLE. IF WE DON'T GO TOMORROW, WE WILL HAVE TO CANCEL THE WHOLE SHOW FOR A FORTNIGHT.

A FEW HOURS LATER, CHURCHILL HEARD THE NEWS...

THIS IS IT, WINSTON! EISENHOWER HAS DECIDED TO GO TOMORROW.

AND SO THE DIE IS CAST!

D-DAY June 6th, 1944
THE GREATEST INVASION IN HISTORY!

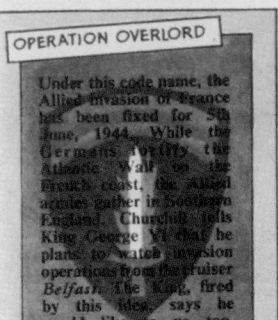

FIVE SPEARHEADS FORMED THE ASSAULT PLAN.

UTAH OMAHA GOLD JUNO SWORD

Montebourg
St. Marc Église
Carentan
Vierville
St. Laurent
Arromanches
Ryes
Bayeux
Meuraines
Douvres

GREAT WAVES OF LANDING-CRAFT AND WARSHIPS AND AIRCRAFT BORE DOWN ON THE NORMANDY BEACHES.

THEN THE ASSAULT!

WELL, MATES, WE'RE HERE!

'AND GENTLEMEN IN ENGLAND NOW A'BED SHALL THINK THEMSELVES ACCURS'D THEY WERE NOT HERE!'

COR BLIMEY! 'ARK AT 'IM!

PARATROOPERS WERE DROPPED BEHIND THE GERMAN LINES.

HUNDREDS OF WARSHIPS BOMBARDED THE COAST.

TROOPS UNDER FIRE DASHED FROM THEIR LANDING-CRAFT.

TO BE CONTINUED

LIVE & LEARN *with* MR. THERM

LET'S HAVE A GAS AIRING-CUPBOARD...

LIKE THIS!

An alcove in a bathroom, or on a landing, can be put to excellent use by converting the space into a gas-heated airing-cupboard, says Mr. Therm . . .

. . . like this one. The same method may be applied to converting an existing cupboard. Before you start, go to your gas showrooms for the airing cupboard gas-heater, and arrange for the gas supply to be installed at the bottom of the cupboard; this includes a control tap, with a restrictor which enables the gas fitter to set the heater's correct gas rate. If the cupboard contains a cold water tank and pipes, make sure that they are well insulated to avoid condensation.

SKIRTING

Start with the base. Make two side pieces, slightly shorter than the depth of the alcove and the same height as the skirting. Cut notches in top edges and front, using a small saw and chisel. Nail to skirtings at side of alcove. Then fit 1 in. by 2 in. battens in the notches and nail them in place.

Cover both the top and front of the base frame with pegboard. Glue the meeting surfaces of frame and pegboard, and secure with ½ in. oval nails spaced 4 ins. apart. Make allowance for a ventilation opening of at least 3 sq. ins. at the top and bottom of the cupboard, says Mr. Therm.

ASBESTOS PLUGGING

A batten is fixed to the wall each side of the alcove, running from base to ceiling. Secure with 2½ in. screws driven into holes which have been filled with asbestos plugging, as shown here. Leave a 1 in. space at the front.

CHRISTOPHER TEMPLE

The front frame is 1 in. by 2 in. softwood. The foot is left open, but an extra rail is fitted across at a distance of 12 ins. below the top. Half joint the four frame members, secure joints with glue and screws, and screw front frame to side battens. Cover top panel with pegboard. NEXT WEEK, Mr. Therm will show you how to finish your gas-heated airing-cupboard.

SUPER DAN DARE ADVENTURE BEGINS TODAY! PRIZES, P.11

EAGLE

EVERY WEDNESDAY

4½d

COMPANION TO GIRL, SWIFT AND ROBIN

DAN DARE
PILOT OF THE FUTURE
SAFARI IN SPACE

HERE WE ARE — ALL SET FOR A JUNGLE JAUNT!

He didn't know it at the time but *Safari In Space* was to be the last Dan Dare adventure Frank Hampson would work on.

WELCOME TO 'MARAKU', COLONEL DARE — MAY YOU HAVE A GOOD HOLIDAY HERE...

THERE WILL BE MUCH FOR YOU TO EXPLORE, AND MANY STRANGE ANIMALS TO 'SHOOT' WITH YOUR CAMERA GUNS.

FRANK HAMPSON

I AM THEREX— I WILL BE YOUR GUIDE. AS YOU SEE, WE HAVE SET UP CAMP AND ALL IS READY FOR YOU. THESE ATLANTINES WILL ACT AS SCOUTS.

WE ARE EXPERIENCED HUNTERS, O COLONEL, THOUGH NONE HAS TRODDEN THE SOIL OF 'MARAKU' BEFORE.

GOSH! ISN'T IT THRILLING, DIGBY, SIR – A *REAL* SAFARI!

EAGLE CLUB

South London T.T. Tournament

Scores of boys converged on two Boys' Clubs in Kennington Oval to spend the day vying with each other for the honour of being the South London Regional EAGLE JUNIOR TABLE TENNIS CHAMPION.

With willing help and assistance from the National Association of Boys' Clubs and officials from the English Table Tennis Association our Tournament got off to an early start, and it was soon apparent that the standard of playing was going to be extremely good. Johnny Leach,

Junior Winner, D. Johnson, and Junior Runner-up, M. A. Blok, proudly display their trophies.

the Tournament's Chief Coach, was again impressed by the skill of the competitors, and found that the under 13's as well as the seniors showed they had a sound knowledge of the game. The winner of the Senior Section was D. Bloy, Runner-up W. Williams. For the Junior Section the winner was D. Johnson. Runner-up M. A. Blok.

Just a reminder to all those who have not yet received their final playing instructions; don't think that you have been forgotten or that your Entry Form has been lost. This is not the case – you will all be informed about your own particular Tournament in good time. Watch for further news soon.

Johnny Leach congratulates D. Bloy, Senior Regional Champion.

NEW YEAR GREETINGS

Our Vice-Presidents are scattered over the world, but they have remembered to send a personal message to every EAGLE Club Member. They wish you all a Happy New Year with good sportsmanship at work, play and on the field. Stick to the rules in your Club Card, they say, think of the other chap – and you can't go wrong.

Left to right: Neville Duke, Stirling Moss, Denis Compton, Stanley Matthews, Godfrey Evans, Trevor Bailey and Leonard Cheshire, V.C.

Is *your* Birthdate here this week?

SEPT 13th 1940 – DEC 14th 1942
MAY 9th 1941 – APR 29th 1943
AUG 3rd 1944 – JAN 27th 1940

You are entitled to a FREE birthday gift if you are an EAGLE Club Member and your birthdate appears in the list above. Choose it from the following list: stamp album, jigsaw puzzle, stationery folder, adventure book, ball-point pen or propelling pencil. Then state your choice on a post-card, giving your name, address, Club Number and the date you were born, and post it to:– Birthday Present (92) EAGLE Club, Long Lane, Liverpool 9.

Your post-card must reach us by Thursday, January 6th. Though the same birthdate may appear more than once, no Member may claim more than one gift.

Manchester Soccer Demonstration

Our first F.A. soccer-coaching demonstration was an outstanding success! Hundreds of Manchester EAGLE Club Members thoroughly enjoyed themselves and took a keen interest in the films and practical coaching demonstrations put on for them.

Fagan, McAdams, and Savage of the City signing autographs.

Excitement really became high when star players from Manchester City and Manchester United took part in one or two friendly competitions, each of which was designed to demonstrate the arts of ball control.

The finale of a heading tennis match brought the EAGLE Club Members to their feet, and the cheering during each rally of this thrilling and skilful game almost brought the house down!

John Berry, Jack Rowley of the United have a heading tennis rally.

EAGLE READER – are you a member of EAGLE Club?

There are many privileges to be had by joining; free viewing and coaching for football and cricket, free treats to many entertainments and special cheap-but-good holiday schemes where you can enjoy the companionship of other EAGLE Club Members.

It costs only 1/6d. to join – and there's a coupon on page 11.

H.M.S. RODNEY VERSUS BISMARCK P.10; SUPER PRIZES P.15

EAGLE

EVERY WEDNESDAY

4½d

COMPANION TO GIRL, SWIFT AND ROBIN

20 JUNE 1959 Vol. 10 No. 25

DAN DARE
PILOT OF THE FUTURE
TERRA NOVA

FRANK HAMPSON.

SPACESHIP AWAAAAY!

One of the last Frank Hampson covers, still showing off his eye for details, action and colour.

GRAVITY'S RISING FAST!

WE'RE IN THE GRIP OF A NEW WORLD, DAN! I WONDER WHAT LIES AHEAD?

MANY THINGS, I EXPECT, SIR HUBERT—AMONG THEM, PERHAPS THE ANSWER TO MY FATHER'S DISAPPEARANCE...

EXTEND WINGS, DIG! AND FOR PETE'S SAKE TAKE IT EASY, OR THEY'LL GO FOR A 'BURTON' WHEN WE TOUCH ATMOSPHERE!

AYE—AYE SIR!

Hobbies Corner

Collecting, Handicraft, Do-it-yourself! Whatever your hobbies, there will be plenty to interest you in the weeks ahead.

Cheese making — THEN

Cheese is one of the oldest foods known to man. Mention of it has been found in early Greek literature, when it was produced in nearly the same way as housewives make it nowadays. Some of the English varieties of cheese that we eat today were being made during the Middle Ages, and this illustration shows it being prepared in the Mid-Eighteenth century.

Cheese making — NOW

During the last war, a uniform cheese was produced suitable for cutting into the tiny ration allowance. Since 1954, when restrictions were removed, the cheese-makers have turned their skill to making the famous English varieties again. Today, however, only 5% of the cheese produced is made on the farm; the rest is made in factories, where cleanliness is all important.

SOME HOME-PRODUCED VARIETIES

COLLECTING CHEESE LABELS

Fromology (the science and study of cheese) is the accepted name for the hobby of collecting cheese labels and, although this pastime is young in comparison with others, it has a wide scope and tremendous interest. A neatly-arrayed album page can look very colourful and attractive, and a further advantage is the small amount of outlay needed to start your collection.

Methods of obtaining specimens vary. Let your friends and relatives know that you are interested in cheese labels, They will catch some of your enthusiasm and will find pleasure in adding to your collection, possibly bringing you back some foreign examples from Continental holidays. Writing to cheese-makers is not generally fruitful, although it may be worth while to visit your local grocer. Other sources are pen-friends and label-dealers.

The Fromologists' Circle was founded in 1952, and now has over 5,000 members. If you write, mentioning EAGLE, to: M. Storey, 331, Horbury Rd., Wakefield, Yorks., enclosing a stamped, addressed envelope, he will send 10 FREE labels and a Bulletin.

MOUNTING YOUR LABELS

Care must be taken when preparing your labels for mounting, as any damage will reduce their value. Difficulty is sometimes experienced when removing them from the silver paper. An easy method in these cases is to insert a strip of thin card between the label and the foil, moving it to and fro and leaving the glue adhering to the label rather than the silver paper. Soaking in water is not a good idea, as quite often this spoils the label's lustre and freshness.

An album with large pages - preferably loose leaves retained by ring clips - is recommended, as this will give a better 'display area' and the opportunity to insert more pages when necessary. You will find that the use of black pages will enhance the coloured labels, while some of the more flimsy types will look crisper on white.

For mounting, nothing beats the stamp hinge, as it allows rearrangement without damage.

NEXT WEEK: MATCH-BOX LABELS

MAGIC IN METER

BY DENNIS MALLET

© Gas Council

The story we are now to tell, Thanks to GAS, turns out quite well!

"It's New Year's Eve! All on parade! What Resolutions have we made?" When good old Dad addressed us thus, Mum answered first: "No flap, no fuss...

"Is what I want on Washing Day— I'll wash our things the *Thermal* way!

"Quite right," responded Dad, "Hear, hear! And fresher food's a good idea. I vow to see that waste is never Seen round here in muggy weather!"

Then Gran chipped in: "My room shall be As warm as warm—just wait and see!"

"I'll learn to cook," said sister Sue. "The simplest way—*that's* what I'll do!"

Then everybody looked at *me*. I meekly said: "I guarantee...

"To wash myself with special care— Provided *Mr Therm* is there!"

THE SHEPHERD KING
The story of DAVID

King Saul's resentment of David, hero of Israel, has reached its climax. Following a warning from Jonathan, the King's son, David is forced to fly to escape death. He seeks refuge in the monastery at Nob, but David's words with the High Priest are overheard by a traitor, who makes a violent dash from the monastery to take the news to Saul...

TOLD BY CLIFFORD MAKINS
DRAWN BY FRANK BELLAMY

TREACHERY! STOP HIM!

TOO LATE! HE HAS VANISHED INTO THE NIGHT.

THAT MAN IS DOEG THE EDOMITE — A HERDSMAN OF SAUL'S. DAVID, YOU HAVE BROUGHT DEATH TO THE CITY OF NOB. GO NOW!

DAWN. THE WEARY DAVID PAUSES TO REST...

I MUST FIND A PLACE TO HIDE. I MUST FIND MEN WHO WILL FIGHT FOR ME AGAINST SAUL — OR ISRAEL WILL PERISH.

SUDDENLY...

WHO'S THIS?

HIS FACE IS FAMILIAR...

WHY, IT'S...

I AM DAVID, SON OF JESSE, NOW A FUGITIVE FROM SAUL. I NEED SHELTER AND SUPPORT!

WE ARE NO FRIENDS OF SAUL'S, BELIEVE ME! WE WILL SHOW YOU A PLACE TO HIDE NOT FAR FROM HERE...

David finds refuge in the Cave of Adullam, near the Valley of Elah, and trusty messengers go throughout the land to rally supporters to his cause.

MEANWHILE, SAUL RAGES IN GIBEAH...

DAVID IS PREPARING WAR AGAINST US! YOU HAVE ALL BETRAYED ME — AND YOU, JONATHAN, MY SON, ARE THE WORST OF ALL!

YOU HAVE DONE DAVID A GREAT WRONG!

YOUR MAJESTY! THERE IS A MAN OUTSIDE WHO HAS NEWS OF THE TRAITOR DAVID! HE IS YOUR HERDSMAN, DOEG THE EDOMITE...

TO BE CONTINUED

ADVERTISING

... serving every boy in Britain

● ● ● ● ● ● ● ● ● ● ● ● ● ● ● ● ●

THURSDAY is 'E-G Day'!

Every Thursday of the year lorries start their journeys across the United Kingdom, each loaded with thousands of copies of EAGLE and GIRL. In all, nearly 1½-million papers go by road and rail – every copy packed with stories, special features and *Advertising*.

Advertising! It's an exciting business and a very important one. In addition to your favourite strips and stories, you can read about a wonderful variety of products and services available throughout the land.

Take a typical copy of EAGLE as an example. There's news of toys and sweets, clothes and careers, cycles and air travel – an amazing mixture of things being planned and made in different parts of the country by people just like your own parents.

If the goods were not advertised, *you* would never know anything about them. In that case, you could never buy them .

Advertising helps to reduce the huge production costs, and so keeps this modest price down to its present level

Without the support of our advertisers, this is what the price would be!

A s *Eagle's* first decade came to a close the publishers still felt the need to justify the adverts. Would readers be prepared to pay almost double for a comic with no sales messages?

EAGLE 26 *September 1959*

As the **scientist** sees it . . .

very week, Professor Steele brings u news from the world of science.

This exclusive EAGLE series tells you some of the most important things scientists have discovered about the universe and the world we live in.

USE A PIN TO DISCOVER WHERE YOU FEEL PAIN

As the scientist sees it . . .

TRANSLATION

I am a Jewish reader of EAGLE and, when reading *The Shepherd King* (10th Jan.), I noticed two words in Hebraic letters on the High Priest's hat. For any reader who does not know what these words mean, the translation is: Holy to the Lord. – *David Young (aged 12), London, N.W.2.*

5/- is paid for every letter published. Readers who want a reply should enclose a stamped, addressed envelope.

DAN DARE SETS OUT ON A THRILLING NEW MISSION TODAY!

EAGLE

EVERY WEDNESDAY

4½d

COMPANION TO GIRL, SWIFT AND ROBIN

28 NOVEMBER 1959 Vol. 10 No. 41

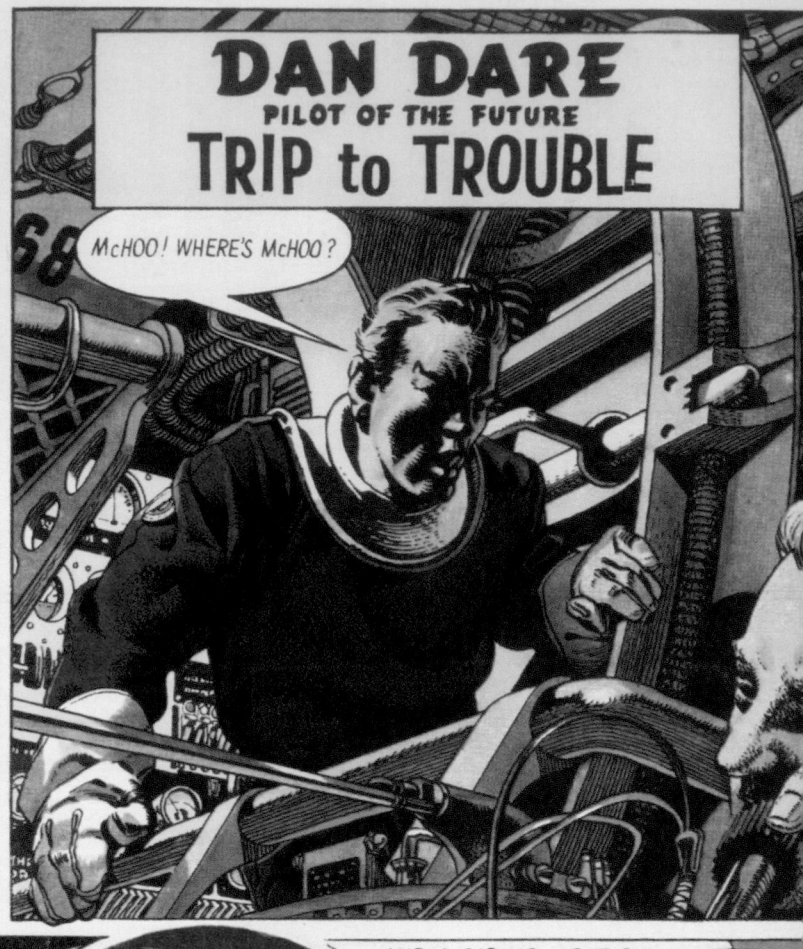

DAN DARE
PILOT OF THE FUTURE
TRIP to TROUBLE

McHOO! WHERE'S McHOO?

By now Frank Bellamy has taken over from Hampson. His style is cleary evident when you compare this cover to his drawing on the Happy Warrior

AND A RIDING LIGHT RUN OFF THE FUEL-CELL BATTERY?

WHAT *ARE* YE BLETHERIN' ABOOT, MON?

THAT ESCAPE ROCKET MY FATHER USED FOR TOUCH-DOWN ON *TERRA NOVA* — WAS THERE A COLLAPSIBLE LIFE-RAFT IN IT?

FRANK BELLAMY

AYE, THERE WOULD BE . WE ALWAYS CARRY 'EM — LIGHTWEIGHT RAFTS WITH SMALL ELECTRIC OUTBOARDS.

AYE — WILL Y'EXPLAIN WHAT A' THIS IS ABOOT ?

SWIFTLY, PREPARATIONS ARE MADE FOR DAN'S NEW VENTURE...

YE OUGHT T'FINISH UP IN ROUGHLY THE SAME SPOT WHEN YOU STRIKE LAND.

THE *NOVADS* NEVER SAW THE BOAT MY FATHER LEFT IN — ONLY A LIGHT FLOATING OUT TO SEA. WINDS AND CURRENTS COULD HAVE CARRIED HIM ANYWHERE BUT, IF WE FOLLOW, USING THE SAME SORT OF BOAT ...

HERE COMES THE LAST ITEM, SIR — AS SOON AS THAT RAFT IS STOWED, I'LL BE OFF!

SAFETY RAFT

STOW WITH CARE

MAGIC IN METER

BY DENNIS MALLET

This story rather neatly shows
A blessing *Mr Therm* bestows!

© Gas Council

QUITE RECENTLY THERE CAME TO STAY OUR VERY POPULAR AUNT MAY; BUT—OH—SHE BROUGHT ALONG AS WELL OUR LITTLE COUSIN, ISOBEL!

THIS GHASTLY BRAT, THOUGH NOT YET THREE, WAS WILFUL TO THE 'NTH' DEGREE; AND, SHOULD HER ELDERS SAY HER NAY, SHE'D SHRIEK AND BELLOW RIGHT AWAY...

...AND, FOLLOWING THE USUAL FORM, HER BEDTIME BROUGHT THE USUAL STORM, WHEN SCREECHES, YELLS AND FLYING TOYS PRODUCED THE MOST STUPENDOUS NOISE!

WELL, ONE FINE NIGHT OUR PARENTS SAID: "WHEN ISOBEL IS SAFE IN BED, WE'RE GOING TO TAKE YOUR DEAR AUNT MAY TO SEE A RATHER THRILLING PLAY; AND, WHILE WE'RE OUT, WE'D LIKE YOU BOYS TO MAKE A MINIMUM OF NOISE— IN FACT, WE THINK IT RATHER FITTING THAT YOU TRY SOME BABY-SITTING!" WE WERE APPALLED— OLD JOHN AND I— BUT, NATURALLY, WE SAID WE'D TRY; AND, HAVING GIVEN OUR DECISION, SETTLED DOWN TO TELEVISION. WE WATCHED ENTHRALLED FOR QUITE A SPELL, THEN *SUDDENLY* THERE CAME A YELL...

OH, NO!

...YOUNG ISOBEL WAS WIDE AWAKE— OF THAT THERE COULD BE *NO* MISTAKE!

WE CHARGED UPSTAIRS TO SEE 'WHAT'S WHAT,' AND THERE THE SILLY LITTLE CLOT WAS BAWLING, SITTING UP IN BED— REFUSING TO BE COMFORTED!

WE DID OUR BEST, AND TUCKED HER IN, BUT DID THIS QUELL THE PIERCING DIN...? NOT A HOPE—THEN DESPERATION BROUGHT A SUDDEN INSPIRATION!

A NICE HOT DRINK AT LIGHTNING SPEED WAS WHAT SHE NEEDED, WE AGREED. WHAT WAS SIMPLER? DOWN I FLEW, FOR ALWAYS IN THE 'FRIDGE', I KNEW, WAS GOOD FRESH MILK— DEVOID OF GERMS— THIS BEING A JOB OF *MR THERM'S*.

I HEATED SOME IN HALF-A-MINUTE, THEN SEIZED A CUP, AND POURED IT IN IT! THIS I RUSHED TO ISOBEL, WHO PROMPTLY STOPPED HER LUSTY YELL AND, HAVING DRUNK IT, FELL ASLEEP— WE NEVER HEARD ANOTHER PEEP!

WHICH ONLY GOES AGAIN TO SHOW HOW MUCH TO *MR THERM* WE OWE!

A FLOATING

THE FLOATING

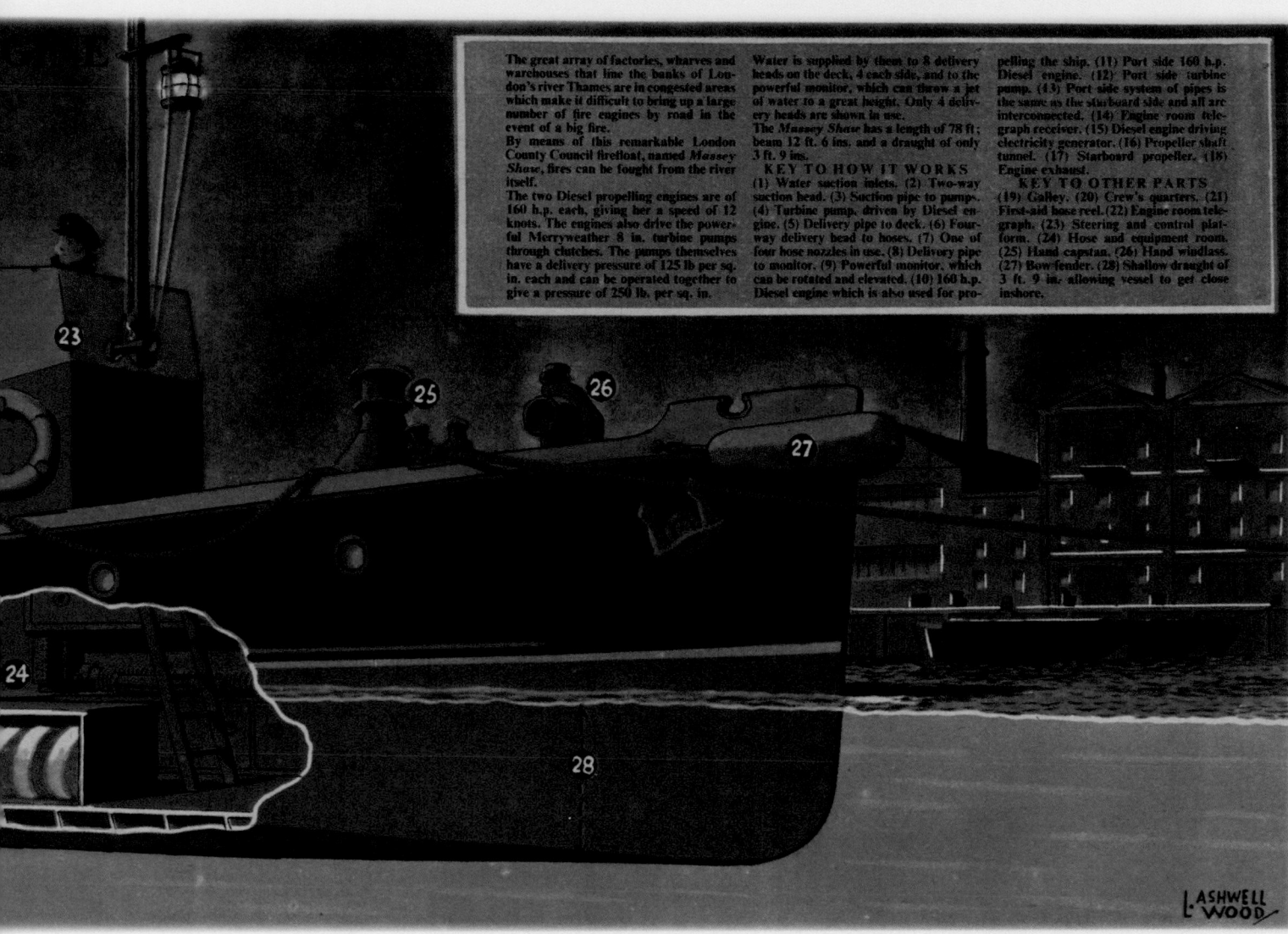

The great array of factories, wharves and warehouses that line the banks of London's river Thames are in congested areas which make it difficult to bring up a large number of fire engines by road in the event of a big fire.

By means of this remarkable London County Council firefloat, named *Massey Shaw*, fires can be fought from the river itself.

The two Diesel propelling engines are of 160 h.p. each, giving her a speed of 12 knots. The engines also drive the powerful Merryweather 8 in. turbine pumps through clutches. The pumps themselves have a delivery pressure of 125 lb per sq. in. each and can be operated together to give a pressure of 250 lb. per sq. in.

Water is supplied by them to 8 delivery heads on the deck, 4 each side, and to the powerful monitor, which can throw a jet of water to a great height. Only 4 delivery heads are shown in use.

The *Massey Shaw* has a length of 78 ft; beam 12 ft. 6 ins. and a draught of only 3 ft. 9 ins.

KEY TO HOW IT WORKS
(1) Water suction inlets. (2) Two-way suction head. (3) Suction pipe to pumps. (4) Turbine pump, driven by Diesel engine. (5) Delivery pipe to deck. (6) Four-way delivery head to hoses. (7) One of four hose nozzles in use. (8) Delivery pipe to monitor. (9) Powerful monitor, which can be rotated and elevated. (10) 160 h.p. Diesel engine which is also used for propelling the ship. (11) Port side 160 h.p. Diesel engine. (12) Port side turbine pump. (13) Port side system of pipes is the same as the starboard side and all are interconnected. (14) Engine room telegraph receiver. (15) Diesel engine driving electricity generator. (16) Propeller shaft tunnel. (17) Starboard propeller. (18) Engine exhaust.

KEY TO OTHER PARTS
(19) Galley. (20) Crew's quarters. (21) First-aid hose reel. (22) Engine room telegraph. (23) Steering and control platform. (24) Hose and equipment room. (25) Hand capstan. (26) Hand windlass. (27) Bow fender. (28) Shallow draught of 3 ft. 9 in. allowing vessel to get close inshore.

FIRE ENGINE

PROFESSOR BRITTAIN *Explains* WEATHER FORECASTING

BOB & JOAN ARE LISTENING TO THE B.B.C. WEATHER FORECAST.

PROFESSOR — HOW DO THEY KNOW WHAT THE WEATHER WILL BE LIKE?

BY MEANS OF A HUGE NETWORK OF EXPERT OBSERVATION POSTS. THESE ARE CONTROLLED BY THE METEOROLOGICAL OFFICE WHICH IS A DEPT. OF THE AIR MINISTRY. THERE ARE MANY TYPES OF OBSERVATION POSTS — SOME ARE SPONSORED BY LOCAL AUTHORITIES & THEY ARE ALL LINKED TO CENTRAL FORECASTING OFFICE BY LAND LINE, TELEPRINTER & RADIO. THEIR REPORTS ARE THUS 'POOLED' TO ENABLE CENTRAL OFFICE TO PREDICT CONDITIONS IN ANY PART OF THE BRITISH ISLES.

JUST HOW IS THE SEA AND LAND DIVIDED FOR PURPOSES OF THE FORECAST? — FOR INSTANCE WHAT DO THEY MEAN BY 'SEA AREAS ROCKALL & MALLIN'? — AND I'D LIKE TO KNOW THE EXACT DEFINITION OF LAND AREAS, SUCH AS 'N.E. ENGLAND', N. MIDLANDS' ETC.

I HAVE HERE, A SET OF MAPS & A CHART WHICH WILL GIVE YOU THIS INFORMATION — IF YOU'D LIKE TO STUDY THEM.

IN SEA AREAS.... ICELAND, FAEROES

MAP SHEWING COASTAL SEA AREAS USED IN B.B.C. FORECASTS, ETC.
A ICELAND · B FAEROES · C FAIR ISLE · D BAILEY · E HEBRIDES · F CROMARTY · G FORTIES · H ROCKALL · I MALIN · J FORTH · K DOGGER · L TYNE · M IRISH SEA · N HUMBER · O HELIGOLAND · P SHANNON · Q FASTNET · R LUNDY · S THAMES · T SOLE · U PLYMOUTH · V PORTLAND · W WIGHT · X DOVER · Y FINISTERRE · V BISCAY.

SUB-DIVISIONS OF LAND AREAS USED FOR DISTRICT FORECASTS

LONDON AREA 25 MILES RADIUS FROM CHARING CROSS	**ENGLAND S.W.** DORSETSHIRE SOMERSETSHIRE DEVONSHIRE CORNWALL	NORTHUMBERLAND **SCOTLAND S.E.** ROXBURGHSHIRE SELKIRKSHIRE PEEBLESSHIRE	& SUTHERLAND. **MID SCOTLAND** PERTHSHIRE **SCOTLAND N.E.** KINCARDINESHIRE	**IRELAND S.E.** WATERFORD WEXFORD KILKENNY CARLOW
ENGLAND S.E. KENT, SUSSEX SURREY HAMPSHIRE BERKSHIRE WILTSHIRE	**WALES S.** GLAMORGANSHIRE BRECKNOCKSHIRE CARMARTHENSHIRE PEMBROKESHIRE	BERWICKSHIRE HADDINGTONSHIRE EDINBURGH LINLITHGOWSHIRE CLACKMANNANSHIRE	ABERDEENSHIRE BANFFSHIRE ELGINSHIRE NAIRNSHIRE CAITHNESS	WICKLOW OFFALLY, LEIX KILDARE DUBLIN **IRELAND S.W.**
ENGLAND E. ESSEX, MIDDLESEX HERTFORDSHIRE BEDFORDSHIRE HUNTINGDONSHIRE CAMBRIDGESHIRE SUFFOLK, NORFOLK LINCOLNSHIRE	CARDIGANSHIRE RADNORSHIRE MONMOUTHSHIRE **WALES N.** MONTGOMERYSHIRE MERIONETHSHIRE FLINTSHIRE DENBIGHSHIRE	KINROSS-SHIRE FIFESHIRE FORFARSHIRE **SCOTLAND S.W.** & ISLE OF MAN ISLE OF MAN DUMFRIESSHIRE KIRKCUDBRIGHTSHIRE	EASTERN PARTS OF INVERNESS-SHIRE ROSS & CROMARTY & SUTHERLAND. **ORKNEYS & SHETLANDS** **IRELAND N.W.**	CORK, KERRY LIMERICK TIPPERARY CLARE
MIDLANDS E. BUCKINGHAMSHIRE OXFORDSHIRE NORTHAMPTONSHIRE WARWICKSHIRE LEICESTERSHIRE RUTLANDSHIRE NOTTINGHAMSHIRE	CARNARVONSHIRE ANGLESEY **ENGLAND N.W.** CHESHIRE LANCASHIRE WESTMORLAND CUMBERLAND	WIGTOWNSHIRE AYRSHIRE LANARKSHIRE RENFREWSHIRE DUMBARTONSHIRE STIRLINGSHIRE **SCOTLAND W.**	GALWAY ROSCOMMON MAYO, SLIGO LEITRIM **IRELAND N.E.** MEATH, W. MEATH LONGFORD CAVAN	MAP SHEWING LAND AREAS USED IN B.B.C. FORECASTS ETC.
MIDLANDS W. GLOUCESTERSHIRE HEREFORDSHIRE WORCESTERSHIRE SHROPSHIRE STAFFORDSHIRE	**MIDLANDS N.** DERBYSHIRE YORKSHIRE, W. **ENGLAND N.E.** YORKSHIRE N.& E. DURHAM	ARGYLE & BUTE **SCOTLAND N.W.** HEBRIDES WEST'N PARTS OF INVERNESS-SHIRE ROSS & CROMARTY	FERMANAGH MONAGHAN LOUTH, ARMAGH DOWN, ANTRIM LONDONDERRY TYRONE, DONEGAL	

MAP SHEWING LAND AREAS USED IN B.B.C. FORECASTS ETC.

ARE ALL THE OBSERVATION POSTS IN GT. BRITAIN?

OH NO! WE MUST HAVE REPORTS FROM ALL OVER EUROPE, EVEN FROM PARTS OF ASIA & N. AMERICA. EACH COUNTRY HAS ITS NETWORKS OF POSTS, AND CO-OPERATE UNDER THE INTERNATIONAL METEOROLOGICAL ORGANISATION, IN PROVIDING REPORTS TO EACH OTHER BY RADIO. — THERE ARE 4 TRANSMITTERS IN EUROPE FOR THIS PURPOSE. THEY ARE SITED IN DUNSTABLE, ENGLAND & PARIS, ROME & MOSCOW. — THE ATLANTIC OCEAN HAS A GREAT INFLUENCE ON OUR WEATHER AND SO —

HEIGHT OF FLIGHTS BY 'MET' AIRCRAFT
———— 18,000 FEET
———— LOW LEVEL

ATLANTIC

A LAT. 59°00'N. LONG. 19°00'W.
B LAT. 52°30'N. LONG. 20°00'W.

THERE ARE ALSO 'FIXED' METEOROLOGICAL SHIPS IN THE ATLANTIC. THIS MAP SHOWS HOW THEY ARE PLACED. BRITAIN MAINTAINS 4 SHIPS (2 OFF DUTY WITH 2 ON). THEY ARE MARKED 'A' & 'B' ON MAP. WE RECEIVE AID FROM HOLLAND IN MAINTAINING 'B'. — NOTE THE ROUTES OF THE DAILY 'MET' FLIGHTS BY AIRCRAFT, WHICH MAKE OBSERVATIONS AT HIGH LEVELS.

THE SHIPS ARE CORVETTES OF THE 'FLOWER' CLASS. THESE SHIPS SERVED AS CONVOYS DURING 2ND WORLD WAR. THEY ARE NOW CALLED 'WEATHER OBSERVER', 'WEATHER EXPLORER', 'WEATHER WATCHER' & 'WEATHER RECORDER' RESPECTIVELY. THEY ARE EQUIPPED TO TAKE SAME OBSERVATIONS AS THE LAND POSTS, WITH THE EXCEPTION OF RAINFALL. THIS IS NOT POSSIBLE AS THE SEA SPRAY MAKES IT DIFFICULT.

SURFACE OBSERVATIONS

1. INSTRUMENTAL MEASUREMENTS
BAROMETRIC PRESSURE, OR HEIGHT OF BAROMETER
BAROMETRIC TENDENCY, OR CHANGE OF PRESSURE DURING THE PREVIOUS 3 HOURS
CHARACTERISTICS OF TENDENCY, OR THE DIRECTION OF THE CHANGE, WHETHER RISING OR FALLING, ETC.
TEMPERATURE OF THE AIR · DIRECTION & SPEED OF WIND · HEIGHT OF CLOUDS.

2. NON-INSTRUMENTAL OBSERVATIONS
VISIBILITY · PRESENT & PAST WEATHER · AMOUNT OF CLOUD · TYPES OF CLOUD (LOW, MEDIUM & HIGH) · STATE OF THE GROUND.

HERE IS A LIST OF SURFACE OBSERVATIONS — BOTH INSTRUMENTAL & NON-INSTRUMENTAL. — YOU ARE DOUBTLESS FAMILIAR WITH THE ANEROID AND MERCURIAL BAROMETER AND THEREFORE WE WILL CONCENTRATE ON THE OTHER FEATURES — I SUGGEST THAT WE TAKE A STROLL ON THE SEASHORE & STUDY THINGS THAT OBSERVERS LOOK FOR.

JUST AS AN OYSTER LIVES ON THE OCEAN BED, SO DO WE LIVE AT THE BOTTOM OF AN OCEAN OF AIR. THE WEATHER IS GOVERNED BY CONSTANT CHANGES OF TEMPERATURE, HUMIDITY AND PRESSURE OF THE WEIGHT OF AIR UPON US. THE WAVES ON THE SEA ARE CAUSED BY THE WIND TRYING TO LIFT THE WATER, BUT THE FORCE OF GRAVITY PULLS IT DOWN. NOW THE AIR (WHICH IS A GAS) IS, LIKE THE SEA, BEING CONSTANTLY AGITATED BY OUTSIDE FORCES, BUT BEING A GAS IT RESPONDS MORE EASILY THAN WATER.
WATER CAN BECOME A GAS OR VAPOUR, AND CAN RISE INTO THE AIR. THE AMOUNT OF WATER WHICH AIR CAN CONTAIN DEPENDS UPON ITS TEMPERATURE — FOR INSTANCE WARM AIR CAN HOLD A LOT OF WATER VAPOUR; AND COLD AIR VERY LITTLE. YOU WILL SEE THAT IF WARM AIR CONTAINING A LOT OF MOISTURE IS BLOWN AWAY BY A COLD WIND, THUS REPLACING THE WARM AIR WITH COLD, THE WATER VAPOUR WILL CONDENSE AND FALL AS RAIN.

AN IMPORTANT EXAMPLE OF THE COOLING OF AIR CAN BE SEEN IN THE FORMING OF DEW. AFTER A HOT DAY, HEAT ESCAPES FROM THE GROUND INTO SPACE. THE EARTH BECOMES COOL & COOLS A THIN LAYER OF AIR IMMEDIATELY ABOVE THE GROUND. THE VAPOUR IN THE AIR CONDENSES AND FORMS DROPS OF WATER CALLED DEW. THE TEMPERATURE AT WHICH THIS HAPPENS IS CALLED 'DEW-POINT'.

IF THE TEMPERATURE IS BELOW FREEZING POINT, WE GET ICE CRYSTALS INSTEAD OF DEW — AND WE CALL THIS HOAR FROST.

ONE OF THE MOST IMPORTANT DISCOVERIES, IS THE FACT THAT WHEN AIR MOVES DOWNWARDS IT IS BEING COMPRESSED & GETS WARMER. WHEN IT MOVES UPWARDS IT IS EXPANDING & GETTING COLDER. AIR MOVING DOWN IS USUALLY CLEAR WHILE AIR MOVING UP IS USUALLY CLOUDY. FROM THIS YOU WILL SEE THE NEED FOR RECORDING TEMPERATURE, ALSO AIR PRESSURE (WITH BAROMETER) AND THE NEED FOR MEASURING THE HEIGHT OF CLOUDS & WINDSPEEDS.

HOW DO THEY MEASURE THE HEIGHT OF CLOUDS AND WINDSPEED?

SEARCHLIGHT BEAM / 90° / 1,000 YDS. / OBSERVATION POST / A

THIS IS EASILY DONE AT NIGHT BY PLACING A SEARCHLIGHT 1,000 YDS. FROM OBSERVATION POST & PROJECTING BEAM VERTICALLY. THE BEAM MAKES A POOL OF LIGHT ON CLOUD BASE. AN INSTRUMENT AT 'OP' ESTABLISHES ANGLE 'A' & GIVES THE HEIGHT — YOU HAVE PROBABLY LEARNT THIS PRINCIPLE AT SCHOOL. IN DAYTIME THEY SEND UP A SMALL BALLOON. THE GAS IN BALLOON IS ADJUSTED TO RISE AT SAY 400 FT. PER MIN. IF IT TAKES 5 MINS. TO REACH CLOUD THEN THE HEIGHT IS 2,000 FT.

THERE ARE TWO WAYS OF FINDING THE SPEED, DIRECTION & MOVEMENT OF UPPER WINDS, AGAIN BY GAS FILLED BALLOONS. THESE ARE FILLED TO RISE AT SAY 500' PER MIN. & ARE MEASURED EVERY MINUTE BY A SPECIALLY DESIGNED THEODOLITE. OF COURSE THEY CAN ONLY USE THIS METHOD BENEATH THE CLOUDS.

TO MEASURE WIND AT GREAT HEIGHTS (ABOVE CLOUDS) THEY ATTACH METALISED PAPER OR NYLON MESH TO THE BALLOON AND 'WATCH' IT WITH RADAR EQUIPMENT.

AIRCRAFT ALSO MAKE OBSERVATIONS OF WIND SPEEDS IN THE UPPER ATMOSPHERE.

HOW DO THEY MEASURE RAINFALL?

YOU CAN MEASURE RAINFALL YOURSELVES — IF YOU HAVE A QUART BOTTLE WITH A FLAT BOTTOM & A DIA. OF SAY 6" AND A FUNNEL OF SAME DIA. (SEE 'A'). IF AT THE END OF A DAY, THE BOTTLE CONTAINS AN INCH OF WATER THEN THE RAINFALL IS 1 INCH. — BUT IF YOUR FUNNEL IS 6" DIA. AND THE BOTTLE 3" DIA. (SEE 'B') THEN THE DEPTH OF WATER IN BOTTLE WOULD HAVE TO BE DIVIDED BY 4, BECAUSE AREA OF FUNNEL IS 4 TIMES THE AREA OF THE BASE OF BOTTLE.

6" FUNNELS / "A" 6" DIA. BOTTLE / 3" DIA. BOTTLE "B"

I SEE — A DEPTH OF 4" IN THE 3" BOTTLE IS EQUAL TO 1" IN 6" BOTTLE.

I THINK YOU UNDERSTAND THAT TEMPERATURE, HUMIDITY & AIR PRESSURE ARE LINKED TOGETHER IN TELLING US WHAT OUR SEA OF AIR IS DOING. WE ARE, IN EFFECT, CHARTING THE MOVEMENT OF THE ATMOSPHERE — JUST AS WE DO WITH OCEAN CURRENTS. OF COURSE WE WANT TO KNOW WHAT IS HAPPENING HIGH UP IN THE ATMOSPHERE, AND SO SOME OBSERVERS USE A DEVICE CALLED THE 'RADIO-SONDE' —

LAUNCHING RADIO-SONDE FROM "MET-SHIP"

THIS CONSISTS OF A BALLOON WHICH CARRIES A SMALL RADIO TRANSMITTER WHICH HAS 3 ATTACHMENTS. THESE RESPOND TO VARIATIONS OF PRESSURE, TEMPERATURE & HUMIDITY. THE 3 ATTACHMENTS ARE SWITCHED INTO OPERATION IN SEQUENCE BY SMALL SWITCHGEAR. AS BALLOON RISES THE RADIO SENDS OUT MUSICAL NOTES WHICH VARY IN PITCH AS THE CONDITIONS CHANGE. THE BALLOON OFTEN GETS AS HIGH AS 10 MILES BEFORE IT BURSTS — WHEN THE INSTRUMENT IS PARACHUTED DOWN.

RADIO IS ALSO USED TO LOCATE THUNDERSTORMS. THERE ARE 4 STATIONS EQUIPPED WITH CATHODE RAY DIRECTION FINDERS. THESE CAN DETECT A THUNDERSTORM WITHIN A RANGE OF ABOUT 1,500 MILES.

PROFESSOR — HOW DO THEY KEEP PACE WITH ALL THE REPORTS FROM THESE NUMEROUS OBSERVATION POSTS?

THE REPORTS ARRIVE IN A SIMPLE CODE FORM, AND ARE IMMEDIATELY RECORDED ON A LARGE MAP. SYMBOLS ARE USED TO SHOW DIFFERENT CONDITIONS, AND VERY RAPIDLY A 'DAILY PICTURE' IS DRAWN OF EXISTING WEATHER CONDITIONS.

LIST OF WEATHER CHART SYMBOLS
BAROMETER · Areas High and Low Pressure (Isobars)
WIND · Direction shewn by arrow
CALM · Shewn thus   TEMPERATURE · In degrees F.
CLOUD SYMBOLS · Clear Sky · Sky ⅒ covered · Sky ¼ covered · Sky ⅓ covered · Sky ½ covered · Sky ⅗ covered · Sky ¾ covered · Sky ⅞ covered · Sky obscured.
WEATHER SYMBOLS · Rain Falling · Snow · Sleet · Hail · Fog · Mist · Thunder · Thunderstorm
FRONTS OR BOUNDARIES between masses of air of different origin are shewn as follows :-
WARM FRONT ON SURFACE · WARM FRONT ABOVE GROUND · COLD FRONT ON SURFACE · COLD FRONT ABOVE GROUND · OCCLUDED FRONT · WARM OCCLUSION · COLD OCCLUSION
NOTE: SYMBOLS ARE PLACED ON THE SIDE OF THE LINE TOWARDS WHICH THE FRONT IS MOVING.

THIS MAP WILL GIVE YOU AN IDEA OF THE TYPE OF CHART USED. IT LOOKS CONFUSING AT FIRST, BUT YOU WILL SOON SEE THAT IT IS A PROJECTION OF THE NORTHERN HEMISPHERE. IF YOU STUDY LIST OF SYMBOLS IT WILL EXPLAIN ITSELF. — AN EXPERT 'FORECASTER' CAN FORM A JUDGEMENT OF THE FUTURE MOVEMENT OF THESE CONDITIONS. HE WILL STUDY THE MOVEMENT OF THE AIR PRESSURES. WHERE THE BAROMETER READINGS ARE EQUAL THEY ARE JOINED TOGETHER BY LINES CALLED 'ISOBARS'. AN AREA OF 'LOW' PRESSURE IS CALLED A 'CYCLONE', AN AREA OF 'HIGH' PRESSURE, AN 'ANTI-CYCLONE'. THE ANTI-CYCLONE SENDS OUT WINDS SPIRALLY FROM ITS CENTRE AND THESE WINDS DISPLACE THE CYCLONE BY DRIVING SPIRALLY INTO THE CENTRE OF THESE LOW PRESSURE AREAS. THESE CONDITIONS WITH TEMPERATURES AND OTHER INFORMATION, TELL THE EXPERT WHAT WEATHER WE ARE LIKELY TO EXPECT, THE 'BOUNDARY FRONTS' EXPLAIN THEMSELVES, BUT I'D BETTER EXPLAIN AN 'OCCLUSION' — THIS IS FROM THE WORD OCCLUDE — 'TO ABSORB'. OCCLUSION MEANS 'THE CLOSING OR OPENING OF A PASSAGE — THE ACT OF OCCLUDING OR ABSORBING'.

MAN IN SPACE

For its first test flights, the X-15 is powered by two small four-barrel rocket engines. Later, a single Reaction Motor rocket of 60,000 lbs. thrust will be fitted. Made of special heat-resisting metals, the X-15 has a wing-span of 22 ft. and is 50 ft. in length.

One of the most exciting aeroplanes ever built is now at the U.S.A.F.'s top-secret Edwards Air Force Base, California, for its initial flight tests. Known as the North American X-15, it is designed to fly at over 3,600 m.p.h. and to climb to a height of at least 100 miles, where it will be above 99.9% of the atmosphere. Later, it may be put into a satellite orbit with the help of a giant booster-rocket.

First pilot of the X-15 is 37-year-old North American test pilot Scott Crossfield, who was the first man to fly at twice the speed of sound. His specially-designed aluminium-coated pressure suit is insulated, ventilated by cooling air and inflatable, to enable him to breathe and to prevent his blood boiling when he is at great heights.

Inside this building, Scott Crossfield has been able to learn what it is like to fly the North American X-15 without leaving the ground, by using the world's biggest whirling-arm centrifuge.

Below, Scott Crossfield is pictured stepping into the gondola on the end of the great centrifuge rotor arm.

you write to the Editor

'BANDIT' SPEAKING

HERE IS a picture of our dog, 'Bandit', chewing over the international situation on the telephone with a friend. He is becoming very intellectual! He is a Staffordshire bull terrier, a breed which is only now becoming popular in England. – *David Lindy, Littlehampton.*

THANKS, Mr. THERM

THE *Live and Learn* series by Mr. Therm has been a great help in providing me with some good fun in building cupboards under the sink, and also the fold-up table. – *Graham Fields, Eastbourne.*

AN EAGLE PRIZE

I HAVE just finished reading the EAGLE novel, entitled *Storm Nelson and the Sea Leopard*, which I found most absorbing and exciting. I won it in a recent EAGLE competition, and thoroughly recommend it for all ages. – *S. Adams, Carlisle.*

STICK 'EM UP!

AS MY brother and I are joining EAGLE Club, we thought you would like to see our photograph. Mum took it while we played a 'Jeff Arnold' game. It is our favourite story in EAGLE. – *Laurence Eddy, Rhondda, Glamorgan.*

5/- is paid for every letter published. Readers who want a reply should enclose a stamped, addressed envelope.

The gondola is fitted out as a dummy X-15 cockpit, in which Crossfield can experience the accelerations of a real flight and check positions of the controls and instruments. The X-15 will be launched from a B-52 mother-plane to zoom four times higher than any previous manned aircraft, gathering data for space flight and to discover how space vehicles can re-enter the atmosphere without being burned up by friction.

THE EDITOR'S CHRISTMAS NIGHTMARE

AFTERWORD

During my 20 years' involvement in the intellectual property the *Eagle* and Dan Dare, I can vividly recall one treasured moment back in 2000 at the production offices of one of Hollywood's leading computer animation studios. It was a unique experience for me in this whole *Eagle* story.

As the executive producer of the CGI television series *Dan Dare – Pilot of the Future*, I was sitting in front of a team of over 50 American animation technicians, writers, and production executives, who were literally about to bring Dan Dare to life in 26 episodes of state-of-the-art computer animation. The average age of this team was less than 30, and they were all highly experienced and talented in their profession in LA, with a string of animated hit shows behind them.

In front of me on the table I laid out a selection of original artwork to give them all an understanding and flavour of where Dan Dare and the *Eagle* began back in the 1950s. This original artwork featured a selection of the original strips held in our archives, together with cover designs by Frank Hampson, Frank Bellamy, and Keith Watson. I was about to explain the unique talent of all the individuals who had been involved in the *Eagle*. However, this creative team seated around me, already knew the history well, they were avid fans of what was created in the fifties. They adored the quality, the design and the vivid colours of the artwork of Frank Hampson and all the artists associated with the comic. They were simply in awe of this artwork, and remember it was the year 2000 and the artwork I was showing was from the fifties and sixties, almost 50 years prior. I knew then that with the British and American writers, the animators, and the production team in front of me, I was about to embark on an amazing experience in producing Dan Dare in the new millennium to a huge global audience. Southport had arrived in California. It was a thrilling and enlightening experience, and the series has now been sold to over 130 countries – so the *Eagle* and Dan Dare is now very much alive to a new worldwide audience, and more is to come.

The whole *Eagle* story is nothing less than remarkable. To think that Marcus Morris and Frank Hampson sat and worked together with a small team, in their Southport studio, built detailed models of the characters and vehicles, and had the imagination to create wonderful, pure adventure stories that the youth of Britain could relate to, is simply inspiring. Soon after publication, the success story began to gather serious momentum. Nearly one million copies were being sold of the *Eagle* comic every week. The youth of Britain simply stopped on a Friday awaiting the next issue of the *Eagle*. As you will have now read: what evil and intriguing plots did the Mekon have up his sleeve? What was the next PC49 or Riders of the Range adventure going to be? What revelations were about to be revealed of the inner workings of the Vulcan bomber and the Nautilus submarine, in the amazing 'cutaways'? And what was Professor Brittain about to explain?

The Eagle Club was truly a 'must have' membership. To be a member enrolled you into adventure, excitement, thrills, and exclusive opportunities. The *Eagle* captured the imagination of a generation in the UK, during the fifties and sixties, in a truly exciting way – exactly what Harry Potter has achieved for a new global generation today.

Personally, I believe that the *Eagle* created the original real Super Hero 'Dan Dare – Pilot of the Future'. Alongside Superman, Batman, Spiderman, and Captain America, Dan simply towers! He will always do so.

I have often thought about what the creators of the *Eagle* would have thought had they entered the name Dan Dare or the *Eagle* into the Internet search bar today and seen the results. It is simply amazing. From a small studio in Southport, to the worldwide web, the story is remarkable and, more importantly, ongoing.

This book has captured the flavour of the quality, adventure, innovation, and excitement of outstanding comic entertainment. It is the first of several new publishing ventures for everybody young and old to enjoy. Next year look out for Dan and the *Eagle* moving into the 1960s.

The words in Elton John's and Bernie Taupin's song, 'Dan Dare (Pilot of the Future)', say it all: 'Can you tell me how old Dan might have done it, if he had been here now'. Well he is certainly here now, together with the *Eagle,* as this wonderful adventure continues.

COLIN FREWIN, AUGUST 2007
CHIEF EXECUTIVE
DAN DARE CORPORATION LIMITED

AUTHOR BIOGRAPHY

Daniel Tatarsky was born in Liverpool nearly 15 years after *Eagle*. Researching this book has allowed him to fall in love with the comic's characters and style in the same way that readers first did back in the 1950s. He is also an actor, and one day he hopes to play Dan Dare's sidekick Digby. The *Eagle Annual of the 1950s* is his second book. He has also written *Flick to Kick: An Illustrated History of Subbuteo*.